Pelican Books
How Israel Lost Its Soul

Maxim Ghilan was born in France in 1931, the son of a French Jewish businessman. He arrived in Palestine in 1944 and by 1948 had begun his association with the Left faction of LEHY, headed by Nathan Yalin-Mor. Hehas been imprisoned by the Israeli authorities on three separate occasions – in 1952 for the possession of secret documents, in 1957 when the secret service tried to frame him for the assassination of Dr Rudolf Kastner, and in 1966 for publishing without censorship revealing articles concerning the Israeli secret service. Maxim Ghilan is a journalist of international renown. He created Israel's first and only tribune of the Left and was, in 1961, secretary general of the Israeli New Left Party. He left Israel in 1969, having been forced to reconsider his nationalist Jewish stand.

To Nathan Zach –
A man of talent
a man of wisdom –
but above all a
man with a heart.

Warmly –

Maxim Ghilan

How Israel Lost Its Soul

Penguin Books

29/8/74
Belsize Park

Penguin Books Ltd, Harmondsworth,
Middlesex, England
Penguin Books Australia Ltd, Ringwood,
Victoria, Australia

First published 1974

Made and printed in Great Britain by
C. Nicholls & Company Ltd
Set in Monotype Times

'I wish it need not have happened in my time,' said Frodo.

'So do I,' said Gandalf, 'and so do all who live to see such times. But that is not for them to decide. All we have to decide is what to do with the time that is given us. And already, Frodo, our time is beginning to look black.'

J. R. R. TOLKIEN,
The Fellowship of the Ring

'How shall a man judge what to do in such times?'

'As he ever has judged,' said Aragorn, 'Good and evil have not changed since yesteryear.'

J. R. R. TOLKIEN,
The Two Towers

Contents

Acknowledgements

This book is dedicated to all those, in both Israel and Palestine, who shall survive the hecatombs in order to live together.

The author wishes to thank those who became, for him, living examples and also those who, by believing in this book before it was written, allowed it to become fact.

Among the first let me mention Fawzy El-Assmar, Sabri Geries, Felicia Langer, Ali Rafi, Nathan Yalin-Mor, Shalom Cohen; among the latter, Judith Ben-Joud, Yossef Firstatter, Yossef Ben-Gal, Patrick Seale and Maureen McConville.

Foreword: The Air-Raid Sirens of Tel-Aviv

This book was born in the early morning of 5 June 1967, when I heard the ululation of the first air-raid sirens and knew the war had started – at last.

For six days I watched people I liked and respected kill other people I liked and respected no less. I was torn at that drastic moment between my very strong wish to be a part of the whole, and my no less strong feelings that such a war was not necessary. I objected to the war even though I then believed – as all Israelis did and most still do – that Tel-Aviv's official broadcasts, which spoke of 'Egypt's offensive against Israel's borders', were true. I believed that Israel's war was defensive, not the preventive war of conquest it has since proved to be.

On 6 June I was about seven weeks a free man. I had been released after serving four and a half months of a secret one-year jail sentence inflicted on me for foiling Israeli censorship and revealing certain aspects of the disappearance in Paris of the Moroccan leftist leader, Mehdi Ben-Barka, which linked it with Israel's secret services, the Shin Beit. I was let out early thanks to the pressure of international opinion, when the news of the secret jailing of two senior journalists – my friend Shmuel Mor and myself – had been leaked out abroad by devious means and published in the *New York Times*.

For this and for other political activities I was also 'punished' in another way: nobody asked me to participate in the war. This is a very real kind of pressure, when a whole country is acting as a single man. An individual asks himself again and again if *he* is not wrong; all the rest seem so obviously to be right and working so busily at their common task of salvation.

But I realized even then that no amount of identification with this sort of 'auto-salvation' could breed in me the paranoid hatred of the enemy, the blindness of thought and singleness of purpose expressed in such familiar dicta as 'My country, right or wrong', 'Everything for the proletarian revolution', 'One Reich, one people, one leader'.

Looking around me, and still believing these Hebrew heroes were fighting *in extremis* – the bloodthirsty enemy having finally decided to attack – I nonetheless knew that something was wrong: perhaps because as a child I had experienced another civil war, in Spain, and since then did not think so much in terms of 'them' and 'us'.

Later, of course, when I became aware of the preventive character of the war, this feeling crystallized into a realization of the inherent phoneyness of both President Nasser's and Chief of Staff Rabin's declarations in the days leading up to the war. I saw that the whole intolerable Middle East argument stemmed from erroneous positions adopted in turn by both Jews and Arabs; from an escalation of words, ideas and actions; and, also, from the fact that totalitarian pan-Arab thought made use of the 'Palestine Refugee Problem' in exactly the same way as pre-war Germany had used its own trauma, the Versailles Peace Pact.

Once again I realized that there was something irrational in the Israeli position which in essence was that 'Not one refugee shall come back'; and in the Israeli readiness to back this position with everything it had – including Israeli lives.

Thus was born my recognition of two basic Israeli facts: the fight for a separate Israeli identity, ready to pay *any* price to stay uncontaminated by the Arabs; and the socio-economic need for a continuing state of war to allow Israel's parasitic ruling class – without par in either the communist or the capitalist world – to continue to feed on the vital essence of the tremendously dynamic Israeli experiment.

There came a time, about ten months after the Jewish victory, when these convictions of mine had to find an outlet. By then of course hysteria had lessened and the uglier facts of the Israeli conquest were coming to light. At the same time the horrifying threats of the Arab leaders and masses on 6 June 'to kill and butcher you all, every old man, woman and child' had been almost forgotten – precisely because official Israeli propaganda made so much of it. So I started to think out the subject of this book, which is, to my mind, fundamental to the existence of some hundred million people in the Middle East and another twelve million abroad.

Later I had to extend my search to that side of the problem I am least interested in – the Jewish identity. For there is no doubt that it is only if separated from the international Jewish question that the Middle East can become what one day I hope it will become: a complex, non-sectarian, multi-cultural and multi-racial United States of the Area.

I have therefore to extend an apology to the Jewish readers in say, New Jersey or Lille, who may be shocked by what seems to them a cynical alienation from a common Jewish bond. But the author no more thinks as a 'Jewish' Jew – whether Zionist or Orthodox – than the early Zionists thought as Assimilated Aryan Jews (in spite of the background of several of them, including a certain Dr Benjamin Herzl).

This is the book of a Middle Eastern patriot, conscious that his loyalty is to a not-yet-born entity. And if somebody says that such an attitude is not realistic, I would like to remind him that the Zionists' attitudes, before their first Basle Congress, were not much more so.

Tel-Aviv – Paris – London
January 1969 – May 1972

1 'The Only Democracy in the Middle East'

Israel is a democratic state. It has an elected President, an elected Parliament of 120 members, a Comptroller with an independent office, democratic laws, a free press – and moreover the millenary commitment of the Jewish People against oppressors, which has made Jews almost everywhere opt for the democratic and parliamentary systems of government.

The Israelis like to talk at length about the government, to protest against it and joke about it. Nowhere will you find the atmosphere of the Eastern-bloc 'People's democracies'.

The law grants freedom of religion and equality to both sexes, to all ages, and to people from different origins. There is no law limiting the right of people to travel abroad. There is, moreover, *habeas corpus*, an inheritance from the British legal system, which was imposed on Jewish-Talmudic, Turkish-Ottoman and Common Bedouin law during the days of the Mandate of Palestine. Even the ubiquitous army is stringently controlled. Military courts must grant full defence to an accused.

In short, a paradise of democracy. 'The only democratic country in the Middle East', as people never tire of telling you in my country. The complete opposite of the Arabic-speaking dictatorships over the border in Syria and Egypt.

Let us see how far this democracy really goes. Let us see if it is more than skin-deep.

*

The first thing to be understood is that the Zionist Establishment, the body of men, groups and ideas which rules Israel, is committed to a double course. It must do all it can for all the Jews of the world, up to and including their immigration to Israel and integration in the country; for the persecution of the Jews throughout the world and the ages is the main ideological – or should we say religious? – drive behind the Zionists' existence. And, equally, it must observe the apparent rules of democracy, since Zionism started as a movement of liberal-national liberation.

As communist bureaucrats torture, kill and imprison workers for the sake of the classless society; as old-fashioned capitalist rulers let people live in squalor and hunger, control them and even beat them over the head, for the sake of man's right to aspire to economic well-being by way of free enterprise; so the Zionist Jew is willing to kill and be killed, to oppress and be oppressed, to threaten and to lie so that Jews may live their life as proud, free men. A contradiction in terms? Obviously. But no sharper or more irrational than the contradictions of other regimes and ideologies.

The State of Israel is Jewish and therefore, according to Zionist logic, it is free and democratic. Jews can't exploit other Jews, can they? Throughout the ages Jews have been victimized by other peoples and nations. They were homeless and had no defenders. Moreover, their efforts to succeed in the face of overwhelming economic and psychological odds caused them more than once to succeed only too well. Their resulting affluence and comparatively superior intelligence provoked a further wave of reaction against them. Thus the dynamics of anti-Semitism were established long ago and went on doing their work through the centuries as long as Jews had incomplete national characteristics and above all no country of their own.

It follows, according to Zionist logic, that anybody lifting his hand against the Jewish State *for whatever reason* is an anti-Semite. It further follows, according to this logic, that the Jewish State must be wary of all other states. Strangers, meaning people of non-Jewish origin, are just a bit dangerous. This has been demonstrated by centuries of Jewish experience.

This attitude, together with a series of socio-economic developments, has created a state of affairs in which Israel, structured on democratic principles, is ruled in a way designed to circumvent the more bothersome – and vital – of democracy's safeguards. Moreover, it is ruled with varying degrees of democratic tolerance, depending on which of the four categories of inhabitant is in question.

The members of the Establishment – and they are the majority of the State's citizens – have the right to full democratic privileges. As it happens, those privileges are not fully used, as the consensus is one of satisfaction with the prevailing situation.

There is also a group of Jews, outside the Zionist Establishment, which is economically exploited and up to a point socially ostracized: the new immigrants before they are absorbed in one of the party-groups which make up Israeli society; and Israeli non-Jews other than those from an Arabic-speaking background.

Thirdly, there are the Israeli Jews who challenge the social structure and political reality of the Zionist Establishment. This relatively tiny political opposition is discriminated against in a number of ways, on the classic pattern of Western capitalist countries. Occasionally they are imprisoned, framed, beaten up (rarely, and then mostly by police dispersing mobs). They have been the target of a few attempts at political assassination (particularly avowed non-Zionists such as Ury Avnery and the late De Haan).

But on the whole, although despised, the non-Zionists and the anti-Zionists are still Jews, still part of the privileged majority. As soon as they repent they are allowed back into the social, economic and psychological fold, as happened to all Jewish former communists who showed themselves penitent during the first fifty years of the establishment of Zionism in Palestine.

Then there are the Arabic-speaking minorities, Moslem, Druze, Christian and others, men and women who identify themselves more or less with the Arab national awakening in the Middle East. They are irremediably condemned by the unwritten laws of the Zionist Establishment to stay outside the pale. They are taken care of, even benefit indirectly from the economic bounty created by the Zionist State. But they are also contained, controlled and frustrated in all matters of independent thought, political organization, and freedom of physical movement. These non-Jewish Arabic-speaking citizens, who according to the law have equal rights, in fact live in an 'invisible' Bantustan, which from time to time in different parts of Israel becomes blindingly visible.

In judging the degree of democracy in Israel, this structure must be borne in mind. One cannot measure an Israeli Arab's freedom of thought by counting how many newspapers exist in Israel and discovering to what extent they are controlled. One must try to find out how many newspapers are owned by Arabs or directed to Arabs, yet censored and controlled by non-Arabs. Similarly one would have to gauge the freedom of thought and movement of the citizens who are neither Jew nor Arab, and of the anti-Zionist Jews.

Israel was established as a haven for the Jewish people and their religion. A haven is a place of safety from the outside world. Therefore it is a place where the outside world is, if not actually barred, at least not made welcome, and not given all the privileges of those who have found their haven. As for those who were living in what has become the Jews' home, there are three possible psychological reactions to their existence: they can be ignored, if and when possible; they can be kept separate; and they can be expelled or eliminated when necessary.

The story of the relations between the Zionist settlers (and after them the native Israelis) and the Arabic-speaking minority of Israel is the story of these three reactions. First Zionism tried, on the whole, to live separately from the Arabs of Palestine – and once it became the economically dominant segment of society, to keep the Arabs out of the settlers' society. At times it tried to ignore them. And in the decisive moments of history – when, for instance, the conflict between the settlers' society and the feudal Palestinian background exploded into war – the tougher and more lucid Israelis opted for the third solution: expulsion. All these brought about a gradual curtailment and erosion of the basic democracy of the State and of the Zionism which preceded the State and overlaps with it.

We must see in greater detail the history of these changing relationships between the Zionists and the Arabs in Palestine, look at the various movements that have grown up in Israel and brought about the growing conflict, and finally examine the effect all this has had on the structures of Israeli society at the present day.

2 The Foundations of Zionism, 1870–1914

The history of Zionist belief starts with the French Revolution and the *Code Napoléon.* It was the old revolutionary turned autocrat who first gave legal rights to the Jews, till then legally considered in Europe a lesser breed of human beings. Napoleon, and the growing tide of liberalism in Britain, broke the external walls containing European Judaism in its ghettoes. Napoleon also foreshadowed Balfour in his wish to allow the migration of European Jews to Palestine.

There remained, even after Napoleon, a good deal of prejudice and discrimination in Western Europe; and, no less important, there remained the twin ideological walls built by the Jews themselves: the belief in their separateness, and the belief that they would reach their promised land only with the coming of the Messiah.

The second wall soon started crumbling when bourgeois 'economic expediency' replaced Catholic intolerance and Protestant puritanism as the political yardstick. As for the first wall, we shall see that it changed in form, but not in content.

Over the centuries, anti-Semitic persecution had pushed the main body of European Jewry towards the less hospitable north-eastern and central-northern parts of this cold continent. The physical climate was severe enough, but the political climate was even more likely to cause suffering to the helpless and the alien. In Prussia, the post-feudal Junker tradition was responsible. In Tsarist Russia it was due to autocracy for its own sake, and the systematic persecution of the innocent minority towards whom the wrath of the majority could be misdirected in order to safeguard authority, law and oppressive order. In Austria-Hungary the classic patterns of anti-Semitism survived. In the Baltic and the northern Balkan countries there still existed the most ignorant, and therefore the most virulent, sorts of religious Jew-hating. Because of the Spanish Inquisition, because of the Italian Renaissance's intrigues, largely based on power in the Church, and because of their isolation from their Oriental and southern mediterranean fellow-believers, the Jews had been forced to migrate towards precisely those lands where they were least well treated – but where at least their physical presence, as nomads or foreigners, was at first tolerated.

Thus it was in the Baltic territories, in the Tsarist empire, and in Bismarck's Germany that the age of liberalism found the mainspring of the European Jews; in other words in the very countries where autocracy was strongest and where the new liberal tradition was seen dimly, as through a veil. But these were also the countries of greatest ferment: the Austro-Hungarian and Russian empires were in the last phase of their imperial might; while Germany was forging a future which seemed golden and was to be, in point of irrational fact, disastrously black for all humanity.

The Jewish way of life, lived out on isolated islands of self-contained culture, tends to extract from the human being what is best in him and what is worst. It has given the world more writers, artists and scientists than any similar segment of humanity; for outside pressure tends to force from gifted Jews more than, or at least as much as, their surrounding fellow-men produce. It has also given the planet more moneylenders, crooked politicians, capitalist exploiters and communist commissars than any other nation – and for precisely the same reasons. Under pressure some become better and genius is shown to exist, while others become worse and villainy is bred. Moreover it is the oppressed who find it most important to be strong and ultimately to wield power.

As strength, power and importance destroy an individual's capacity for thinking rationally, and acting in accordance with rational thought, it is no wonder that the anti-Semites who needed pretexts for exploitation and oppression had powerful examples of the 'bad Jew'. Similarly, inside Judaism, the expounders of the 'You put us apart from all other peoples' school found plenty of examples of Jewish 'superiority' to feed their self-esteem. Rational examination of the psycho-economic causes of the Jewish Question disappeared almost completely behind the smoke-screen of partisan views, inferiority/superiority complexes, and the need to justify cruelty, hatred, fear and exploitation.

This interplay of feelings and actions was particularly strong under dictatorial conditions. In comparatively little time the Jewry of Russia, Poland and the Baltic and Balkan territories found it impossible to continue to live quietly there. The feeling of being stifled became progressively stronger as more and more Jews became acquainted with French Revolutionary and Napoleonic liberal ideas, and applied them to their own fate. At the same time, more and more Jews abandoned the religious tradition of their forefathers. The great divide between the Western bourgeoisie and its religion was only a thin, disguised crack in Eastern Europe, and among the doubly isolated Jewish communities there it dwindled almost to nothing. Almost, but not quite.

First the liberal revolution impinged on Eastern European consciousness, then it undermined the already disintegrating foundations of Jewish self-contained religiousness. The acceptance of liberal ideas was, in a way, easier for the isolated European Jews than for other Europeans: most Jews had kept, or had been kept, away from the agricultural and industrial sources of European life, and were thus pushed towards commerce and finance. Their experience of capitalism was, on the whole, more intimate than that of the rooted, surrounding middle classes. So, when liberalism – with its goals of separating the autocratic church from the autocratic state, and transforming the latter into a 'popularly' controlled organism – came to Eastern Europe as an idea which was to launch the first Russian revolution, the Jews were among the avant-garde of the upheaval.

There is thus a dialectical pattern in the Jewish awakening and liberation from the bonds of frustration caused by the double ideology of territorial 'return' and supernatural deliverance. First liberalism fought against Christianity's unity of state and religion in the West. Liberalism then came to Eastern Europe and created an upheaval in ideas among the oppressed. The Jews grasped liberalism as a way out of their double quandary. The younger Jewish generation refused to content itself with the goal of liberalism and went further – either towards emigration, or towards an ideology of total social revolt, such as socialism then was. In this way the Zionist revolution was born.

In a word: the moment religion disappeared as the main goal, the spirit of the times – liberalism in the West, revolutionary socialism and anarchism in Eastern Europe – came to replace it in the breasts of the younger Jewish generation. According to the degree of their continued identification with their cultural (Jewish religious) background, or their rejection of it, the European Jews became believing or semi-religious emigrants farther West; or liberal nineteenth-century revolutionaries against autocracy; or Zionists; or, in the more extreme or oppressed cases, socialists.

The spectrum of revolt was, then, quite variegated. Its motivation, however, was simple enough: like the rest of Europe, European Jewry was freeing itself from the moorings of an outdated belief-morality. It happened that for the Jewish people in the Diaspora this liberation involved a reappraisal of the whole *Gestalt* of Jewishness; a reappraisal, painful and traumatic as it is, which has not been concluded to this day.

For Jewish belief remained, in a way, as important as ever. Two thousand years of living landless and fanatically devoted to the precepts of a state-oriented religion gave strong predominance to the characteristics of Judaism that can be considered universal (the same characteristics which inspired the inception of Christianity): a reasonable (for the epoch) code of ethics; a definite feeling that right is right and wrong is wrong; a conviction of the moral superiority of 'us' as opposed to 'them'; and the willingness to incur pain, suffering, shame and discomfort to win what Jewish ethics proposed as a recompense to the virtuous.

Where does such a viewpoint lead when the source of belief disappears? Jews in Western Europe tried to assimilate, with a vengeance. This often provoked violent reaction from anti-Semitic and other auto-centred nationalist or Christian movements, but until the advent of Hitlerism in Germany Jews in

Western Europe did remarkably well as a liberated part of the bourgeois society of the nineteenth and early twentieth centuries.

The gradual disappearance of religious belief as a basic component of national separateness was as marked in Western Europe as in other parts of the world. But while assimilation to the Western way of life was a normal part of the evolution of advanced capitalism, in Russia, Poland and the Baltic lands in the early twentieth century the Jews had to assimilate to the *revolutionary* reality of these areas:* Tsarism still exploited the existence of the Jews to misdirect popular fury against these tortured minorities, as did the anti-Semitic rulers of the rest of the Slav, Balkan and Baltic countries. The Jews had now the choice of dying, escaping or fighting the system.

Two movements loomed large on the East European Jewish scene: Poalei Zion, or the Toilers of Zion, a Zionist-socialist movement later to become the syndicalist Israeli Labour Party; and the Bund, a Jewish-socialist movement which decried emigration to Palestine, asking instead for recognition of the social and cultural rights of the Jewish proletariat as a class belonging to a separate people, with its own language, Yiddish, and with a separate culture and even separate economic interests.

The importance of the role played by Jews in the revolutionary upheavals of Eastern Europe was due in no small measure to the fact that many of them were workers: the phenomenon of the rich Jew was, proportionally, less apparent than in the West. Many Jews in Western Europe already belonged to the intermediary-exploiting classes, and many of them in Eastern Europe of the same period to the classes which were economically most exploited – often in the most barbarously cruel fashion. But in spite of this, all the Jews acted at times as a group, as a separate people or element, producing internal class-contradictions of their own, but also with common interests. And this united but helpless separateness, which presented so tempting a prey to all and sundry

* A similar thing happens nowadays to the Jewish communities of South America in social ferment. It seems that a capsule-like community is condemned to live outside the framework of its time's changes – and pays, inevitably, the price in xenophobia and suffering.

caused non-Jewish fanatics and exploiters to regard the Jews as a convenient scapegoat. The exploitation-cum-witch-hunting relaxed only when the Jews proved by means of physical violence that they were not going to submit to it.

There was, then, a double aspect to the Jewish problem. One part, the cultural-psychological, remained constant throughout historical evolution; while the other part, the economic, changed with changing circumstances from the age of slavery to early feudalism, to monarchy, to early capitalism, to imperialist capitalism, and state capitalism. The Jews remained 'a problem' because their national personality remained separate.

For a long time this was due to religious fanaticism, which kept them separate and suffering, but also alive as a people. Thus, as always in history, belief fulfilled both a positive and a destructive role. In the later years of the nineteenth century, religious motivation largely disappeared; many Jews stopped believing their redemption would come from the efforts of the Messiah.

From that moment on, these Jews faced a choice: they could try to identify with their surroundings – as the liberal assimilants of Western Europe did, but usually at the cost of their national and historical characteristics; or, in the absence of the Messiah, they could 'liberate' themselves – that is, create the conditions under which normal (whether bourgeois or socialist-revolutionary) life could be lived. This, too, involved abandoning their separateness. Hence, in the late nineteenth and early twentieth centuries, many assimilated Jews of Western Europe completed their integration by adopting one of the main attributes of bourgeois success – the Christian faith. In an age which separated belief and politics (if not church and state), this adoption was often purely formal, as in the case of the Jewish German poet Heinrich Heine. None the less it should be stressed that, while subjectively the capitalist or liberal individual had freed himself both from the need to believe and from the limitations which belief imposed on his use of the means of production (and on his enjoyment of their fruits), society as a whole was – as society generally is – two steps behind individual expediency. Autocracy was still rampant, the state throughout Western Europe still paid lip-service to Christianity. It was expedient for 'liberalized' Jews to leave behind their anyway redundant religion.

This abandonment, however, created a deep feeling of outrage among the rest of the European Jewish community: those, for instance, who did not profit directly from liberal capitalism; those who remained believers; those who naturally identified the Jewish capitalists who had turned Christian from reasons of expediency with the rest of their oppressors or class enemies; and those who, while wishing to preserve their separate identity – their 'us-ness' in the face of a provedly hostile 'them' – had become disenchanted with the belief which was basic to their separateness.

A quandary had been created. To those who refused to give up the props of belief, but had enough sanity left to be aware of the changes in the society which surrounded them, the solution was evident. It was Zionist nationalism. It is usually from a partial ability to see things, while another part of the brain remains obscured by prejudices, that revolutionary movements arise.

Zionism was no exception to this rule. In a way Zionism was the Jews' 'liberal revolution', affirming the Jewish separate entity while taking a leaf from the liberalism of Western Europe; but it was liberalism as seen from inside the cage in which the Jews had been confined.

In time this borrowing from liberalism was fatally to influence Zionist ethics as far as the Palestinian population was concerned. It should be understood why this was so. As we are not in search of a villain, it would be futile simply to condemn early Zionism as 'colonialist' or 'settler-minded' in its outlook (although it was self-confessedly both these things). What must be understood is the Zionist Jews' place in the chain of oppression, cruelty and reaction. Its place was not at the beginning of the chain. Archaic belief on one hand, and the cruel class-and-race exploitation they had suffered on the other, gave rise to the liberal brand of settler-capitalism-cum-Zionist-socialism of the Jews of Palestine.

The economic ideas changed, and the Jews adapted to them, each according to his own class interests. But the fatal triplets – belief, separateness and oppression – remained. In a world intrinsically opposed in its cultural structure to international integration, it was impossible for most Jews to become 'internationalists' in the fullest sense. The beliefs, behaviour, languages and enmity of those belonging to other (and more numerous) in-groups forced even the most revolutionary Jews to a continuation of their separateness. And indeed how could it be otherwise under the pressure of so many different in-groups, all totally self-centred, egotistical in the strictest sense of the word?

Since 'separate' surroundings were necessary for the evolution (or auto-liberation) of the Jews, it was only natural that the assimilated and emancipated turned towards their past. The lore of the ancient has a particular fascination. Religion may dwindle in importance. The teachings of one's childhood remain important even after they are outgrown.

What was more natural, then, than that the Jews should turn their eyes towards Zion, the Zion they had prayed for as children, or for which their parents and their parents' parents had prayed, as a symbol of all that was free and entirely their own? The Holy Land, the Promised Land, the Land of Israel was an inseparable part of the dreams of the Jews. And woe to the man who tries to stand in the path of another's dreams.

*

Having tried to understand why Zionism appeared and what forces provoked its appearance on the world scene, let us see how the Zionist whirlpool prepared the creation of the State of Israel – a new, changed version of Jewish identity in the past, of Jewish identity in the Diaspora.

1870: The first Jewish agricultural school, Mikweh Israel, was founded. The first Jewish colonizers, no more than a cultural minority going to its source of inspiration, installed themselves in Turkish-ruled Palestine. The Jewish population of Palestine, including religious mystics who had lived there for centuries, was by 1895 less than ten per cent of the total population of Moslems, Christians, Armenians, Turks and so on. In approximate numbers there were 47,000 Jews and 453,000 others, mostly Arabic rather than Turkish speakers. At least 350,000 of the total could be called 'native Palestinians', that is people born in the country, and whose parents were born there.

1895: In a quarter of a century, the movement of Liberal Jewish Revolution had exploded in Europe and elsewhere. A first Jewish settlers' village, Petah Tikwa, was created in 1878. In Western Europe Pinsker published the Zionists' Manifesto: *Autoemancipation*. Zionism started to become a comprehensive political movement. It was strengthened by the climactic, anti-Semitic Dreyfus trial in France, which awakened monarchist, nationalist and anti-liberal feelings against that symbol of 'alien' influence, the French Jews, who, being a new cultural element, once they were naturalized wholesale by means of the Crémieux legislation under Napoleon, enriched and changed the texture of European life. A non-religious Jewish journalist from Vienna, Theodor Herzl, was present at the trial. He got the feel of his times and transferred the feeling to the Jewish population of Europe through his political invention: Zionism, the transplantation of Jewish modernization and cultural assimilation to a single country. A trickle of emigrants followed his advice, and the utopian design laid down in his book, *Der Judenstaat*, the Jews' own state: they emigrated to the old country of the Prayer Book. The settlers' villages of Rishon Letzion, Zihron Yaakov and Rosh Pinah were founded.

At this point some 26,212,900 *dunams* of a total Palestinian area of 26,320,000 *dunams* were either in the hands of the Turkish rulers or in those of Arab feudal landlords, many of them living outside the country's borders. The enormous majority of the people actually living on the land, the *fellahin*, were for all practical purposes serfs. Nonetheless, they lived there, on and off the land, as the parents of many of them had lived there before them for untold generations. There were also a number of migrant Arabs, a minority of small landholders, and another of city-merchants. The number of Jewish settlements by 1895 was fourteen.

1900: The Zionist movement became the movement of national liberation of the Jewish people, in Europe and elsewhere in the West. Some first fissures appeared in the coherent national-liberal ideas of Herzl when they clashed with the religious and traditional heritage of the more conservative Jews. His 'I do not care' attitude towards the site where the Jewish state should be created gave way to an acceptance of the dictates of national obsessions. In 1897 the first Zionist Congress was held at Basle, and there the first religious and traditionalist voices were clearly heard. The congress adopted a programme stating as its aims the organizing of large-scale Jewish colonization in Palestine, the fight for an international acknowledgement of the Jewish right to exist in Palestine, and the creation of a permanent Zionist body. In 1898 Herzl met the German Kaiser, Wilhelm II, in Constantinople. The Kaiser refused to help the Zionists and pushed forward, instead, the Palestine colonization plans of the German religious Templaı sect.

At this point Herzl, like the whole early Zionist movement, was still under the influence of 'European' ideas and concepts: the 'indigenous' population of the Asian and African continents were considered as second-class human beings, at that time; liberal revolutionaries in the West did not yet consider granting equal rights to peoples with unequal cultures and technologies. Colonization, development, are the 'white man's burden'. The deep hypocrisy of economic exploitation and cultural exclusiveness hid behind the slogans of keeping aloft the twin flags of culture and religion. The Zionist movement was unaware of this interplay behind the scenes of Western imperialism. It simply adapted itself, as any 'good European' movement would, to the facts at hand, and was supremely opportunistic in its revolutionary aim: the independence of the Jews. Only the Western powers could help a dispossessed people. And the indigenous population of Palestine, of which they had only a theoretical knowledge, could be humanely dispensed with; later Herzl was to write:

> When we occupy the land, we shall bring immediate benefits to the state that receives us. We must expropriate gently the private property of the estates assigned to us. We shall try to spirit the penniless population across the border, by procuring employment for it in the transit countries, while denying it any employment in our own country.
>
> ... The property-owners will come over to our side. Both the process

of expropriation and the removal of the poor must be carried out discreetly and circumspectly. Let the owners of immovable property believe that they are cheating us, selling us more than they are worth. But we are not going to sell them anything back . . .

The voluntary expropriation will be accomplished through our secret agents. The company will pay excessive prices. We shall then sell only to Jews and all the real estate will be traded only among Jews. To be sure, we shall not be able to do this by declaring other sales invalid. Even if this did not run counter to the modern sense of Justice, our power would not suffice . . .

For the voluntary expropriation we shall have to use local subagents who must not know that their employer himself is a secret agent who takes instructions from the centralized 'Commission for Property Purchases'. These secret purchases must be carried out *simultaneously*, as upon the pressing of an electrical button. Our secret agents, who will appear over there as purchasers on their own account, will receive the signal: *Marchez!*

. . . If we move into a region where there are wild animals to which the Jews are not accustomed, big snakes, etc., I shall use the natives, prior to giving them employment in the transit countries, for the extermination of these animals. High premiums for snake skins, etc., as well as their spawn.*

A humane, intelligent and utopian scheme of settlement and exploitation; but all the same, a settlement of a non-indigenous population *in place* of the indigenous population. The basis of Zionism, the very root of the Jewish movement of Liberal Liberation, was the expropriation of the natives. Even at its inception, the Palestinian-Israeli problem was not one of who shall rule but rather of who shall live in the land.

On the other hand, Herzl was quite aware of the need for a secular, non-religious, albeit solely Jewish state. His revolutionary movement was pitted against the very roots of Jewish belief; he could not know that the sheer weight of two thousand years of psychoses, superstitions, persecutions and beliefs could sink his liberal ideas without trace.

In *Der Judenstaat* there is a letter by Herzl:

* *The Complete Diaries of Theodor Herzl*, edited by Raphael Patai, translation by Harry Zohn, Vol. I, pp. 88, 89, 90, 98.

> ... Shall we, then, end up with a theocracy?
>
> We shall not. We shall not give free reign to our clergy's theocratic inclinations. We shall know how to confine them to their temples ... they must be venerated as becoming to their distinguished role – but in matters of the state that appoints them, they must not interfere. Otherwise, they will create internal and external problems.*

Here he is again, the liberal-revolutionary thinker, caught in the whirlpool of a period of change, but without any deeper insight into its psycho-cultural roots.

1901: For the first time Herzl 'went native' and directly approached Abd-El-Hamid, Sultan of Turkey and Caliph of Islam. He suggested financial help to develop the natural resources of the Ottoman empire. In return he asked for Jewish mass-immigration into Palestine. One might surmise that the first part of his scheme was designed as a two-bladed sword: to attract Jewish capital to the Zionist idea, and to attract the Sultan's attention to the Jews' plight. But the Sultan rejected Herzl's scheme, and in addition refused to grant a charter to a 'Jewish-Ottoman Colonization Association for the Settlement of Palestine and Syria'.

1902: The Zionist Organization's Executive asked Great Britain to grant rights to autonomous Jewish settlements in certain parts of the Sinai desert – which had and has a very sparse indigenous population† and which, at that time, was quite unconnected, politically, with Egypt.

But negotiations broke down. At this point, there was already a British appraisal of the possibilities of exploiting the Arab feudal leaders. The Turkish Sultanate, which was also the ally of an enemy nearer home, the German Kaiser, caused British policy to be most careful in its dealings with the Arabs – and the embryonic Zionists.

1903: The British government offered the Zionist movement, which was fast becoming a powerful lobby in the British Isles,

* *The Jewish State*, 11th edition.

† A 1968 Census carried out by the Israeli army found only 35,000–40,000 migrants in the whole of the peninsula, most of them Bedouin, some Mongol. To this one must add a few hundred Egyptian administrators who escaped during the war.

the territory of Uganda, for the establishment of a Jewish National Home. The sixth Zionist Congress agreed, by a vote of 295 to 175. Herzl was for the offer. Only in 1905, after the death of the visionary leader of Zionism, was the Uganda offer definitively rejected by the Zionist movement. Chaim Weizmann, later first President of Israel, wrote on this episode:

> Among the arguments put forward against this scheme was the fact that the few white settlers, mostly English, who were already in Uganda, would fight against a Jewish influx into their territory, which would not accommodate more than a very limited number.*

Of the black natives of Uganda, as of the Palestine natives, not a constructive word. The logic of Western culture runs true to the spirit of Western liberalism.

1904–6: Revolution in Russia. The crudest form of anti-Semitism was used, once again, by the Tsarist repression as one means of turning aside the mounting flood of popular anger. Untold hundreds of thousands of Jews fled westwards. It is estimated that some *five million Jews* emigrated from Russia, the Baltic countries and a few other central European territories to America and other places at the end of the nineteenth and the start of the twentieth centuries. They included what is now called in Israel 'the second Alyah', the second wave of organized Zionist immigration: it was East European, socialist, formed of men and women who tried to throw away their artisans' or pedlar's heritage and went to Palestine to become 'tillers of the soil and builders of roads'. They brought with them a truly radical approach to many problems – but except in a few cases this approach was confined to the framework of the Jewish exclusive entity. There was very little actual mingling with the native Palestinians. Mutual distrust, and the fact that the European Jews were confined for so many centuries to the Ghettoes, added to this ideology and to economic differences. This 'second wave' of immigrants to Palestine was to some extent the result of official British policy: in 1906 Parliament, at the insistence of the prime minister, Lord Balfour, passed a bill restricting specifically Jewish immigration

* *Trial and Error*, Chaim Weizmann, London, 1950, p. 115.

into Britain, thus closing one more door on the Russian victims' faces.

In 1909 Tel-Aviv, the first purely Jewish city, was created near the port of Jaffa. In 1911 Deganiah, the first Kvutzah or non-communistic cooperative, was founded. Jews living in the Western world and naturally attracted to Western civilization started betting on the ascendancy of the West – and particularly of France and Great Britain – in the Levant. As history was to prove, they were right. They had all the necessary equipment to succeed – except friends: they still suffered from the dislike and discrimination inherited from the ages of Christian cultural exclusiveness in Europe. This dislike, and sometimes the *Realpolitik* considerations of the imperialist West, hindered their task considerably. The Western powers, and Great Britain in particular, were not loth to try to exploit both Jews and Arabs for their own advantage in the Middle East. In 1914 Chaim Weizmann met Lloyd George, the Chancellor of the Exchequer, and Herbert Samuel, then President of the Local Government Board. 'The Zionists gave us a definite promise that if the Allies committed themselves to giving facilities for the establishment of a national home for the Jews in Palestine, they would do their best to rally Jewish sentiment and support throughout the world to the Allied Cause,'* wrote Lloyd George about this and other meetings. The proposal was clearly viewed with favour by both British statesmen.

It is important to note this point. Some anti-Zionist writers and politicians have voiced the simplistic idea that in the first phase of its existence, from 1897 to 1914,† political Zionism was oriented towards Turkey as well as Germany. This is incorrect. Turkey was for the Zionists as a whole, and for Herzl and Weizmann in particular, part of the Levant, an Oriental and despotic power with which one might at best come to terms in order to 'expropriate Palestine gently'. The Kaiser's Germany was something else again: it was the cradle of German-speaking culture,

* *Royal Commission Report*, Jerusalem, Government Press, 1937.

† See particularly the Maptzen Programme, *The Other Israel*, Tel-Aviv, 1968.

which was – through Yiddish, which is strongly influenced by the German language – the culture then nearest to most of the European Jews, including Theodor Herzl himself. It was also the only country which had direct influence on the Ottoman Porte. Thus what appears to be a 'Turkish' orientation was, in fact, a matter of strategy used *against* the 'wily oriental' Sultan.

Although Zionism was decidedly pro-Western, through its links with rationalism and liberalism, there was a further consideration. In the words of Max Nordau, a writer and politician, and Herzl's deputy in the Zionist movement, 'our aspirations point to Palestine as a compass points to the north, therefore we must orient ourselves towards those powers under whose influence Palestine happens to be.'* Therefore the orientation of Zionism was, and remains to this day, towards the Western world, and whatever power happens to be at its head. One might treat with Abd-El-Hamid, the Sultan of Istambul and the Caliph of all Islam; but one would surely find a backing for one's economic enterprises in the West. And as Great Britain and France were, through the more liberal character of their society, less Christian-dominated and less closed to 'strangers' such as the Jews, the enemies of the Kaiser also found themselves under pressure from the Zionist movement, a pressure that some of them, including the old-style militaristic imperialists of the War Office, resented and despised, but which was viewed more hopefully by Lord Balfour, and the bright young men of Whitehall, and later of the Arab Office, then starting to make their impact on British policy. For after Abd-El-Hamid's refusal to contemplate Herzl's offers, and since powerful interests bound Germany to Turkey, the Zionists and some Allied statesmen discovered they had, possibly, common interests.

1914: Herbert Samuel, the second practising Jew to hold ministerial office in England and then President of the Local Government Board, addressed a Zionist Paper to the British Cabinet. He stressed the political and military advantages to be gained from a predominantly Jewish Palestine. The *Manchester Guardian* adhered to this line in 1915, so becoming the first non-Jewish publication to give sympathetic expression to the ideas of

* Mentioned in *The Other Israel*, op. cit.

Zionism. In Britain the main overt arguments for a Jewish Palestine were the defence of the Suez Canal and the route to India, the need to counteract Turkish influence on the Islam-believing Arabs and the rest of the indigenous population of the Levant, and the humanitarian need to help the most persecuted – and yet Christian-revered – 'race' to find peace at last. The post-Victorian mind quite seriously believed that by helping Zionism – by helping oneself to a biggish slice of the Levant – one might assist Ahasuerus, the Wandering Jew, finally to find a place of rest.

Underneath this romantic picture lay less noble considerations. The role of modern Western imperialism in the Middle East has been that of an 'intermediary', or 'helpful' power which encroaches gradually upon the former exploiters of the Levant giving its protection, assistance and advice to one part of the area against the other in order to end by ruling both directly. The bad experience of the Crusades, by which the Western Europeans had tried with catastrophic results to supplant the indigenous population of the Holy Land, for the benefit of Christian settlers, had given the later planners of Western imperialism their lead: Lord Palmerston refused the alliance with Egypt's Mohammed Ali who offered his aid 'against Russia', preferring to 'protect' Egypt directly and thus to set aside its cotton produce for the factories of the British Isles; France applied the *Mission Colonisatrice* to Algeria, and after a short interregnum conquered the country and colonized it directly, thus furthering her metropolitan economy and relieving the poorer and semi-feudal French provinces, where manpower was so cheap that people lived below subsistence level. In 1840 Britain 'helped' the Ottomans against her main enemy of that time, imperial Russia, and became firmly entrenched in Egypt and Syria. From 1882, when Anglo-French troops destroyed the force of the first 'Arab Junta man', Ahmed Arabi, first Sir Evelyn Baring and then Lord Cromer installed themselves as British Agents, in reality absolute rulers of Egypt, their armed forces backing every command. In 1899 Britain brought off a similar coup in the south, in Africa. When the back of the religious insurrection of the Mahdi had finally been broken, the Sudan came under the 'joint rule' of Britain and Egypt – the latter still under the control of a British Governor General, 'appointed by the Khedif'.

There was plenty of experience to show imperial Great Britain and colonialist France the way to further penetration into the Middle East. Unfortunately for these powers – as for the Zionist movement – the First World War was altogether the wrong moment to attempt further incursions: the local population had awakened very gradually and slowly, it is true, but awakened all the same to the possibility of its independence from foreign powers.

Thus we reach the most crucial age for the future of Palestine: the years just before, during and after the First World War. It was a time when various middling to big imperialist powers struggled to expand their sources of raw materials, to magnify their ego, and to create in the colonies second-class human beings 'in their own image'. It is against the background of this imperialist struggle that the devious politicking of British, French, Turk, Jewish Zionists and Arab neo-feudalists must be seen. Meanwhile the indigenous population of the eastern Mediterranean coast – now Syria, Israel and the Lebanon – looked on helplessly, held by the twin chains of foreign-exploited relative prosperity and political backwardness. The fact that this relatively fertile area has always been a thoroughfare of imperialist interests made the coastal zone more prosperous than the inner, arid areas of the Middle East. On the other hand, as so often happens, political militancy awakened among those who were most backward: the Bedouin and Arab chieftains of the arid zone. This probably happened because they were, as true desert sons always are, much less dependent upon their own, precarious, sources of subsistence: the plain-pastures and sedentary agriculture of the oases and fertile spots. Some of them even had a tradition of living by the sword, as marauders and parasitic attackers on the city-dwellers and their caravans. Their independent and rebellious spirit was further sustained by the fact that it is much easier to cow and submit a man who has an income, a trade and a fortune, than one who has a sword and a camel.

The true areas of political might, on the other hand, ran at the beginnings of the twentieth century much farther north and much farther south: the first through Cairo, which, although Arab in culture and Turkish by political fiction, was at the start of the First World War the seat of Lord Kitchener, *de facto* Governor of Egypt, whose title, British Agent, reflected admirably his true task; the second axis of political might still ran through Constantinople, where the Porte ensured ruthless and quite parasitic Turkish rule over a biggish segment of the Eastern world. From there the lines of power ran on northwards, and were lost in the shadows of intrigue, fastened thoroughly as they were to the interests of Wilhelm II of Prussia and Germany. Imperial Russia, too, looked with an anxious and envious eye towards the Dardanelles and beyond; keen to occupy, if the chance was only given her, the southern coasts of the Black Sea and particularly the Straits of the Dardanelles, which alone ensured Russia an armed naval thoroughfare to the Mediterranean Sea.

But even without the Tsarist player's decisive influence, the Middle Eastern playground of 1910 and after was no less passionate and no less confused than the checkerboard of the 1970s. Palestine, in particular, was neither the 'empty area' which some Zionists wished it to be nor part of the 'Arab state in the making' the pan-Arab propaganda tried *post factum* to make it seem. It was simply a subdeveloped area, rather nearer the European continent than some, in which a number of forces tried to make themselves felt. One of them was an alliance of indigenous forces and tribes, which the neo-feudal rulers tried to turn into a united area – a single absolutist Arab kingdom – and this by fighting each other as well as the infidels, and by encroaching upon each other's feudal holdings.

The prosperous coastal area, and particularly the Syrian part of the coast, were both less independent than the desert-rulers' fiefs and more given to political intrigue and plotting for freedom. This reflected their greater mercantile and intellectual development. In the Arab camp, then, there was a clear-cut difference between the holders of military power – the rulers of the inner territory's Bedouin tribes and the Arab officers in Abd-El-Hamid's army – and the politically conscious and economically developed coastal area city-dwellers. It took the despoilation of almost the whole Palestinian population to allow the latter to develop their own awareness of the need for arms and power. So much for 'political awareness' *per se*.

One can easily understand why this coastal population, Arabs, Armenians, Assyrians, Druzes, Christians of half a dozen hues, even Blacks, did not at first oppose – indeed, welcomed – the first waves of Jewish immigrants. For them, in spite of the warning of the community-rulers and extremist pan-Moslem propagandists, this was just another industrious and well-rooted component of a multi-national, multi-denominational population. For most of these pedlars, artisans, middle-class shopkeepers and small landowners, the political implications of Zionism were, as yet, pretty unclear; and the increasing number of Jews, who anyway had never entirely left the country and had been present in Palestine throughout the ages, if in very small numbers, was somehow reassuring. They were supposed to be, and felt by many to be, a bridge towards the West. It is interesting to note, *en passant*, that the relatively prosperous Sephardi, or Eastern Jews, with their knowledge of Levantine usage, were highly regarded, while the dispossessed Russian- and Polish-born immigrants were somewhat despised and mistrusted. In today's Israel the exact contrary happens: the Western-born Ashkenasis, the 'Europeans', are the supposed harbingers of culture, while the Sephardis and Oriental Jews – although in a slight majority – are mistrusted and considered in need of re-education. This is today particularly true of Jews from Northern Africa and Iraq.

The Zionists, however, were not just a pack of additional pedlars coming to an underdeveloped area. They were a revolutionary vanguard, the spearhead of a conquering army. Their aim was to settle *and to replace* the indigenous inhabitants although 'without hurting them', as Herzl wrote. They were totally unaware of the psychological, economic and social background of the native, exploited lower classes. Moreover the fluid delineation, under Turkish rule, of the areas' boundaries and inner 'borders' justified, up to a point, the shrugging-away of the national 'ownership' of a given area. Had the aim of Zionism been simply imperialistic – domination of the area, and integration of the natives in a Jewish-led commonwealth – there is little doubt that the confrontation with the Arabs would have been weaker and perhaps short-lived. But as their aim was colonization and a settlers' state, a polarization of all 'Arabs' – or Arabic-speaking indigenous inhabitants – against the 'foreigners' was inevitable. Indeed it is only due to the triumph of Arab feudal independence elsewhere – specifically in Iraq, the Nejd, Hedjaz and Transjordan – that the confrontation did not become, from the first years, violent and radical. As it was, the various neo-feudal rebels thought Palestine was but one bit of the hoped-for feudal Arab kingdom; and if that bit fell to Great Britain no great harm was done; it would be taken back when Britain finally left. The facts were different, and three generations of militarily strong, economically supported and politically conscious Palestinian Zionists and later Israelis changed the picture with the utmost finality. The United Arab Kingdom did not make its appearance in the Levant, and rather more modest feudal estates had to be cut off from the dead body of the former Turkish dominion; each Arab ruler, each imperialist Western power, carved himself his slice. Zionism too sliced away, increasingly, patiently and prudently; and the native inhabitants of Palestine thus became bereft of their own natural surroundings, virtually expropriated, the 'Wandering Jews' of the Middle East. Thus history went full circle; and the final irony of Jewish destiny was made apparent.

3 Arab Nationalism in Palestine before 1920

Against the tide of Zionist immigration blew the eastern wind of Arab nationalism. As happens when two elements fight, a tremendous storm blew up and to this very day it has not abated. But this storm did little to stop the gradual rise of the tide. On the contrary, it has persistently threatened to destroy both warring factions; and the stronger the forces deployed, the bigger this threat has become.

It is important to understand what this pan-Arab, or simply Arab, nationalism was and now is. This question, not needed in discussing the emergence of a national revolution in the European West, is necessary and basic to an understanding of the emergence of feelings and forces of a national entity which was previously conditioned by belief – in a similar, if not parallel, way to that which has conditioned the evolution of Israeli nationalism.

While the cultural trappings of Zionism, and indeed the sources of its patriotism and belief, are five thousand years old, Arab belief is 'only' some thousand years old: 1390-odd years old,to be exact. This gives it a – comparatively – strong malleability.

Moslem history starts with the rallying of some dwellers of the Arab peninsula, both idolators and Jews, to the standard of a new Prophet, Mohammed Ibn-And-Allah, who gleaned from Judaism and Christianity a good deal of material, applied it to his own brand of puritan teaching, and proclaimed the result as God's own revelation. In Islam, the coupling of information, communication and belief was complete, even more totalitarian than in Judaism or Dark Ages Christianity. Furthermore, as it evolved, the Moslem doctrine of total predestination brought about such absurd concomitants as the injunction not to teach anything outside a meagre curriculum of Koran readings, writing and some basic arithmetic. It took the half-Persian half-Arab Caliph of Baghdad, Abd-Allah El-Mamoun, son of the fabled Haroun El-Rashid, to abolish, in A.D. 812, these limitations and open the 'Arab world' wide to synthesis with other cultures, as the Arab population had long ago begun to mix ethnically with its conquered and with allied foreign peoples. But by then the pattern of suspicion and intolerance had been set by almost three hundred years of imperial expansion. This heritage of suspicion and of hate of all 'infidels' was to become through the centuries both the pretext for economic domination and the main stumbling block of succeeding Arab imperial dynasties, the parallel to the Jewish 'You chose us out of every people' feeling; it is indeed the basic limitation to the intermingling and cooperation of Islam with other nationalities in the Middle East to this very day.

It began with the wandering desert-tribes of Hejaz, and later of the Nejd, in what is now Saudi Arabia. From among them Mohammed gathered his followers. Islam, together with the extremely precarious economic conditions of the Arab peninsula's dwellers, brought about a mighty wish for conquest and expansion. The basic mentality of the Bedouin desert-pirate only too readily adapted itself to the needs of the religious Islamic crusades, while the conversion of the assailed and at times exploiting commerce-islands of the deserts, the oasis-cities of Arabia, into hinterland bases of the new empire was also a natural development.

As long as Islam was the new driving force of a quasi-national identity, religious in content but imperialistic in its economic implications, all was 'normal' and well for the Arabs. The Abbasid dynasty was a neo-feudal organism, and its conquests and victories over Christians, Persians and Egyptians were a 'normal' development of history. But as the territory covered by the new belief-imperialism became too big for efficient communications, the usual fragmentation of power appeared, and a new dynasty was created and built up its own framework of reference, in its confrontation with the Christian West, in Spain and France.

Meanwhile, back in the country of 'origin', Arabia, another new dynasty, the Omayyads, was in ascendance.

There, the influence of the Persians made itself predominantly felt; in the West, in northern Africa and Spain, the Jews and converted Christians became a healthy addition to the till then 'pure' Moslem way of life. The mixtures proved to be a blessing to the Caliphate of the East and the Arab reign in the West. In fact, each time the so-called Arab world was able to leave, or forced to move out of its narrow Moslem frame of reference – while being driven on by this selfsame belief to further conquests – the Arabs evolved a further step. In general, it can be said that the Middle East in its totality, and the Arab culture and rule particularly, benefited most strongly when cultural and genetic cross-pollination took place.

As far as politics go, the Middle East continued to be the thoroughfare and hunting preserve of one imperial power – home-bred or foreign – after another. After the armies of old, the various Moslem sects now erected their own dynasties and short-lived kingdoms. In each case the domination was in the name of Mohammedan belief, and in each case it was accompanied by extreme cruelty, exploitation of the conquered, and the total oppression of all 'infidel' minorities. Only two identities were exempt from *total* repression by Islam: the Christians and the Jews, who, according to Moslem belief, do not have to be converted as long as they pay tribute. This was a very convenient religious rule in an area in which Christians represented strong Western powers, militarily and politically able to use persecution of its co-believers as a pretext for further crusades; and where the Jews were among the richest merchants of the Arab countries. It may also have been adopted because of Mohammed's own background, which was strongly influenced by both Judaism and Christianity; but the fact remains that, as so often happens, the political and economic interests and the precepts of belief coincided for the ruling classes of the Arab world.

Thus, the exclusiveness of Arab belief was, in two important points, dissimilar to the belief of the Jews of the Diaspora: first, it was the belief of a victorious, religious, conquering imperialism, and as such used as a tool of repression and not only as a tool of defence. Second, it was a prolesytizing belief, assimilating into itself believers from other creeds and tolerating in its midst the existence of two competing religions – Judaism and Christianity. Were human history a rational process of evolution rather than a tragi-comedy of accumulative aberration, Islam might have developed to become the main ideology of the West. Unfortunately for the Arab identity, there were a few built-in brakes in its belief: and as political force and geopolitical rule became stronger and more extended, the natural need to keep the past with them, not to let things change, and above all not to let any kind of alien influence alter their identity, first eliminated the drive for further influence exerted by the Arab's belief; and, later, exchanged the consolidation of temporal power for the rule of belief alone. Islam's religious fanatics, such as the 'Moslem Brotherhood', are quite right to say that, once the asceticism of primitive Mohammedanism was checked, decay set in: because of their precarious and ascetic way of life, fanaticism was the natural framework for the imperialism of the desert-Arabs; but the ascendancy of the Abbasids and Omayyads, while culturally beneficial in the extreme, led inevitably to the usual political decay and fall of self-centred cultures, whose ruthlessness is limited by their economic interests and pleasures. The fragmentation of the Arab empire, and the softening of the Arab's *mores*, took care of the more dynamic features of Arab expansion.

As for the more negative aspects of Islam, they were enough by themselves to condemn the Arab world to a subordinate role in history. The rules of Islam had been lifted from other religions and re-invented by Mohammed for the specific needs of a half-nomad, half-feudal society. The nomads were the dynamic element of this revolution, its revolutionary class, as it were. After Islam triumphed and went on to become the standard-bearer of an imperialist society, the puritanical precepts of the Arabs' belief had to be used as a class-instrument not by the 'desert revolutionaries' of Bedouin blood but rather by merchants who had become aristocrats and by deputy warlords who lived in the shade of these rulers and occasionally supplanted them.

As happened to Judaism and to Christianity before it, Islam's social purpose changed with society itself: not because somebody debased a religious belief but rather because belief follows the lines of least stress in social structure – being a conservative instrument of power, it naturally adapts itself to the ruling classes, even when these change with the changing economy and the politics of a given area. Islam's main drawback, from the Arabs' own viewpoint, was that its aggressive proselytizing ensured imperialist confrontations with ever wider foreign powers; and yct it had built-in brakes, which precluded the development of education and culture according to the unhampered needs of a merchant-imperialist society. To this must be added, of course, further layers of reaction, of conservatism and of ignorance, the product of hereditary rule – and the fragmentation of the Arab empire into roughly three areas of influence: the Arab-Persian countries; the Eastern, or coastal-Mediterranean, including Egypt; and the Spanish and North African civilization.

The birth of Arab belief-driven imperialism happened at the end of the European Dark Ages. In the West, the Renaissance, with its liberated technological and economic drive, was in the ascendant. If one has to choose between two fanaticisms, the Christian and the Moslem brands of belief, the Moslems were undoubtedly the more interesting. But over the centuries Islam continued to be a hindrance to both technological and political growth, while becoming the main instrument of the Ottoman rule over the Arabs and the rest of the Middle Eastern peoples (as well as some of the European ones). Europe, on the other hand, had been able to overcome the more galling restrictions of Dark Ages Christianity. The West successfully penetrated the Middle East, and has not left it since. It was, in terms of dynamic strength, the 'better man'.

Roughly, one may sketch three different eras of Arab identity, identical with the historical development of Arab imperial and religious might and decay: the three periods during which Arab identity, as it exists and develops today, was formed.

The Arab Crusades (c.A.D. 571–800) – from Mohammed's coming to the decline of the Abbasid dynasty in the East and of Omayyad rule in Spain and the north-western coast of Africa. This era was one of religious identification, in which other national and religious identities were drawn into the whirlpool of the politico-religious *Umma-El-Islam*, the 'Nation of Islam', by being either assimilated or dominated by it – and at times just by co-existing in its midst. The Arab language and the majority culture of Islam became the main instruments of communication and cooperation and the means of enjoying leisure and luxury, on the intellectual level. Inevitably, religion tinted this leisure-and-work culture of a multi-national society gone Arab; but the cultural patterns of the Bedouin stayed dominant, the background and backbone of the songs, poetry and philosophy of the empire. On the other hand, Islam became a restraint which did not allow the Abbasids to evolve as dynamically in the cultural field as they did politically. It was only thanks to their intermingling with the Persians, Jews and Christians of their conquered territories that the Abbasids were able to stage a cultural comeback and to flourish in an intercultural commonwealth, although this too was dominated by the old limitations of Islam to which the rulers paid lip-service and in which their downtrodden, semi-feudal vassals believed rather more sincerely. This was, if one wishes, the era of the Arab resurrection, an era comparable to the European Renaissance. In Spain this Arab Renaissance came early and was even more dynamic. The Omayyads evolved in Western surroundings, and were less bound by Arab-Bedouin tradition. They saw more of the modern world than the Abbasids and thus were able to intermingle, culturally and ethnically, with the West, to accept wider influences than their Eastern cousins.

In this era the Arab identity evolved from that of desert tribes to a dominant culture applied to several and varied peoples. To some extent it welded them together in two separate political areas, very different from each other in their agrarian, commercial and social situations. Belief was the main guideline, but economic-imperialist (and before that, economic-mercantile) interests predominated among those who were used by the standard-bearers of Islam, and became, in turn, its exploiters for their own class-purposes. Because of its theology, which not only supposed predestination but also favoured hereditary rule of a kind rather different from the European feudal and monarchic system (it was *not* always the elder son of a Bedouin sheikh or caliph who was *elected* to become his father's inheritor) Islam did not bring about the fusion of all Arab-dominated territories into a single state-area, not even in the Middle East. Indeed, religious belief and ethnic background continued to be the mainstreams of separatist identity in this zone. The 'original Arabs', Bedouin raiders and migrants, became the harbingers of Islam and thus evolved effortlessly into the dominating class – although mingling with slaves and other subjects of non-Arab descent. This made the 'racial' interpretation of the 'Arab world' meaningless. Not so culturally: through the twin fetters of belief and aristocracy, the rulers held fast to Islam, its language, its traditions and its accompanying *mores*; any non-Arab cultural heritage was suspect in their eyes, rejected or grudgingly assimilated into Islam-dominated culture.

In the Arab world even more clearly than in medieval and Renaissance Europe, two identities existed, super-imposed on each other. The Arab concepts of *Qawmiya* and *Wataniya* thus evolved: *Qawmiya* being the identity of the Arab nation as a whole, and *Wataniya* that of each Arab country, people, or political grouping, separately. As Professor Uzzi Ornan has pointed out, the *Wataniya* were roughly the nations which had been conquered by Islam but refused to accept its rules: 'Though most of them eventually converted to Islam, they preferred to keep their own culture and to preserve their sovereignty. They did not want to become absorbed by the tiny Moslem ruling class which manned the government and its agencies and which spoke no language but Arabic.'*

The Age of Submission (*c*. 800–1798) – from the start of Arab imperialist decay and fall to the incursion into Egypt of Napoleon Bonaparte, who awakened the Middle East to the need for change: politically, this was an age of disintegration. Egypt seceded from the Caliphate. The Shia minority rebelled against the Sunni-

*'Western View of Arab Nationalism Based on Semantic Misunderstanding', an article by Professor Uzzi Ornan, *Jerusalem Post*, 31 December 1970.

Moslem majority in Iraq, and Turkoman palace-guards became the rulers of the Eastern part of the Arab kingdom. The rigid class-structure of Omayyad rule gave way to a more pliable structure under the Abbasids – but the rigidity of religious belief continued to be total. This directed ethnic, national and social revolt along the lines of religious heresy. The Shiites, the Mutazilah and the Kharajite sects fought the centralized power of the Abbasid dynasty. Sufism appeared, influencing the philosophy of the Arabs, and through them of mystic thought in the West to this very day. The primitive-communist sect of the Ismailis made its appearance in Persia and Iraq. Likewise, the rebellion of the 'Arab Spartacus', the Zanji slaves' revolt, took place in Basra and Syria from 868 to 883; the slaves' army was finally defeated at great cost by a Turkish army. The Turks and Turkomanes became, for the first time, the ascendant force inside Islam. This was a turning-point: the Turks had a totally different culture and a non-Arabic language, and their identity was, therefore, impervious to the up to then arabizing influence of Islam. Indeed, the Turks and Mamelukes reversed the Arabs' main ideological weapon. The Arab empires disintegrated because of cultural stagnation and economic inability to adapt their trade to international patterns, and also because of a breakdown in communications; the Arabs stubbornly kept on urging trade as a side-line of their imperialist-religious conquest. The Turks, or rather the Turkomane sons of the Arabs' former slaves from Central Asia, were there to inherit the power of the Abbasids as early as 842. Having been held apart from the Arab ruling military-aristocracy, in language as well as in caste, their influence was tyrannical, and became in fact parasitic. A pattern which was to be repeated ten centuries later, during the Ottoman decline, set in: agriculture, neglected by the Arabs, was now pressed out like a half-dry lemon by the Turkish-speaking rulers. Moreover, while the Arabs exploited the proselytizing role of Islam to incorporate into their lower classes the non-Arab and non-Islamic populations of their conquered territories, the Turkish-speaking rulers simply exploited these lower classes, Arabs and non-Arabs alike. Their rule in Egypt, which they easily won from the Arab-Fatimid dynasty implanted there, and Turco-Seljuk rule in the East brought to a close the era of Arabic-speaking and Arab-cultural domination in the Middle East.

From this point on Arabic became the uniting language of the oppressed in the Middle East. In opposition to it we shall see again and again how an extraneous language became the lingua franca of the rulers and a symbol of Levantine prestige: Crusaders' old French, then modern French, and later on English, not to speak of the imposed language of the Ottoman administration, Turkish. All these imperialist conquerors had similar approaches to the area: they wanted to rule it, to exploit it, in some cases to develop it – from outside. There was no wish to create an indigenous exploiting class, culturally associated to the Turks or to the West, i.e. a local infrastructure of power. A lower, or executive, class of exploiting 'bosses' and administrators was created and occasionally used by the proselytizing Arabs and helped them develop and expand. Indeed, it was only when these tactics were stopped by the limitations of Islamic belief that the impetus of Arab imperialism decelerated. The West, intruding into the area, only wanted 'educated ones', i.e. people able to understand and accept the West's commands. The indigenous population was *ipso facto* 'barbarous', and had to be 'educated' before it could be trusted with even the crumbs of the ruler's power.

During the age of Arab submission the use of Arabic became fragmented to a high degree. For a dweller of the *Maghreb*, or 'West' (i.e. northern Africa), it was almost impossible to understand an Egyptian or a dweller of the *Mashrak* (or Middle) 'East'. Only written Arabic kept its pristine original form through the changeless writings of the Koran. Thus Islam, the instrument and framework of Arab imperialism, became the instrument for the preservation of a separate – and downtrodden – Arab identity. For a while a further parallel course was laid between the destinies of the Jewish nation and that of the Arab *Qawmiya*: both were kept alive, at times only in a state of cataleptic hibernation, through the re-application of an old belief to new purposes.

The Birth of Arab Nationalism (1798 onwards): to begin with, the introduction of a semi-Western brand of nationalism was artificial, i.e. not adapted to the natural evolution of the area. Mohammed Ali, in nineteenth-century Egypt, and Hussein I of Mecca later on, both learned from the West; both adopted the idea of a limited modern Arab state, although without relinquishing their old belief. Indeed, what the Holy Land was for the bourgeois-liberal Zionist revolution, the reawakening of Arab splendour was for the despotic Arab liberation. Anthony Nutting once observed that 'by a strange coincidence the leaders of the two most important rebellions against the Ottoman Empire – Mohammed Ali and Hussein of Mecca – proved to be as maladroit and facile in their dealings with the British and French as they were masterly in outsmarting their Turkish rulers'.* This is no coincidence at all. Both Hussein and Mohammed Ali were fighting a battle against the neo-medieval framework of Ottoman imperialism which, as local representatives of the Ottoman Porte, they knew intimately. Naturally enough they looked upon the West as the ally from the future come to help them destroy their enemies of old.

Historically the neo-feudal despots Mohammed Ali and Hussein helped the coming of the modern brand of exploitation, imperialist penetration from the West. Trying to liberate from foreign control the lands in which they ruled, in order to strengthen their own power, they opened the way to far stronger forces waiting in the wings for the opportunity to destroy Turkish might and replace it efficiently.

At the beginning of the twentieth century totalitarian rule was exerted over the Middle East by the Ottoman Porte, a Moslem but separatist-national imperialism. Christian education and Western commercial interests were somewhat rudely awakening the Arabs. Ambitious and able men started to exploit this situation both to consolidate their power and to express the frustration caused by foreign rule. These men were either 'foreigners' – non-Arabs or Christianized Arabs influenced by the West – or, as in the case of Hussein of Mecca, they were the leaders of migrant tribes, whose economic interests were not jeopardized by a possible upheaval and who could therefore still identify the old

* *The Arabs*, Anthony Nutting, London, 1964.

religion with their own ambitions. Thus, except in the desert tribes of the Arabian inner peninsula, the Arab revolt started from above, from among the actual and potential despots. It was autocratic in character and non-popular in essence, at times even half-foreign.

This fact is no less relevant than the exclusivist nature of Zionism to the understanding of the Palestinian–Israeli confrontation of today. The fact is that the Arab revolution, although much less exclusive in spirit than its Zionist counterpart, was totally undemocratic both in character and in origins. Repeatedly, the revolution was instigated by the wielders of class-power: Mohammed Ali in Egypt, Sherif Hussein of Mecca, the Egyptian army officers of Neguib and Abd-El-Nasser, the armed forces of Iraq and Syria, and so on. Moreover, no separation of religion and state is evident in the Arab revolt, as it was in the revolt of Atatürk Kemal Pasha in Turkey, when Ahmed Tevfik Pasha was at last deposed in 1920 from his post as last Grand Vizier of the Ottoman empire. On the contrary, Islam was the backbone both of Arab neo-feudal despotism and of absolutist Arab socialism. Islam is the state-religion, and at times of stress, whenever the Zionist enemy endangered Arab cooperation – as in June 1967 – a *Jihad*, or Moslem Holy Crusade, was declared from El Azhar's Mosque in Cairo and all believers in Islam were called – albeit in vain – to fight the enemy.

Into the situation thus created by the end of the nineteenth century, first by foreign rule and then by the solidarity of the suffering and the prop of religious belief, was stretched the 'helping hand' of the Big Western Brother, Britain or France. Into the hiatus created by the breakdown of the Turkish empire, with the weak but effective help of the Arab revolt, also stepped the Zionist revolutionaries, anxious to blow life into their separate ideals, to live their own exclusive life in an area they blithely supposed to be devoid of 'modern' aspirations for independence and self-assertion. This immediately identifiable force, Jewish Zionism, blinded the autocratic Arab revolutionaries to the dangers from their main enemies, the British and French efforts to dominate the area. We have seen in history what the protectors of the Middle East did to it. There is little doubt what the new ones wanted to do. But the Arabs' reaction to Zionist presence, in the twentieth century, is certainly not the first instance of a nation rushing into a bear's embrace to escape the tearing claws of an eagle.

Inside the general framework of the Arab awakening, there appeared the problem of the separate Palestinian entity, which is not only the spearhead of the Arab–Islamic fight against Israel, but also the harbinger of a separatist national consciousness, no less real than that of the Israelis. The Palestinians, like the Israelis, only recently developed a separate personality; indeed, they have done so only because of their isolation from the rest of the Arabs and their expropriation by Zionism.

Until the end of the nineteenth century the identity of the population of Palestine could in no way be considered that of a united, separate and cohesive community. Its interests were as one with those of what are now the Lebanon and Syria. With the exploitation of the so-called 'capitulatory rights' granted by Turkey to the Western powers, a marked European cultural influence made itself felt in this coastal area. Palestine in particular, being the Holy Land of the Christian faiths, became a centre of cultural-religious and therefore political agitation. Missionary schools and other beneficent bodies run by the churches took upon themselves the task of 'educating' the native population, that is of adapting it to the external European identity. On the cultural plane, it was this religious-political indoctrination which created the 'Levantine mind' so despised and yet so ruefully admired in the West: by superimposing Western cultural values and knowledge on deeply ingrained Eastern psychological patterns of behaviour.

Palestine was by no means the only area in the Middle East in which this happened. In the Lebanon too, among other countries, with its abundant and fertile lands and prosperous mercantile communities, the levantinization of the natives was carried out. The same thing happened in Syria. While this process of acquainting the local population with Western 'values' was going on, the Levant was in the peculiar situation of being politically dominated by the Ottoman Porte, which as far as possible exploited it economically. Thus, the values of the *Frengi* (Europeans) became for many a Levantine, who first tasted modern nationalism through his acquaintance with Christian civilization, identical with freedom. Liberalism once more manifested itself as a 'culturally liberating' factor, while it was busy fortifying the economic bastions of imperialism.

The confusion of the local Arab intellectual class, or, to use the Arab idiom, of the 'educated ones', was reinforced by their having been left in comparative peace as a national entity by the Turks. Indeed in spite of the obvious hostility of the Porte's Viziers towards them, the Arabs were never forced to mingle with the Turks, to shed their identity. On the contrary, they were held, as it were, in abeyance. Thus, when Christianity, a new convert-seeking faith, brought to the local population the benefits of westernizing culture, there was no innate contradiction between the nationalist fervour of the early Arab awakening and the fact that the awakened were mostly Christians.

In Constantinople itself a group of Arab military leaders serving the Porte organized themselves as early as 1875. The same thing happened in Damascus. In 1847 the Société des Arts et Sciences was formed in Beirut, and in 1868 the poem 'Awaken O Arabs!' was read at a secret meeting by Al Yazeji, one of the founders. Nassif Yazeji, as well as other precursors of modern Arab nationalism – men such as Butrus Boustani, and Nejib Azouri – were Christians.

Then the League for the Arab Fatherland was founded by Nejib Azouri. In the first decade of the twentieth century pan-Arab nationalism became crystallized in the coastal area, and the creation of the Syrian Scientific Society was the first expression of modern Arab romantic nationalism (1847) as it was finally followed in the creation of twin secret societies, born in Syria and Constantinople: El Fatat, a civilian outfit, swiftly associated with a 'free officers' military group, the El Ahd. In 1913 the first congress of Arab nationalists was held in Paris, as an outshoot of the activity of these bodies. This congress resolved to avail itself of the help of the Western Powers against the Turks.

We have seen some cultural reasons why the Arab nationalist awakening takes place in the coastal area and why it is so strongly influenced by Christian activists, in spite of Arabism being a pan-Islamic movement. There are other economic reasons for this, too.

The centre of a culture is, obviously, an economically prosperous region. The coast provides the merchant-basis from which spring the local upper classes, the mercantile potentates or the land-*Effendis*. The latter hold power thanks to a centralization of fertile-landownership. In Egypt as late as 1947, only five per cent of the land is cultivable and five per cent cultivated; in Iran the figures are ten and three; in Saudi Arabia four and two; in Jordan, that is, eastern Palestine, nine and five.

In Lebanon, however, sixty per cent of the land is cultivable and forty-four per cent cultivated; in Syria twenty per cent is cultivable although only eight per cent is cultivated; and in Israel, after Zionist colonization, twenty-two per cent of the land is cultivated out of a possible thirty-five per cent. A commercial economy, coupled with a neo-feudal agrarian system in the more fertile areas, breeds the cultural prosperity of the few, who, in turn, breed nationalist and separatist feelings.

On the other hand, it is the fate of the coastal area to have the same enemies as the arid and backward desert area – and also the same cultural-religious heritage. So to begin with, separatist feelings, compounded by fear of outsiders and pride of identity, directed themselves along the age-old belief-chiselled path of Islam and Arabism. The fact that Turkey indiscriminately exploited all these areas reinforced this development. Nevertheless there was an urge for truly national, separate identities: the Druzes in Syria and the Lebanon revolted early in the twentieth century, though to no avail. In 1860 it was the Christian Arabs who rebelled against the Druze feudal overlords, and were slaughtered by them. The Maronites preferred French tutelage to the independence of Lebanon in a common framework with Moslem-Arabs.

At the end of the nineteenth century, the feudal structure of the coastal economy started to disintegrate in the Lebanon and in

Palestine because of the encroachments of the Western powers upon Constantinople's financial empire. In 1909 the El Kathaniya Arab Society was founded in Constantinople by the partisans of an Arab kingdom within the framework of the Ottoman rule, somewhat on the lines of the Austro-Hungarian empire; the crisis was somewhat hastened by the fact that the Ottoman empire was bankrupt. In 1913–14 the Ottoman national debt was 63 million pounds sterling, while foreign investments in the empire were as follows: 24 million pounds sterling by Great Britain; 3·3 billion francs by France; 1·8 million marks by Imperial Germany.* There exists a correlation between the disintegration of the economic and cultural power of the Turks in the Middle East and the awakening of pan-Arab nationalism, although the former was not caused by the latter.

While imperial Turkey, the 'sick man of Europe', lay dying, the various entities which would have liked to supplant it gathered to tear pieces off the Porte's flesh. The dream of a united Arab kingdom represented but one of these vultures. Obviously this dream was most cherished by those feudal suzerains and sheikhs who had some claim to a hereditary throne – which meant, in the Moslem tradition, Mohammed's descendants. The Hashemites or Beni Hashem tribe was one of these. Sheikh Hussein of Mecca was the main pretender to this exalted position; but so also was Abd-El-Aziz Ibn-Saud (who was to become the ruler of Saudi Arabia); as was his main and ultimately defeated rival, the Sheikh Mohammed Ibn-Rashid of the Nejd.

On the least anachronistic plane there were the secret society of the Arab officers of the Ottoman army, El Khataniya, which wanted a united kingdom of Arabs and Turks; and the El Fatat, which wanted complete Arab independence and was by far the most important. Its sister organization El Ahd is centred mainly in Syria and Lebanon, with offshoots in Palestine. But even this group, which had been in intimate contact with Western education and ideas, was still thinking on the lines of an absolutist monarchy, Arab rather than Turk. The ideas of these groups were a

*I am indebted for many facts in this chapter to Nathan Weinstock's *Le Mouvement Révolutionnaire Arabe*, Maspéro, Paris, 1970.

partially enlightened mixture of absolutism and liberalism such as, at that juncture, could only appear in an area far behind the political and economic evolution of Western Europe.

When the First World War broke out, the tug-of-war between various imperialist interests for the spoils of the Ottoman empire became more serious. Great Britain in particular had the firm intention of strengthening her positions in the area – which were already based on total control of Egypt – by availing herself of further bases in the north, and particularly by controlling the coastal area of Palestine and Syria. Unfortunately for the interests of the British War Office, France not only was the ally and partner of Britain in her venture against the Kaiser and the Sultan, but had strong entrenched interests of her own in Syria and the Lebanon, such as the 'protection' of the Christian-Arab Maronite community there. France, like other imperialists, used the 'protection racket' to fight off other vultures.

Since its conquest by the Turks in the sixteenth century Palestine had been a separatist, if not separate, area. The conglomerate of religious sects and belief-inspired interests was even greater here than elsewhere in the Levant. Napoleon, that first Gentile Zionist, had proclaimed in Gaza, as early as 1799, that the Jews should rebuild their historical fatherland there; but on an exclusivist Jewish basis his call was not to be answered till the Zionist Congress of Basle. Britain, which protected the Ottoman Empire in the nineteenth century against the encroachment of the French, had already one piece of bounty to boast of – Egypt. Britain had no particular wish to follow in the footsteps of the *Mission Colonisatrice* of Napoleon, and of the Bourbons, who fought for direct French rule over the Levant. Rather, the British wanted to create additional puppets through whom they would extend their economic domination and the military control which would allow a link with India, through the Suez Canal and the overland territories of the Levant, Persia and Afghanistan. Lord Stanley is said to have declared, as early as 1867, that Britain would gladly destroy the Turks' hold on the Levant, but 'the trouble is that we do not know what we shall put in their stead'. In 1912 Kitchener laid down the goal of cutting off the Levant's coastal area up to the north of Haifa and Acre from the Turks, by creating there a 'British influence area'. 'We need an Anglo-Arab dyke to stop the Germano-Turk flood', he is said to have stated plainly.

The destruction of the local craft industries by the implantation of Western manufactured goods, and the subordination of the merchants of the coastal area to Western imperialist interests, destroyed the social structures of Levantine smallholder-capitalism. The neo-feudal economy of these areas had already started to disintegrate in the nineteenth century with the Ottoman Porte's decision of 1858 to take over the lands from absentee *Effendis* in order to tax directly the serf-*Fellahin*. Weinstock* gives southern Iraq as an example, an area where no agrarian reform has been carried out to this day and which therefore is quite typical of the neo-feudal conditions which then existed in the whole of the Levant – and still exist in part of it: the income from lands is divided, by and large, as follows: government taxes, 10 per cent; absentee owner or *Effendi*, 40 per cent; sub-tenant, usually the local sheikh, 7·5 per cent: overseer, 2·5 per cent; *Fellah*-serf, 40 per cent. Weinstock adds that this 40 per cent is not enough for subsistence and quotes the significant corollary that most children in that area die before the age of ten.

Thus at the start of the First World War the scene was set. The revolutionaries of the coastal area were feudal oligarchic interests, the Arab officers of Turkish despotism and the Christian-educated rich intellectuals, usually the sons of the local mercantile bourgeoisie. The masses were either illiterate serf-peasants or, farther inland, no less illiterate tribesmen, somewhere between brigands and herdsmen. This was the tortured, hardened, embittered and ignorant mass which ought to carry out an Arab revolt. It was obviously not yet capable of doing so. The British helped the Arabs and the Jews to win some independence, in order to supplant the direct Ottoman autocracy with an indirect industrial-capitalist suzerainty of the area.

Striving for this goal, Britain was unscrupulous. Moreover, the various trends of British imperialism combated each other: the

*op. cit.

Indian Office of H.M. Government, for instance, was strongly against supporting the Arabs, a policy which might cause trouble with the Hindu majority of India; the Cairo-based Arab Office of Hogarth, Lawrence and Clayton schemed for the creation of a real, or if necessary fictitious 'Arab Revolt' in the Levant. As Lawrence and others showed so graphically, it turned out to be a fictitious one: the 'Revolt's' leader, Shiekh Hussein of Mecca's son Feisal, was allowed again and again to gather the fruits of English and French conquests, and when he obtained victories of his own this was invariably due to the support of the British naval and air forces, which destroyed the cumbersome Turkish land forces. When Damascus was captured by Australian troops, the city was even evacuated later on, to allow Feisal's Arabs to 'conquer' it all over again. An ever more grotesque episode of a similar nature occurred at Deraa.

But let us not anticipate. The British purpose was, it is true, to gain the Arabs' help in throwing out the Turks and ensure the population's goodwill to the implementation of modern industrial and military imperialism from the West; but by no means did Great Britain strive for a truly strong and united Arab force: not because such a totalitarian Arab monarchy would be a tyranny – on the contrary, centralization of local power would have helped Britain in her bid for control of the area; but rather she was afraid of a new, Arab, Ottoman-style despotism with teeth and claws, which might strike a bargain with somebody else. Britain was guided in her policy, on the whole, by the old 'divide and rule' dictum. It is with this in mind, ultimately, that the contradictory promises to Arabs and to Jews must be seen.

When the First World War broke out, the propaganda and political struggle were directed in the Middle East by the British Cairo Military Headquarters. Lord Kitchener's successor, Sir Henry McMahon, the Chief Commissioner for Egypt, took it upon himself to start negotiations with the Sherif of Mecca, Hussein Ibn-Ali of the Beni-Hashem tribe, towards mobilizing the help of the Arabs throughout the Middle East against the Turks. In the Sudan, Moslems were already in arms against the British empire, and so were Mohammed's believers in India, Afghanistan and nearby Persia. One of the Arabs' most respected leaders was Hussein. McMahon had instructions from London to neutralize him, if possible to engage his services, by promising recognition of the Arab peninsula as an Arab state with sovereignty over the Holy City of Mecca after the Turks had been driven out with Arab help. As the British empire did not dream, at first, of creating an independent Jewish state, but rather a Jewish presence, or National Home, peopled by Westerners in the service of the empire, it always opposed total Arab independence: 'The Shereef of Mecca has communicated to the Authorities', wrote Sir Edward Grey, Foreign Secretary of Great Britain, to Sir James Rodd, British Ambassador in Rome, on 21 September 1916, 'his desire to make himself independent but had insisted upon knowing whether we were prepared to recognize an independent Arab State. We were, of course, prepared to do that if he succeeded in establishing his independence; for all we were pledged to was that the Moslem Holy Places should remain in independent Moslem hands.' A bit ambiguous, as might be expected of any diplomat worth his salt, but clearly showing Great Britain's true intentions.*

The British position was more clearly expressed by Lieutenant-Colonel Sir Gilbert Clayton, Director of Military Intelligence in Cairo and one of McMahon's chief advisers, who wrote at that time: 'To set up a great Arab State . . . was never my idea . . . The conditions throughout Arabia, Syria and Mesopotamia did not allow of such a scheme being practical, even if anyone were so foolish as to attempt it . . . The object we have to aim at is, I consider, to work to preserve all the various elements in the Arab territories very much in the same position as they were before the war, but minus the Turks. In this way we shall have an open field to work in.'†

In other words: to supplant the Turks by British – and if there

*CAB/37/155/33 Grey to Rodd, cited by Isaiah Friedman, 'The McMahon–Hussein Correspondence and the Question of Palestine', *Journal of Contemporary History*, London, Vol. 5, No. 2, April 1970.

†Clayton to Jacob Arden, 11 March 1916. Cited by Isiaah Friedman, op. cit.

be no other choice, by Franco-British – imperialism, while keeping the clock back in the Levant, was the precise aim of British military action and diplomatic endeavours there. In order to do so, Britain was willing to mobilize, at one and the same time, the influence of affluent Western Jewry and of the rebellious Arabs of the Levant; provided, of course, no 'great Arab State' would be created by chance as a result of these endeavours. But a great Arab kingdom was precisely the hope of the Sherif of Mecca. Hussein, a feudal lordling, dreamt of becoming a feudal king, the Orient's Charlemagne.

Both the Arabs and the British empire were living behind the times, the Arabs roughly in the age of medieval knights, and the British and French imperialists in the age of the robber-barons of early capitalism. As so often happens in politics, the times had changed but the man in charge did not understand how. This was to bring about the immediate decline of French power in the Middle East and the gradual decline of Great Britain as an imperial power there. What grew up in Palestine in their stead was, up to a point, the result of the clash of these cultural legacies, used to prop up brutal economic needs – but encroaching upon the latter and making their standard-bearers blind to the experiences of the past.

After the allied conquests and the farcical feudal-Arab triumphs, the real struggle for power started. In the Hedjaz and the Nejd, Ibn-Saud, supported by the British India Office, was the ultimate victor over his rival Ibn-Rashid; Britain was to acknowledge the existence of his Saudi Arab kingdom in 1927. Hussein of Mecca, who played a double game with Turks and British till the very moment the latter gave him decisive backing and arms and were shown to have the upper hand, had long discouraged the coastal Syrian nationalist leadership, in exile in Cairo, where it held endless and pointless talks with the British Oriental Secretary Ronald Storrs up to the outbreak of the war. Hussein warned the Syrian militants against agitation hostile to the French – as his interests were now vested in British and French overrule. On 11 August 1917 Hussein even sent a telegram to the pan-Arab nationalist leader El-Faruki asking him not to concern himself with Syrian matters. Later Hussein asked El-Faruki not to denounce the Balfour Declaration, which granted the Jews the right to found a national home in Palestine. All was going well for Britain and her plans.

The bourgoisie of the coastal area took all this lying down. Astonishingly, as this area was by now very well developed intellectually: it had, for instance, 286 newspapers (31 in Palestine, one of which was the anti-Zionist *El Karmel* founded in 1903; 87 in Syria; and 68 in literate Lebanon) as compared with 70 in what is now Iraq and 6 in Hedjaz. The sheep-like adherence to the leadership of the Arab officers of the Porte turned nationalists and later of the desert-chieftain Hussein of Mecca can only be explained by the mixed non-integrated character of the coastal elite: belief and origins still counted more than economics and local feeling, there; irrational pride and belief were abetted by personal greed and the fear for one's possessions, strengthened by the great hunger in Syria, caused by Turkish oppression and Arab and Druze landowners' hoarding of grain and food during the First World War. This famine gave the coastal Arabs a taste of what could happen if they stepped out of line. Besides, of course, the whole cultural-historical tradition of the Arab civilization was absolutist; indeed, there was some kind of identification between the glory of the past and the might of the absolute leader, warlord or Caliph.

Thus, when Hussein later proclaimed himself 'King of all Arabs' – evoking the hate and hostility of Ibn-Saud in Hedjaz – he had the help of the El Ahd officers contacted in 1915 by Hussein's son Feisal in Damascus. It was in Syria that Hussein was going to found his kingdom – as the British were quite content after the war to encroach upon the promised Syrian fief of their French allies, as allotted to them by the Sykes-Picot agreement, which parcelled the Middle East into French (roughly northern) and British (roughly southern) 'zones of influence'. But the French did not take the challenge lying down. Following the example of Britain, which occupied Mesopotamia in 1917, against the letter of former agreements, the French threw Hussein out of Syria and occupied the country. They ruled or dominated

Syrian and Lebanese politics till the Second World War, when Marshall Pétain's collaboration with Hitler gave Britain a pretext (and good military reasons) to throw their French rivals finally out of the Middle East.

Meanwhile Britain, busy trying to set up a straightforward colonial administration in Iraq, was forced by the Euphrates-valley tribe-risings to set up a Husseini monarchy ruled, for all practical purposes, by the 'wily fox' and pro-British schemer, Nuri El-Said. The official monarch was Feisal, son of Hussein. Britain had also obtained, in July 1920, the Mandate over Palestine and Transjordan from the disciplined League of Nations. In the west, a Jewish and pro-Zionist High Commissioner, Lord Samuel, was appointed in Palestine to watch over the empire's interests; in the east, Abd-Allah, another son of Hussein, was allowed by the British to seize power over all of Transjordan, where a number of so-called 'kingdoms', in reality feudal tribe-strongholds, had appeared after the rout of the Turks. One of them was the short-lived 'Kingdom of Moab', as it has been called by the British adviser, Major Alec Kirkbride, with a 'fine sense of history'.*

* Christopher Sykes, *Crossroads to Israel*, pp. 52, 54–5.

4 The Stillbirth of 'Palestine', 1920–39

The creation of the emirate of Transjordan was welcomed by the British who, after containing the growth of united Arab totalitarian rule by the creation of a Jewish National Home along the Mediterranean, endeavoured to contain the undue expansion of this Jewish home to the east by creating a new Hashemite stronghold under absolute British control. Thus for the first time the territory of Palestine itself was divided by arbitrary borders and much of the Palestinian population, as well as the wandering tribes of Eastern Palestine or Transjordan, were brought under the formal rule of a Hedjaz-born descendant of the Prophet. Abd-Allah was supported in power by a Bedouin guard, the Arab Legion, trained and commanded by British officers, the leading and best-known of whom was Sir John Glubb.

In spite of the new borders which grew to crisscross the Middle East, the indigenous population of the area circulated freely – even more so, as new areas of prosperity developed and formerly prosperous areas declined, such as the Hauran zone in the north, from where migratory workers moved into Palestine. As for the indigenous population of the Palestinian coastal area, it prospered at first because of its commercial relations with both British and Jews and also because of its suddenly central position. That is to say, the bourgeois, commercial and landowning classes prospered; as for the *Fellahin*, the tenant-landworkers, they were systematically deprived of their living and of the land which was 'theirs', by work and birth, through the voluntary and rapacious sale of land by the *Effendi*-landowners to the Zionist colonizers. The Zionists not only bought the land, they also developed it immediately, changing the very ecology of the country and continuously creating *faits accomplis*. It was this impact on the old way of life, this multiple and complex change in the life of the coastal area of Palestine, together with the influence of changes elsewhere in the Arabic-speaking world, which gave first impetus to the growth of a home-born Palestinian nationalism, in the sense of the *Wataniyeh* of the old Arab empire. In spite of its aristocratic-religious prestige, the indigenous bourgeoisie of Western Palestine, which was quite levantinized by the early twenties, would have preferred a different kind of ruler over Abd-Allah – and the development of a Bedouin-born upper caste in Transjordan, in accordance with the old Moslem custom of taking a Praetorian guard from elsewhere, made West Palestinian separatism even stronger. It was in 1920–21 that Palestine acquired a separate national personality, an identity of its own. Undoubtedly, Zionism was the strongest factor that influenced the conception of Palestine. Sykes writes:

> ... Since November 1917 throughout these lands between Africa and Turkey, Zionism had been a subject of angry preoccupation among the Arab nationalists, but had hitherto taken second place to the agitation for a United Syria. With the disintegration, without hope of restoration, of United Syria, the order of preoccupation was reversed and Arab nationalism began to find fresh impulse in the wrongs of the Palestinian Arabs. In the words of H. V. Temperley: it may be remarked that had the Sherif's son, the Emir Feisal, not been ejected from Syria by the French, much less might have been heard of his father's claims to Palestine.*

Palestine's original dwellers got used to the new situation – and to the new borders. Their identity was emphasized by the exclusivist 'invasion' of the Jews, who tried neither to mix with them nor to assimilate them into Jewish society. Pan-Arab awareness, meanwhile, continued to develop due to the greater literacy of the coastal plain's population, while in later years the radio and particularly the transistor-set were to contribute powerfully to relieving the feeling of isolation of the Palestinians and later still of the Israeli Arabs.

The bitterness of deprivation of what they considered their

*Sykes, Crossroads to Israel p. 56

exclusive heritage and the totalitarian tradition of Islam-dominated Arab thought forced the Palestinians to the right of the political spectrum. This was not always so. In 1921 a delegation of the 'Moslem-Christian Association', which endeavoured to represent 'all Palestine's Arabs', was received by Secretary of State Winston Churchill in Jaffa. Heading it was Mussa Kazim El-Husseini, former Governor of Jaffa and Mayor of Jerusalem under the allied OETA or military administration. This delegation expressed strongly anti-Zionist views, rejected the Balfour Declaration and asked for an end to Jewish immigration and the appointment of a government by the British, a government which would be 'answerable to a popularly elected Parliament'. Churchill refused, but went on to say that the Balfour Declaration ensured the creation of '*a* Jewish home, not *the* Jewish home'. This, he added, did not mean a Jewish government to dominate the Arabs of Palestine. And Churchill concluded: 'The present form of Government will continue for many years. Step by step we will develop representative institutions leading to full self-government . . . but our children's children will have passed away before this is accomplished.'

This was not only a typical Churchillian sop. The initial British pro-Zionist impetus had been blunted. One of the first acts of the High Commissioner, Lord Samuel, was to introduce Hebrew as one of the official languages; but more important politically, he also introduced in 1920 the Transfer of Land Ordinance, the first of a series of restrictive laws, which endeavoured to protect the *Fellahin* or land-tenants from deprivation. This Ordinance was to no avail, any more than the further Land Ordinances of 1932, 1933, 1934 and 1940 were to be (the last one being purely political and anti-Zionist rather than a social-reformist piece of legislation). The Palestinian and Lebanese or Syrian *Effendis* who held lands in Palestine contrived to make them unsuccessful. Sykes retells how in one single huge land-deal eight thousand land-tenants were 'compensated' for the loss of land, home and work at the rate of £3 a head. At this time the *Fellahin* were still some thirty-five per cent of the country's population.

Politically, then, things turned in Whitehall in a direction somewhat less sympathetic to the Jews. For the Colonial Office, the initial act of allowing Zionist immigration had fulfilled almost all its purposes. Now at the Cairo conference of 1921 it was time to go on to serious matters and carve up the Middle East into puppet-kingdoms ruled by Arabs and dominated by Great Britain. For this the feudal leadership of the Arabs had to be conciliated; the more advanced bourgeois elite of Palestine was of less import. In March 1921 Lord Herbert Samuel rigged the elections to the post of the Mufti, or Moslem religious authority in Jerusalem. Samuel invented a new title, 'Great Mufti', to counterbalance the title of 'Great', or 'Chief' Rabbi which survived under Turkish rule as the 'Haham Bashi' ('Chief Wise Man') responsible for the Jews. Under Samuel's pressure Haj Amin El-Husseini, another feudal chief, was elected over the heads of several other candidates who got more votes than he did. Haj Amin had played a role in the 1920 disorders in Palestine and had been condemned *in absentia* by the British to fifteen years in jail. It is probable that the Mandate administration hoped to blunt his zeal by co-opting him into actual co-rulership. But this choice turned out to be not only fatal to the British but also a turning-point which actually caused the stillbirth of independent Palestine.

The British tried to complete by this co-option the web of collusion with their own interests, the web they had started weaving with the Balfour Declaration and which had almost been finished two years before in January 1919 when Feisal, then still pretending to the throne of the 'Kingdom of all Arabs', signed an agreement with the Zionist leader Chaim Weizmann which stipulated that all necessary measures should be taken 'to encourage Jewish immigration into Palestine, provided the Arabs obtain their independence' as demanded by Feisal. In other words, the young Arab leader was ready to pay for a new British-protected feudal throne not only with subservience to Britain but also with the existence of a Jewish province – or half-independent National Home – in Palestine. In the same year, and indeed in the same month of January 1919, the World Zionist Organization had submitted a memorandum to the peace conference called in

Paris after the First World War. In this memorandum three demands were made: recognition of the historical title of the Jews to Palestine as a national home; establishment of Palestinian boundaries including southern Lebanon, Mount Hermon, Aqaba and Transjordan; establishment of a British Mandate in Palestine. Added to these demands were things already promised by Britain: fulfilment of the Balfour Declaration; promise of expanded Jewish colonization in Palestine; creation of a representative council of the Jews in Palestine. The Zionist goal – a Jewish state with an eventual minority of non-Jews instead of a common non-religious, non-racial state – was already clearly stated by Dr Weizmann himself, answering the questions of the American Secretary of State, Lansing: 'I define the Jewish National Home to mean the creation of an administration which would arise out of the natural conditions of the country – always safeguarding the interests of non-Jews in the country – with the hope that, by Jewish immigration, Palestine would ultimately become as Jewish as England is English.'*

It was this goal which was achieved in Israel, albeit by use of rather more violent and devious means. It was this goal which Feisal, and Abd-Allah, agreed to, in the fond hope that it would not hurt their feudal ambitions in the Arab kindgom they hoped to extend to the whole of the Middle East, the 'Jewish national home' included. It was also this goal which the British Mandate at first encouraged, then resisted, when Zionism became a force quite independent of the role which Britain had assigned to the Jews in the Levant.

As a matter of fact, it was only the bourgeois, indigenous Palestinian leadership which agreed with the Zionist goal; the gradually deprived agrarian populace, gradually driven out of the country into urban areas, rebelled under the leadership and agitation of the most extremist and fanatically Moslem elements. Palestine was the only part of the Middle East where the British empire made mistakes at that time, but there it made two at once: it underestimated the drive of the Zionists, and it underestimated the religious fanaticism of the Moslem Palestinians as

* *Trial and Error*, Chaim Weizmann, London, 1950.

a catalyst for their gradual emergence as a separate entity. This, and the frustration caused by the appearance of Arab independent states in the surrounding – and to the Palestinian mind much less cultivated – areas, created a curious mixture of Arab identification and specific Palestinian feeling, which was not only the first glimmering of an independent Palestinian *Wataniyeh* nationalism but also a source of indignation and inspiration for the rest of the Arabic-speaking nations, a goad to their frustrated pride and a 'reason' to ignore the political facts which emerged later with the creation of an Israeli entity.

One should not suppose that the growth of a new Jewish society in Palestine was entirely damaging to the Palestinians. In a pattern later to be confirmed by the structure of the State of Israel, the industrialization of Zionist society and the increased productivity of its agriculture gave considerable marginal benefits to the Arab-Palestinians – though usually to the better-off classes. Psychologically, their being kept 'outside the pale' by the Jews, as the Jews themselves had been kept by the Gentiles for two thousand years, caused them to become aware of their increasingly isolated – and independent – identity. The trouble was simply that here was one society being supplanted as the chief entity of its native territory by another. The fact that this other entity was both more advanced in culture and technology and generous enough by nationalist standards to allow for co-existence with the Palestinians as long as they kept to themselves did nothing to assuage the pain and the humiliation of the latter.

From the first, the Palestinian reaction to Zionism was total rejection. This, it might appear, was wise in view of the subsequent creation of a racialist, exclusivist Zionist state. In fact it was utter foolishness. Several times the Palestinians could have obtained some sort of British-protected compromise, which would have led sooner or later to the creation of a bi-national state or at least of a confederation of a Jewish and an Arab protectorate under British rule. The systematic rejection of any compromise with Zionism, indeed of the acknowledgement of the existence of Jewish and later Israeli political existence in Palestine, was the main beam supporting the contrived edifice of Arab aspirations and pride in this country. When it fell in 1948, the whole building went with it.

We have already seen the first rejection, during the meeting between Mussa Kazim and Churchill. In 1922 the newly formed Arab Congress of Palestine boycotted the British-directed elections of a Legislative Assembly for Palestine – which would have ensured at least some kind of Arab representation. In the same year it rejected any cooperation with a planned Advisory Council which was to be nominated by Lord Samuel. At this juncture the Zionist leadership would have accepted such an arrangement, as even three years later, in 1925, there were only 33,801 Jews in Palestine – three per cent of the total population. In 1923 the Arabs rejected another of Lord Samuel's brainchildren – the creation of an Arab Agency, to counteract the growing strength of the Jewish Agency for Palestine. The same year the Anglo-Transjordan agreement was signed with Abd-Allah, a document to be superseded in 1928, under High Commissioner Lord Plummer, by an actual Treaty. Abd-Allah had nothing to lose and much to gain by such an agreement – and was afraid of the encroachments of his main rival in the Arab world, Ibn-Saud of Hedjaz. The Palestinians, with 97 per cent of the population 'on their side' thought they could allow themselves to be intransigent in a similar situation.

The never-never-land quality of Arab politics was encouraged by Hussein of Mecca's declaring himself, in 1924, 'Caliph of all Arabs' – without ruling a single inch of territory. This nonetheless strengthened the Moslem-fanatic politicking of Hadj Amin El-Husseini, in Palestine. His bourgeois rivals, the Nashashibi and other 'Notable' families, lost more and more ground. Meanwhile, from 1925 on, a comparatively huge influx of Jews reached Palestine from the persecutions in Poland and Lithuania and the renewed repression in Russia by the Bolshevik government (which put, among others, the Jewish Bund party, not to speak of the Zionists, outside Soviet law). In this year alone 34,386 new immigrants arrived, and this allowed the Great Mufti's clique to foment violent reactions not just through the use of nationalist slogans – which would have been incomprehensible *per se*, at that juncture, to many of the poorer Palestinians – but rather by dint of the most rabid anti-Semitism, echoing the *Fellahin*'s social, religious and national frustration.

Meanwhile things went on developing in the surrounding countries: in 1927 the French repressed another Syrian rebellion; the same year Saudia was officially acknowledged by the British; while in 1926 Iraq had officially become a British protectorate, rather than a colony. In Palestine, on the other hand, only the Jews developed politically.

In 1928 for the first time the Palestinian Arabs had second thoughts about total rejection of the *status quo*: the Arab-Moslem-Christian Congress unanimously accepted the idea of parliamentary government for Palestine – which it had rejected before – and handed a memorandum to this effect to the departing High Commissioner, Lord Plummer. But now it was the Zionists who said 'let's wait'. They had understood that time would play into their hands. That same year Hadj Amin El-Husseini pushed aside the pro-forma leader of the Palestinians, Mussa Kazim, who was almost eighty, and the Mufti's Supreme Moslem Council became, *de facto*, the ruling unofficial body of all non-Jews in Palestine. It put into effect a two-pronged campaign of anti-Semitism and non-cooperation with the British administration. A forged photograph of the Omar Mosque flying a Jewish flag caused riots where the cries of '*Jihad!* Holy War! Kill the Infidels!' were heard once again. An incident over the installation of a barrier, to separate in accordance with Jewish tradition praying men and women, caused a recrudescence of the riots along the Jewish holy of holies, the wailing wall, which was under nominal Arab ownership.*

Things got worse. In 1929 the Zionist leadership mobilized Jewish solidarity throughout the world and created an extended

*This photographic falsification was, in a way, prophetic: in 1967, when the Israelis conquered the Old City of Jerusalem, just such a flag was flown over the Omar Mosque, put there by the paratrooper shock-troops which entered the compound of Haram-El-Sharif. Likewise, in a gesture which was more pettily vengeful than religiously correct, the barrier was rebuilt by the Israeli Military Rabbinate along the wailing wall, following the Six Days War.

Jewish Agency apparently to co-opt non-Zionist Jews into the body responsible for the *Yishuv*, or Palestinian Jewry. However, the six members which should have been representative of non-Zionist Jewry were in fact full members of the Zionist *Vaad Leumi*, or National Committee.

To gradual political and agricultural encroaching by Zionism, the Palestinian Arabs responded with anti-Semitism and violence. This, in turn, encouraged the growth of Jewish impatience and of the right wing 'Revisionist' brand of Zionism; during the 16th Zionist Congress of 1929 Chaim Weizmann had difficulties in overcoming the Revisionist opposition, which gained ground under the leadership of the brilliant orator and thinker Wladimir Zeev Jabotinsky. Meanwhile, the Moslem Supreme Council's exhortations were followed by the Arab masses: the majority of the Jewish population of Hebron was massacred.

In September 1929 Britain again changed horses in midstream; the Arab riots had done their part to convince the Mandatory authorities of the danger which lingered – for the British rulers – in a continued pro-Zionist policy. The Hope-Simpson Enquiry Commission and Lord Passfield's report were negative towards the Jewish position.* In December 1930 Britain called Jews and Arabs alike to a round-table conference to prepare constitutional government for Palestine.

Observes Sykes: 'As in the past, Jewish refusal or boycotting of a constitution was in too direct opposition to Jewish liberalism to be undertaken without the danger of a radical party-split and of perhaps fatal loss of sympathy in the world. As before, the Arabs saved them.'† They simply refused to 'sit at one table with the Jews – and thus the whole constitutional issue was postponed, not to be opened again till six years later'.

This headstrong policy was pursued by the Palestinians in 1931. At this point the Zionists' 'Arab policy' practically disappeared; rupture between the two communities was complete. The Arabs under the Mufti's nationalist-religious mouthings started a policy of anti-British endeavours, since their violent activity against the

*A Labour government had meanwhile taken the reins in Whitehall.

†Sykes, op. cit., p. 129.

Jews had proved unsuccessful. This was not, as some historians abundantly gifted with hindsight have pretended, an anti-imperialist struggle: it was a struggle either for the conquest of British protection, or for the supplanting of Great Britain by another European and pro-Moslem power.

As for what the 1929 riots did to the Zionist mind, let us once again consult Sykes:

> Zionism, by the early thirties, had undergone some changes. It was still essentially what it had been in the first days after the war, idealistic, modernist, devoted to liberal and socialist beliefs, opposed to violence ... hitherto most Zionists, for all their murmurings against the regime, respected the Mandate and even felt some gratitude for its work in their behalf. The events of 1929 changed this. Jews found it hard to maintain the former loyalty to a regime which, moved to action by a bloody aggression against Jews, had ended by trying to limit and (to their minds) to cripple Jewish endeavour in the Jewish homeland.*

In 1931 the first pan-Arab (and Islamic) congress against Zionist colonization was held in Jerusalem. By then, the Mufti's work in Palestine and enmity to Britain and to France in the Middle East had resulted in a certain sympathy to the anti-British and anti-Jewish elements rising in the West. The congress itself once more totally and unconditionally opposed the Jewish state-to-be. It was reflected in the Palestinian streets by disturbances which once more took the form of typical pogroms. The British government, by now more alarmed by the Moslem riots than by Jewish pressure, turned its coat once more and shelved Lord Passfield's anti-Zionist White Paper.

By then polarization was complete, and the Zionists and Mufti racialists had adopted totally opposed positions. If any single year could be picked out as the point of no return it would be 1929. The early thirties were consequently the era in which an independent and bi- or multi-national Palestine was stillborn. In 1932 the Zionists warned the High Commissioner, Lord Wauchhope, that the revival of constitutional plans and the creation of a democratic, proportional Legislative Council common to Arabs and Jews would be, as they delicately put it,

* Sykes, op. cit., pp. 131–2.

'as much against Arab as Jewish interests'. The stiff-necked aristocrat disregarded the warnings or threats of his 'charges'. On 10 November 1932 he served the League of Nations notice that he would create just such a Legislative Council. He also enacted a Local Government Ordinance which allowed the Arabs to grasp firmly the reins of local power in those towns in which they held a majority; and the Jews to consolidate themselves in their new colonies and towns. Polarization now became political: the common bonds of Jews and non-Jews were weakened, the bases of separatist existence officially sanctioned by the Mandate, development was connected but separate and, worst of all, it went on under the twin banners of the two racialist ideologies. Nationalism became a disguise for far older, far more dangerous psychoses.

As if to underline this by a further blow to the Palestinians' pride, the Constitutional Republic of Syria was created in June 1932 in neighbouring Damascus. It was more or less independent – and totally authoritarian. But this certainly did not worry the Palestinians, caught in the cross-currents of racialism. They worried about their lack of *independence*, not their lack of *freedom*.

In 1932 Chaim Arlozoroff, a leader of Labour Zionism, was assassinated on the beach at Tel-Aviv. Some accused Revisionist-Zionist terrorists, who were duly brought to trial. Others accused the Palestinians. The fact is that Arlozoroff was the last Zionist politician of both renown and power who tried to reach some kind of cooperation with the Palestinian non-Jews. His death opened the way to the devious politician who was to dominate the scene for the next thirty years: David Ben-Gurion, who inherited the mantle of Arlozoroff's power but opposed his ideas.

That same year a far more catastrophic event took place far from Palestine's borders. On 30 January 1933 Adolf Hitler was declared Chancellor of Germany by the ageing German President Hindenburg. The Arabs took heart: maybe Britain would be confronted with a power strong enough to dislodge her from the Middle East. They also initiated a boycott of Zionist and British goods.

The first effects of Hitler's rise to power on the Middle East made themselves felt in 1934–5. What is now called in Israel the 'Third Alyah', the immigration of thousands upon thousands of Central European Jews, mainly from Germany, had begun. Jewish immigration in 1931 had actually declined somewhat. In 1932, when armed struggles were going on in the streets and beer-cellars of Germany, and Nazi slogans were being painted on Jewish shop-windows, immigration doubled and reached 9,533. In the years of Hitler's coming to power it tripled again and reached 30,327. In 1934 42,359 immigrants arrived in Palestine. In 1935, when the Nazis legislated the Nürnberg Laws, 61,854 immigrants arrived – mostly European Jews.

In October of that same year the Arabs rose once more in Palestine – but this time they directed their rage against the British Administration alone. Under their by now acknowledged leader, the Mufti Haj Amin, they rioted. Twenty-six Arabs were killed, 187 injured; only one British subject was killed and twenty-six wounded. But most remarkable of all, not a single Jew was killed or injured.

At this point, without losing its racialist background, Palestinian nationalism seems to have jelled into a half-conscious national anti-imperialist feeling. Incidentally, one man, already the victim of pan-Moslem nationalism, now became an actual martyr of the Arabs' fighting: the venerable Mussa Kazim, so cavalierly pushed aside by Haj Amin, was hurt in the Jaffa street-riots of that year and died shortly after, probably from shock, in the ninth decade of his life.

In that same month of October the Zionist extremists started a counter-riot in Tel-Aviv against the limitations on mass-immigration. Hitler's shadow, looming large on the wall, gave an ideal pretext to growing Zionist extremism. In Europe and the U.S., no thought at all was given to the problem of menaced European Jewry, now coming totally under the sinister shadow. Great Britain herself admitted only 3,000 Jewish escapees from Nazism between 1932 and 1935.

Meanwhile the Palestinians had understood that the demographic balance was changing to their detriment. A deputation of Arab mayors went shortly after this to the High Commissioner and demanded the Legislative Council they had rejected years before. Nothing came of it. In 1934 the Municipal Law was passed and elections were held, and one of the Mufti's stalwarts, a member of the Khaldy family, defeated the leading contender in Jerusalem, Ragheb Bey Nashashibi, a member of the levantinized 'land-bourgeoisie' and an opponent of the Mufti's fanatics. Haj Amin and his partisans publicly declared that they would 'annihilate' the Jewish National Home if they ever reached political power in Palestine. The Jewish Agency informed the High Commissioner that it was totally opposed to constitutional reform and to self-government – which, being proportional, would give a natural majority to the Arabs.

In 1935 the Mandatory power did its best to save the situation. Legislation protecting the small tenant-cultivator or *Fellah* was published – to no avail. A Legislative Assembly composed of fourteen Arabs and eight Jews (representing the by now 28 per cent Jewish minority in Palestine) was also put forward. The Zionists once more declined. They also started to buy arms abroad. Discovery of one case of arms-smuggling provoked violent Arab reaction. As unimaginative as the Mandate authorities, the Palestinians now harped on the slogan of a Legislative Assembly. Their 1935 delegation was headed by the Mufti himself. However, inside the Palestinian-Arab camp not all were in favour of such a council. A debate raged on the question of whether this might give some foothold to the Jews. The Zionists profited from every anti-Semitic slogan of the Mufti's men, organized propaganda abroad, appealed to public opinion in Great Britain and elsewhere. Meanwhile, the apparent prosperity of the Middle East ended abruptly with the Italian invasion of Ethiopia and the disruption of stability in the Mediterranean basin. Fascist broadcasts in Arabic increased. Totalitarian popularity was also evident in the Arab countries.

The depression had an almost immediate effect on the Palestinian situation. Several guerilla chieftains arose, most of them non-Palestinian soldiers of fortune. One was a Lebanese, Fawzy El Kaoukji. He assassinated Arabs who cooperated with the British or with the Jews and enlisted workless Arab peasants and layabouts. Sale of lands by the *Effendis* to the Zionist funds had brought an exodus of peasants to the towns; but in the mixed towns, such as Haifa and Jerusalem, the Zionist leadership now allowed for little employment of Arabs by Jewish firms: immigration was at a record level, recession was strong, and mutual hate and distrust were stronger than ever. Each side now had good prextexts to care 'for its own people only'. But it is worth remembering that hate and distrust on both sides preceded the situation in which mutual exclusivism became a fact – as did the Zionist slogan of 'Hebrew Labour Only'.

In April 1936 the Palestinian parties created the Arab Higher Committee, which, like the Moslem Council which preceded it, was under the Mufti's thumb. It called for a general strike, which lasted for six months and was the Palestinians' first genuine grass-roots revolt. It accounted for 1,351 victims, among them 305 dead: 187 Moslems, 80 Jews, 28 British, 10 Christian Arabs. Britain armed the Jewish auxiliary police; and the Palmach, or Jewish Shock-Troops, were created by Orde Wingate. Riots and battles raged unabated till June, when moderate Arab leaders called in vain for a truce. Nonetheless in July, 137 Mandate civil servants tried again, and presented a document listing the minimum demands of the Arabs. This moderate step was taken at the instigation of Britain's main feudal Arab supporters in the Middle East: the Emir Abd-Allah of Transjordan and Iraq's Foreign Minister Nuri Said. But the rebellion was now beyond the control of far-removed feudal lordlings, who lost their authority over Palestine when they proceeded to hack out elsewhere their own separatist fiefs. Fighting continued. In September 1936 British troop reinforcements arrived from abroad. The Mandatory power had decided to stop the rebellion at any price. At the end of that same year the rulers of Iraq, Transjordan, Saudi Arabia and the Yemen asked the Arab Higher Committee for Palestine to stop fighting and believe in 'the good intentions of our friend Great Britain'. The General Strike was accordingly called off – but only because the populace had been cowed and bled white. The Peel Commission arrived on 11 November 1936, giving Arab moderates cause for hope. The Arab Higher Committee, however, typically decided to boycott the inquiry. It only sent representatives to the Peel Commission's fifty-sixth session, on 12 January 1937. No less typically the Mufti, at the head of a group of nine Arab Higher Committee men and one secretary, invoked purely religious grounds for his opposition to the Jewish National Home. He spoke of an apocalyptic day in which the Jews would build their third temple on the ruins of the Omar Mosque if they were not stopped.

The irony of this line is that at this juncture there was almost no direct religious motivation in Zionism. The mysticism of modern Israeli extremists was still confined to a thin outer fringe of extreme Revisionists and Zealots. The Mufti spoke out of his own racialist feelings. Zionism had kindled in the Palestinian nation the worst fires of hate, just as Arab racialism, together with the Hitler massacres, gave the Zionist movement a lasting trauma, making its leaders impervious to non-separatist humanitarian viewpoints.

The Mufti also suggested an Arab-British pact; demanded the prohibition of sale of land to the Jews and a stop to Jewish immigration; and went so far as to imply that a solution would have to be found to the 'too numerous, 400,000 strong' Jewish community in Palestine. In the light of the Mufti's subsequent collaboration with Adolf Hitler, his visits to the extermination camps and his creation of an Arab-Nazi unit for the Germans, there is little doubt that, had the Arab Higher Committee taken power in Palestine under Haj Amin, there would have been something remarkably like the 'final solution' of the European Jewish problem, as carried out by the National Socialists.

That same year the British government thought it had no way out but the partition of Palestine into a Jewish and an Arab-Moslem state. Professor Coupland offered this to Chaim Weizmann. Weizmann even met Lebanon's president Eddé, who hailed him as the 'first President of the Jewish Republic' – a thing which Weizmann was to become, in due time. On 7 July 1937, through the publication of the report to the Peel Commission, Britain declared the Mandate unworkable and British pledges to both parties unreconcilable. Imperialism had lost another round, but the Palestinian people was not fated to profit from its setback.

In 1937, 97 Arabs were killed, 149 wounded and 816 arrested. The Jews created an organization for illegal immigration – Mossad Alyah Beit. The League of Nations asked Britain for a detailed partition plan. Some voices of sanity were raised, however, against partition – even if from imperialist interests, rather than humanist logic: partition would create 'two racially totalitarian states side by side in what we now call Palestine', Sir Archibald Sinclair stated in the House of Commons on 20 July 1937. Lord Samuel proposed an Arab Federation consistent with British interests, comprising Saudi Arabia, Iraq, Transjordan, Syria, Lebanon and Palestine, giving the Jews the right to settle in both Transjordan and Palestine. The two basic errors of all later ideological and political programmes for the settlement of the Jewish-Arab struggle in Palestine were already evident in this first year of partition plans: either the problem was seen in the light of exclusivist and racialist needs and values, or the interests of imperialist powers were considered the most important. The problem of Palestine as an emergent independent entity was scarcely considered, either by the king-makers of the West or by the supposed victims on both sides of the barricades.

As the pan-Moslem leadership and the Zionist policy of exclusivist settlement consolidated the racist, pan-Arab character of the Palestinians at that stage, so the rebellion of 1936 consolidated the hitherto submerged maximalist tendencies of Zionism. At the 20th Zionist Congress of August 1937 the Peel report was rejected as too little and too late. Sykes reminisces:

> In a press interview the chairman of the executive of the Jewish Agency, Ben-Gurion, said: 'the debate has not been for or against the indivisibility of Eretz-Israel. No Zionist can forego the smallest portion of Eretz-Israel. The debate was over which of two routes would lead quicker to the common goal.' When Dr Weizmann was asked about the exclusion from the proposed State of the South and the Negev, he remarked more enigmatically: 'It will not run away.'

The minimalist Professor Magnes, who advocated a bi-national Jewish-Arab state but was also an avowed Zionist, was shouted down at a meeting of the Jewish Agency's council. Not to be outdone, the Arab Higher Committee also rejected in its totality the Peel report on partition. Anti-Zionism was the order of the day in the Arab world. On 8 September 1937 it became the flag of the pan-Moslem camp: the Mufti as the saviour, the Axis powers a possible ally, and Britain and the Jews – not the Zionists any more – the 'hereditary enemy'. The 400-man-strong pan-Arab conference meeting at Boudan made the following resolution:

> Palestine is an integral part of the Arabian homeland and no part of this territory will be alienated with Arab consent ... We must make Great Britain understand that she must choose between our friendship and the Jews. Britain must change her policy in Palestine or we shall be at liberty to side with other European powers whose policies are inimical to Great Britain.

In Palestine the rebellion went on. Lewis Andrews, Commissioner for Galilee, was shot down together with his escort outside the Anglican church in Nazareth. In October 1938, nineteen Jews were killed in Tiberias. In 1938 Franklin D. Roosevelt called the Evian conference in order to find a solution to the Jewish-European problem. Nothing much resulted from it. In November 1939 the St James Round Table conference was called by the British government, the prototype of the talks to be held later, with the help of mediators, between Jews and Arabs – both in 1949 in Rhodes, with the help of U N mediator Ralph Bunche, and in 1971 in the U.S., under the sponsorship of Gunnar Jarring.

On September the Second World War broke out.

*

The Palestinian rebellion went on until the end of 1939. In the battles, 3,122 Arabs were killed, 110 hanged by the British, 1,775 injured and 5,679 arrested; 329 Jews were killed, 857 injured; 135 Britons were killed and 386 injured. In May 1939 the White Paper was published, and in July Palestine's doors were closed to all but a token number of Jewish immigrants. Zionism became outspokenly militant, the Irgun started fighting the British in August 1939, and in December Winston Churchill declared himself for a Jewish state.

The Palestinian rebellion was unsuccessful as an instrument of national liberation. First, because in spite of its grass-roots character it never crystallized into a popular movement with social aims – in spite of the fact that the expropriation of the *Fellahin* was a class-phenomenon, the *Effendis* remaining in the cities (at that time) or in their homes abroad, and getting comparatively huge gains from the losses of their poorer countrymen. The fact that an exclusivist, racialist fanatic like Haj Amin El-Husseini took the leadership of this revolution totally eliminated any popular advantages which this mass revolt might have brought to the poorer Palestinians. In fact, in 1936–9 the Palestinian masses acted precisely as the Israeli masses acted in and after the 1967 war; they fought, died and were maimed in the name of a racialist ideal of intolerance, under pretext of fighting for their survival; and allowed fanatical zealots and exploiters to accumulate profits and personal advantages in the process. They also gave the racialists of the other side an advantage which was to be exploited to the hilt by the more extreme Zionists.

The Palestinian masses did so because of the mutually exclusivist character of the fight, a struggle which was real, motivated by cultural and psychological fears, deep-seated and not to be overcome at these times. Much time will have to pass, in fact, before they can be overcome, and then only by a gradual elimination of cultural and national differences between these two peoples of one country. Till then, the danger of mutual destruction or total expulsion from this land is extremely real for both sides, and no amount of ideological slogans will make it less so. Nor will any kind of identification with one of the mutually exclusive goals: an Arab Palestine or a Jewish State of Israel.

One might ask oneself why belief helped the Jews develop a militant nationalism, and ruthlessly overcome the opposition under the Mandate and after, while it limited the endeavours of the Palestinians and crippled their hopes of an independent national entity for so many years. The answer may be that the Jews did not use their old-fashioned belief blindly and tenaciously; rather, under the influence of Western liberalism, belief underwent a change, became the basis of their modern and state-centred nationalism, fanaticism clothed with the trappings of modern 'logic' and using the language of twentieth-century political dynamism. The Palestinian Arabs, on the other hand, under the fatal leadership of Haj Amin El-Husseini, went directly back to the old teachings, called for a *Jihad* or holy war, and generally behaved as if the 1920–50 Middle East was still the stamping ground of Haroun El-Rashid and Abd-Allah El-Mamoun. They had not the benefit of modern economics, sociology, politics and technology; nor that of Western diplomatic thought and usage. At the time the Husseini Moslem fanatic assumed the leadership of the Palestinian entity-in-the-making their nationalism was up to a point instinctive, and of course deeply religious; but politically superficial. Also, Islam somewhat diluted the involvement of the Palestinians with nationalism in one country, centred on one territory – till it was too late. With Zionism, Jewish belief concentrated their efforts; with the Palestinians, belief dissipated them.

5 Jewish Liberation Movements up to 1942

The growth of the movement for liberation of Jewish Palestine from British Mandatory rule has to be seen against the background of the contradictions within the ruling Establishment. This Jewish Establishment, intelligent, able, industrious and extremely careful, had developed as we have seen a 'state inside a state', infinitely better organized, both economically and politically, than the Arab one.

Already the usual contradictions of a state developing a capitalist economy had appeared in Jewish Palestine, but adapted to the particular syndicalist variant of capitalism which grew up there. This may also explain why it was the so-called 'Left' – leaning heavily on trade-union funds and organization, as well as on the Kibbutzim – which had most success in industrializing, in pay-as-you-go business, and in creating export enterprises. This 'Left' fought an economic battle with the 'private enterprise' brand of commerce and industry in the Jewish sector of the pre-war years, and was able to gain on it, little by little but all the time – owing to the fact that the industrial complex of the Histadrut, the main trade union, was able to prevent strikes as well as being equipped to get the fattest and juiciest prizes from the Mandatory authorities whenever some development project was tendered, military camps built or roads laid.

Thus, without relinquishing the socialist-Zionist ideology it had inherited from the idealism of the first settlers, the Left developed through the 1930s a full-grown 'capitalist' complex. It considered strikes as attacks upon its authority and damaging to the 'Jewish interest'. It fought for the exclusive use of Jewish labour while the capitalist Jewish Right, being poorer and less privileged, had to make do with whatever it could afford and therefore tried to get the cheapest labour possible – this being, in the Palestine Mandate, Arab labour. So, up to a point and for its own reasons, the Right favoured economic co-existence with the Palestinians, while the Left fought it with utter intransigence.

A number of fights ensued between the Right and the Left, which was simultaneously a capitalist employer, that is an exploiter of the workers, and a 'defender' of their interests. The Left was able to checkmate the private-enterprise wing of Zionist capitalism, using all the time the slogans of 'Jewish patriotism', but not forgoing for a moment the closest coopcration with the imperialist authority of the British Mandate Administration.

When the Second World War broke out, this cooperation took on a further and deeper-seated aspect: the Jews of Palestine found themselves on the side of the Allies – including the British empire. Great Britain, the greatest sufferer among the Allies after the fall of France in 1940, was also the Mandate Administrator, taking with one hand the right of free immigration, but giving with the other the bounty of economic development and internal Jewish predominance to the authorities of the Zionist Establishment. Britain was also the great protector, the arch-ally – but not for the Zionist Right.

The free-enterprise branch of Zionism had been waiting, all the while, for the right moment to impose its ascendancy. It had the greatest charismatic leader of world Zionism – Wladimir Zeev Jabotinsky. It had a programme for maximum immigration and occupation of the total area of Palestine and Transjordan. It also had on its side a considerable segment of the American Jewish community as well as of the East European one, which was becoming, in the thirties, under Stalin's rule, more and more disenchanted with Soviet socialism.

This was reflected in the home front in Palestine. It was also reflected in the relations between the paramilitary 'defence' organizations. Originally, there had been only one 'defence' or Haganah organization. Haganah was born in an idealistic atmosphere, hostile to military, or even paramilitary, ideas. The need to defend the colonies established by the Jewish labour wing, and the hamlets created by the followers of the free-enterprise wing, led in the end to the formation of a guild of watchmen, or militia. The Zionist movement had some pretensions to establish independent political and economic organisms, and, for their protection, such a military arm, although abhorrent at that time to most of the Jewish leaders – and to Dr Chaim Weizmann above all – was deemed a necessary thing.

The precursor of the Haganah in pre-Mandate Palestine was an organization called simply 'The Watchman' or Hashomer. It was indeed just that: a unit of gun-carrying horsemen, who watched the fields and protected the Jewish inhabitants from the depredations of marauders and highwaymen. Some of these were Bedouin nomads who pilfered whatever they could lay their hands on, in the time-honoured way of the *Bedawi* tribes. Others were *Fellahin*, land-labourers deprived of their livelihood when the *Effendis* sold their fields to the Keren Kayemet or Jewish National Fund.

The Haganah or 'Defence' was created in 1920, under the guidance of men who had fought in the Jewish Legion with the British armies in the First World War. Its founder was Eliahu Golomb, who was a Labour man. So was the first commanding officer of this secret defence body of the Jews in Palestine. In fact, as the chronicler and journalist Haviv Knaan has explained,* at that time the Haganah was not much more than an armed fist of the Histadrut syndicate.

The first commanding officer, Joseph Hecht, had immigrated from Russia in 1914. He had worked in the fields, 'conquering the soil' from the Arabs, and draining the marches of the badly kept land the National Fund had just bought. He was one of the first volunteers to the Jewish Legion and later kept secret arms caches for the Hashomer watchmen. In 1921 he directed the defence of the Agricultural School of Mikweh Israel, under siege by rebelling Arabs, and after this success he began helping Eliahu Golomb, one of the most gifted Labour leaders, to organize a defence body.

Hecht came from Eastern Europe at a time when *Konspiratzia*, or the art of secret intrigue, was at an apogee there. As a result

* *Haaretz*, 5 April 1970.

he saw his new task as the creation not of a military but rather of a political and class organization: a Russo-Jewish mixture of workers' council, clandestine party and secret society. In this spirit he formed the 'secret army' of the Jewish community during the crucial and blood-covered years 1921 to 1929.

Hecht filled his men with a no-nonsense belief in 'doing things and doing them well'. He indoctrinated everybody with the need for utmost secrecy – secrecy not only from the *Goyim*, the Gentile, that is the British Mandate and the Arabs, but also from the bourgeois, that is the free-enterprise wing and nationalist element among the Jews.

On the other hand, Hecht never hesitated to perform any action to fulfil what he conceived as his 'Party duty'. At this time a reaction to the earlier pro-Zionist attitude of the British Administration had set in, as it repeatedly did, and Lord Plummer, the High Commissioner for Palestine, had tried to reach some kind of agreement with the leaders of the Arab nationalists, including Haj Amin. It was a time when for men of Hecht's uncomplicated views it was easy to see any viewpoint which was not Zionist-Labour as a defection and a betrayal.

He therefore planned, organized and helped to carry out the political assassination of a well-to-do Jew from Holland, Dr Israel De Haan. Dr De Haan, a religious Jew and a socialist, had come to Palestine as an ardent Zionist. However, after a short trial-and-error period he changed his mind and became strongly anti-Zionist. With the help of the ultra-religious Zealot community of Jewish Jerusalem De Haan made contact with the leadership of the Arab nationalists. The Zionist leadership saw in him a 'traitor' – and Hecht took it upon himself to carry out the proper sentence for treason.

Reactions to the killing were violent. The involvement of the Haganah in the De Haan assassination was never *legally* proved, but a section of the Jewish leadership disapproved of the deed – or of the scandal which followed it. And since Hecht was not altogether effective as a military leader, owing to his lack of formal military schooling, he was quietly eased out and asked to 'keep away' from defence matters for a year.

This was particularly useful to the Jewish leaders as negotiations had begun for the inclusion of the free-enterprise men in the Haganah command. At the end of the negotiations it was agreed to give them fifty per cent representation. Hecht judged this a 'class betrayal' and tried to organize a putsch in which the other officers declared that they would have only him as their commanding officer. The putsch failed, the Right adhered to the Haganah, and Hecht left security matters forever. He died in April 1970, at the age of 76, a bitter, lonely and forgotten man who tilled his earth and spoke but seldom to his neighbours in the small fishing village of Michmoret.

As for the right wing, its partnership in the Haganah was of relatively short duration. In the thirties it broke away to form the Haganah Leumit, or 'National Defence', which the young and talented David Raziel was to run in due course. Later this body became better known as the Irgun Tzwai Leumi ('National Military Organization') and, abroad, simply as the Irgun.

The Haganah was, as we have seen, clandestine. And with good reason. Officially the British Administration did not tolerate the carrying of weapons by private citizens. But just as the British often closed one eye when investigating the existence of the armed Arab irregulars, so the authorities also knew of the activities of the Haganah, and indeed used this organization again and again as an 'auxiliary police'. These Jewish *Gaffirim* were almost exclusively Haganah members, all of them armed with British guns. They did their bit in the rebellion of 1936 and later.

From time to time, worried by the too rapidly increasing influence of the Jewish sector, the Mandatory Authorities gave free rein to the Arab counterpart of the *Gaffirim* and even went so far as to disarm units of the Jewish auxiliary police – which were immediately set upon and killed.

In 1939 the fight against the White Paper, which severely restricted Jewish immigration into Palestine, became the rallying-point of all those Zionists who did not accept the theory that there was an affinity of interests between the British Administration and the emerging Zionist Establishment. The rallying-point, indeed, of *all* Zionists: apart from the solidarity and feelings of unity awakened by the White Paper, the syndicalist leadership saw the growth of its industrial power curtailed by the shortage of Jewish labour, while the Arab rebellion made any change in its 'Jewish labour only' policy unthinkable. It also saw the beginning of the holocaust in Europe. It was, however, torn between these arguments and its fruitful cooperation with the Mandatory Authorities.

The Right could afford to be more logical. It was not kept back by avowed or non-avowed vested economic and psychological interests in the Mandate. Neither was it the ruling element in the Vaad Leumi, the National Committee of the Jews in Palestine. So it had every interest in challenging the existing order. *Ki Sheket Huh Refesh* – 'silence is dirt' – Jabotinsky had said. And the Right, directed by powerful 'Revisionist' Zionists in Palestine and abroad, started fighting the British Mandate.

This was not a fight for the *expulsion* of Britain from the Holy Land. Even Jabotinsky never saw Great Britain as an enemy. For one, he had fought in the British army as an officer. He also always maintained that he had to fight the British to make them see that the Jews – and particularly the Right Zionist wing – were the only ally Britain could trust in the Middle East; a sentiment echoed in Golda Meir's declarations of the late sixties and early seventies, that Israel is the only trustworthy friend of the US in the area.

But England had other, more important interests in the Zone, at that time: the route to India; oil in the Persian Gulf; the African Front, threatened by Rommel's armies; the possibility that an Arab betrayal would thrust a dagger in the backbone of the Allied forces in the Middle East; and above all, the fear that an additional million Jews would almost certainly provoke another Arab revolt, more successful than the attempts of 1921, 1929 and 1936–9.

For embattled Britain, the main thing in the first years of the Second World War was to keep the *status quo* in the Middle East, to have her back covered. This Britain could achieve only by checking the growth of the Jewish population of Palestine on the one hand, and by using this Jewish element, on the other, to help her block any possible pro-Nazi revolt – as happened during the revolt of Rashid Ali El-Keylany in Iraq.

However, it was much too late in the day for Great Britain to keep her finger in the dyke. The world war which made this *status quo* necessary also gave the Jewish element a chance to develop its industrial capacities to the utmost. There were six hundred thousand Allied soldiers and personnel in the Middle East, cut off from their natural supply bases. The logistic problems of the fronts in the Middle East and northern Mediterranean, Africa and southern Europe became one further factor to facilitate the growth of the Zionist brand of capitalism.

Private enterprise developed hugely. But it was the highly technological and efficient instruments of the Histadrut which had to fulfil the main tasks of building military camps and fortifications, laying roads, and creating virtual new towns, almost overnight. Such bodies as Solel Boneh and Koor, respectively Israel's biggest building and industrial complexes today, got off the ground then.

For the first time in the Zionist Establishment's history the economic interests of the Left power-élite became almost identical with the political interests of the British. And this allowed the subterraneous development of a nationalist consciousness in the Right wing of that Establishment. So were created the first real contradictions inside Palestinian Zionism.

A fissure appeared between the interests of the Jews in Palestine and those of their rulers, both Jewish and imperial. Up to that point the Zionist-socialist Establishment had lived, as it were, in a hothouse of never-never politics. They ran their Kibbutzim according to the precepts of utopian communism, but the *Fellahin* who worked the land until the Kibbutzim bought it from its feudal Arab owners they shooed away like so many tsetse flies. In this the Left had been persistently opposed by the private-enterprise sectors. The Right acted to defend its own class-interests. It needed labour for the evolution of such 'non-Left' hamlets as Rishon Letzion, Petah Tikwah, Hadera and Rehovot. But these villages and townlets, as well as the small Jewish land-holders and industrialists, were far weaker than the Histadrut.

This body *was* the Establishment, or at least its main tentacle. And a prosperous Establishment – upper-class in spite of its idealistic, even utopian, beginnings – would not rock the boat. When the British Mandate was threatened in the early forties by the 'right-wing' activities of the Zionist Revisionists and the Stern group, it was the 'socialist' Left which gave every assistance to the Mandate imperialists – to the point of kidnapping Irgun and Stern freedom-fighters and holding them in Kibbutz prison cells or simply delivering them up to the CID (in the Palestine of the forties this meant 'Colonial Investigation Department', which was notorious for its methods and more than once charged with torturing terrorists and even murdering them).

While the Right was fighting for independence, the Zionist-socialist ruling élite fought only for more immigration of European Jewry. From time to time the Haganah – for all practical purposes the military arm of the 'Left' Establishment – blew up bridges or organized clandestine immigrant landings. In all other respects it cooperated closely with the British authorities.

It was this double background of Left reluctance to adopt national-revolutionary attitudes, and of the underprivileged position of the free-enterprise Right, which led to the most misunderstood fact in the history of Israel's fight for independence: that it was the Right which first and foremost fought for liberation from imperialist rule. This nationalist fight was progressive, revolutionary and beneficial for the Jews of Palestine. Indeed it should be remembered that most underdeveloped countries start their struggle for progress with an ultra-nationalist movement, a movement of national liberation which is, as often as not, chauvinist, and also often led by the sons of the landowners and the rich – the 'young intellectuals'.

Because of its particular circumstances, Israel developed a variation of the normal process. Israeli society evolved from a people with limited national attributes but with a national goal; through a phase of utopian socialism; through a further period of capitalist acquisition of power bases and of emerging industrial society – in which the traditional roles of Left and Right were reversed – to the point where, caught in the crossfire of history and blood, the *whole* Jewish community was drawn into the fight, ensuring finally the predominance of the syndicalist class at home. But while it lasted it was a fight for national assertion. It became a fight for survival. And it gave birth to the State of Israel.

Against this background of awakening national consciousness – as opposed to Jewish-Zionist consciousness – appeared the first fighting and committed anti-imperialists in Israel. They came from the extreme right. The men who declared themselves to be 'not Zionists but Land of Israel Nationalists' were ultra-extremists. They have entered history as one of the most dreaded and most hated 'terrorist gangs' – Lohamey Herut Israel, 'the Fighters for the Freedom of Israel', known to one and all as the 'Stern Gang' and in Israel simply as Lehy.

The story of Lehy is rather simple – and strange. In the late thirties the Haganah or Defence Organization had been split by the militants of the Revisionist Zionist movement under Jabotinsky, who became commander-in-chief of the rightist splinter, Irgun. Soon two young men were at the head of Irgun, David Raziel and Abraham Stern, both in their late twenties or early thirties. Both were born in Poland, both Jewish mystics, both very practical politicians and tacticians, who were able to weld a disciplined paramilitary body from a shadow army of hesitant defenders of townlets from the pogroms.

Up to that time the syndicalist utopians of the Labour movement, which controlled the Haganah, had a rather shame-faced approach to military matters. Contemplating the cheerful ultra-militarism of the Israelis in the early seventies and the almost mad worship of the average Tel-Avivi for *his* air force, *his* tank corps, or *his* current commander-in-chief, it is hard to believe that thirty years ago the leadership of the Jewish community in Palestine hated war and military trappings, and indeed the very idea of creating an army. What they wanted instead was a popular militia of workers and Kibbutzniks – dominated by the latter.

Here, as in many other facets of day-to-day life, the nascent nationalism of the Revisionist Zionists opposed a concept of its own to the 'official' image promoted by the Labour leadership. Jabotinsky started extolling the virtues of uniforms, conscious discipline, weapons, and the rest of the nationalist paraphernalia so dear to the chauvinist *rinascimiento* which swept the Right of the European continent in the twenties and thirties, as it swept Asia, Africa and even parts of South America later on.

Jabotinsky was in no way a fascist. In economic matters he supported plain old-fashioned free enterprise. On the contrary, it was the 'Labour' camp which evolved towards a corporative regime. But Jabotinksy was no doubt influenced by the reaction to communist and socialist ideas then sweeping over Europe. In the late thirties, before Hitler's death camps and the horrors of the Second World War, but after Stalin had claimed three million victims and after the Moscow purges, it was not so blind a viewpoint as might be supposed. Without being fascist, Jabotinsky compared the triumphant sweep into power of nationalism in Germany, Italy, and Spain with the Left hold over the Jewish Establishment, both in Palestine and throughout the Zionist movement abroad. He drew the simple conclusion, and declared that Zionism too must become militant, nationalist, and conquering in its ideas and actions. In the early seventies, of course, this is the official view of the Israeli government and the Establishment of both Israel and world Jewry.

The results of Jabotinsky's new policy were astonishing. The Revisionist party swept through large segments of Jewish communities everywhere. It should be noted that the nearer to the Russian border the bigger the influence of the Revisionist Zionists was. Polish Jews, for instance, before their almost complete destruction by Hitler, were greatly influenced by Jabotinsky, and his movement encompassed not only the most able but also the most idealistic of the young men there.

Two such were Raziel and Stern. When they emigrated to Palestine, they became part of the active young leadership of the Revisionist secret army. Under the influence of Abraham Stern, who took the *nom de guerre* Yair – 'the one who shall lighten the path' – Raziel gravitated naturally towards the post of commander-in-chief of the split-away Irgun.

And then three fateful things happened. In 1939 the war broke out. In the same year the British government published the White Paper prohibiting the further entry of Jews into Palestine, except for a quota of 40,000 a year who were to get 'special certificates'. And in 1940 Jabotinsky died of a stroke, thus beheading the forceful nationalist movement.

It has already been said that Britain's entry into the war created a dichotomy in the economic and political relationship between the Palestine Zionists and the British government. Where once the Zionist leaders had the stronger influence with the British, if never their total sympathy (for after all this active, Westernized, competent minority had the insolence to *compete* with British culture, instead of just accepting its gifts), now the White Paper was published a *rapprochement* was made between the British and the Arab neo-feudal leaders, for reasons already explained.

The Zionist Establishment, however, was still there, and, being there, was in a position to supply much of the technological, industrial and commercial demands of the Allied armies, now bivouacked in the Middle East and logistically cut off from their sources by the Nazi U-boats and the advancing Axis armies all over Europe and Africa. So the British treated the Zionists of Palestine just as the Gentile communities of former ages treated the Jews of the Ghetto: they discriminated against them, disliked them, tolerated them – and used them. And the British in turn were used by the embittered and isolated Jews for their own purposes.

These purposes of the Zionist Labour Establishment were the consolidation of the economic and political power of national-syndicalist Jewish power in Palestine; the exploitation of the war-boom, a temporary but vast source of income; and the further tightening of Labour's grasp upon the whole Jewish-Palestinian population. Thus, thanks to the British empire, the Histadrut emerged as the dominant economic power in the Zionist camp: the Haganah acquired excellent military training in the ranks of the British forces;* and kindled by the White Paper,

*Almost all the senior officers of the Israeli defence forces from 1948 to 1967 saw active service under Allied Command in the Second World War.

the agitation in Palestine and abroad for the immigration of further Jews went on tirelessly. There were of course psychological pressures for the liberation and emigration of all Jews to Palestine, even before 1939; but the campaign of 1939–47 was incomparably stronger than before – being waged as it was against the double background of Nazi camps in Europe and of a dynamically expanding corporative-capitalist economy at home.

However, the Zionist Labour leadership was determined not to kill the goose which laid such golden eggs – the British Mandate. In spite of its slogan 'A Hebrew State!' always accompanying the cry of 'Free Immigration!', much was done in those years by the Labour leadership to contain the movement of national liberation, then gaining impetus in Jewish Palestine. In the ranks of the 'Right', the situation was ripe for such a revolution. The cooperation between Labour and the British was quoted as a 'good bad example'. Jabotinsky always believed – as did Ben-Gurion – that the British Mandate was wrong in 'trusting the Arabs' and that a pro-British Jewish State would do much more for imperial interests in the Middle East and on the route to India. This belief helped to propagate Zionist-Revisionist ideology in London.

But such is the inner dialectical logic of a national revolution – or a social revolution, for that matter – that this state of affairs soon gave way to a somewhat timorous and hesitant militancy against the British Mandatory authorities, even inside the Labour sector; particularly after the gates closed before the immigrants' noses and the first details of the mass deportations of Jews to the *Nacht und Nebel*, 'Night and Fogbound' Death Camps, were known in Palestine.

On the other hand, when the leaders of the Zionist Establishment called on the young Jews of Palestine to join the ranks of the Allied armies, Irgun gave up its short-lived first war upon the Mandate. A kind of truce was sealed between the 'terrorists' of the Irgun and the British army. The gates of the internment camps opened, and many Irgun members left prison to become fully-fledged British soldiers, with their commander David Raziel at their head. Indeed, Raziel fell in action in 1943, operating as a

British Commando in Iraq, where he helped put down the pro-Nazi revolt of Rashid Ali El-Keylany.

When the Zionist revolutionary movement had degenerated into the ruling economic Establishment of the Jewish community in Palestine, Irgun had become for a short while the main instrument of Jewish national liberation. Now it was quiescent. The torch had to be handed on to somebody. But – to whom?

Ultimately the torch was not handed on, but grabbed violently from the weak fingers of the Irgun, whose leaders already wore British uniform. The hand which took it upon itself to carry on the struggle for national freedom – the national freedom of a *new* nation – was that of Abraham Stern–Yair.

Yair and some of his fellow commanders created a schism in the Irgun. In clandestine meetings in Israel and abroad, he spoke before the Irgun leadership and told them succinctly that 'The enemy is the one who rules in your country.' This lapidary definition, equally applicable to social and national causes, equally abrasive for 'bureaucrats', 'capitalists', 'fascists' and 'professional revolutionaries', was understood by Yair to mean that although Nazi Germany was the enemy of the whole of the Jewish people the fact that Britain had imperial interests in Palestine made her the immediate, and indeed necessary, target of the National Liberation Movement of the Land of Israel. All this was based upon a dreamy, mystical and almost religious conception of history, of the past and the future of the Land of Israel.

Yair's ideas were not well received by either the higher or the lower echelons of the Irgun underground. When a war is on, when your people are dying, in concentration camps and on the front line, it is difficult to remain rational, it is difficult to understand what must be done to allow a country and its population to survive, or to allow them to continue fighting, in the 'right' way and for the 'right' goals. The Revisionist underground men turned their backs on Abraham Stern and his friends.

They went on their way, anyway. They created a small, tightly-knit underground and, as is almost inevitable in such an organization, developed a strategic theory of terrorism, carried out individually against individual targets: that is, assassination, bank-robbing for logistic purposes, and bomb-throwing at administrative and military targets.

This kind of action, tolerated by freedom-lovers when done by a 'popular' movement as *part* of its activities, is on the other hand loathed by the same progressive circles when carried out by a national liberation movement which is cut off from society, from socialist theory, and which moreover uses neither the alibi of revolutionary war nor the camouflage of wider political action. But, at specific moments in history, and in the face of the total incomprehension of the masses, direct action is the only possible political argument. At such times one must act, and *show* by acting.

In the Palestine of 1940–43, however, the incomprehension was too complete. In spite of the White Paper, the British Administration were still the 'good guys', the ones fighting Nazism. Nobody, and particularly not the Labour camp, tried to analyse the situation in the light of a conflict of self-interests.

The only group which could have done so, the outlawed Communist Party, had become politically 'unclean' by justifying the Ribbentrop-Molotov pact of non-aggression between Germany and the USSR. Its analysis, partially true but biased, doctrinaire and bigoted, failed to impress any segment whatsoever of the Jewish population; while, by not participating in the national liberation movement of the Jews – at first Zionist, and later run by the Fighters for the Freedom of Israel – it denied itself any role of importance in the political scene of the forties.

So the Lehy men were hunted down and killed off like dogs. Both Haganah and Irgun gave lists of Lehy members to the British CID – which promptly jailed or killed them. Sometimes Haganah men themselves handed the freedom-fighters to the Special Branch. Subsequently they were tortured to give information, in a series of cruel episodes of which we are sadly reminded when we hear of the tortures of the seventies, in the special jail of the Tzrifin Camp belonging to Israel's Military Police. Yair knew that his days were numbered in such an atmosphere. He prepared the continuation of his work, coldly and detachedly, on both ideological and practical bases.

First he wrote a series of mystical commandments, the *Ikarey Hageulah*, or *Principles of Liberation*, intended for the liberation of the whole of Palestine and culminating in the building of the Third Temple of the Jews.* On the practical plane, he created a chain of command capable of carrying out his work after his death. For he had no doubt at all about his fate.†

One of the men charged with carrying on was a young engineer, also Polish born, who had been active in the Irgun even before the split. His name was Nathan Friedmann-Yellin, and he took upon himself the underground nicknames of Gera and Mor. After the creation of the State of Israel he changed his name officially to Nathan Yalin-Mor. In the sixties and seventies he became one of the foremost fighters for Palestinian self-determination and for a lasting peace between Israelis and Palestinians.

But all that lay in the future. In 1942 nothing looked more remote than a Jewish majority in Palestine. The Labour-dominated Jewish minority was prosperous but isolated, and those struggling to separate land-of-Israel consciousness from world-wide

*It must be stated at this point that some leading figures of Lehy disputed the authenticity of this document, claiming that Dr Israel Scheib-Eldad – about whom more later – had prepared the document for the consideration of his leader, Yair, and that it became 'Yair's' when found among his papers, after his death. However, given Abraham Stern–Yair's religious-nationalistic background, there is no reason to doubt his being capable of preparing such a document. Yair, a brilliant scholar of classical history, well versed in both the Latin and Greek classics, was always a dreamer turned activist. He was also a man gifted with the charisma of a prophet, and the analytical genius of a born leader. But he was in no sense a 'non-Jewish Hebrew', as so many Israel-bred figures are today – Moshe Dayan for one. His background was thoroughly Judaic.

† One of the stanzas of *Hayalim Almonim*, 'Unknown Soldiers', the hymn of the underground written by Yair – who was also a gifted poet – is:

When we fall and we die
Inside houses, on streets,
We shall be buried quietly and in silence.
But thousands and thousands of others shall vie
For the right to fight and to die, for ever.

Zionism were regarded as 'gangsters' and 'wild beasts'. Indeed, the leaders of the Zionist Establishment said publicly that whoever hunted them down or handed them to the Mandatory authorities would be doing a service to Jews everywhere. The fact was that the Establishment was just as afraid as the Mandate administrators of this murderous maverick group.

Then British Military Intelligence put into effect an ingenious plan which almost wiped out Lehy. An *agent provocateur*, purporting to 'act in the name of Mussolini's Fascist Italian government', proposed a deal to Lehy: if they fought the English, the Italians would help them to create a Jewish state. Yair vacillated. He did not accept this extraordinary offer – which he probably considered genuine – but thought about it. Meanwhile British Intelligence broke the story: the 'Stern Gang' was in contact with the Fascist enemy. And the last gap in public opinion closed against the small band of freedom-fighters.

One should not judge Yair too harshly for considering, even for a few days, the false 'Mussolini offer'. The isolated, idealistic and fanatical leader had to do *something* if he was to go on fighting in the face of the total enmity of the people he was trying to liberate. Also, he had a very good precedent – which is worth recounting.

In 1937–9, two years before his death, Jabotinsky saw the danger in which the Jews of Europe stood. He conceived a plan of 'evacuation of European Jewry' which would create a *fait accompli* and bring Great Britain to accept the Jewish State as a self-imposed but willing ally of British imperialism in the Middle East. The plan consisted, quite simply, of invading Palestine.

Jabotinsky planned to arm and train one hundred thousand young European Jews from his most loyal fief – non-Soviet Eastern Europe. This was made possible by a strange agreement which illustrates Jabotinsky's genius for juxtaposition. In those days Poland was ruled by the chauvinist, even neo-fascist Pilsudsky Party, noted for its anti-Semitism. It had organized several pogroms, claiming that the Jews were 'the main evil of Poland' – always the claim of fascists and racialists who cannot reach the roots of the real troubles of their countries. Jabotinsky started talks with them. If the Jews were the main evil of Poland, he said, why not help us to evacuate them? You don't need pogroms. They will go voluntarily.

The astonished Pilsudskeans found themselves in a political and diplomatic discussion in which they were out-manoeuvred at every step. The result was a secret agreement: the Polish regime would arm and train an army of Irgun men, which would leave Poland and take with them not only their families but many other Jews.

It is possible that, in agreeing to this, the Pilsudsky regime was not only acting from anti-Semitic considerations, but also dreaming once more the old Slavic dream of an outlet of political and naval influence in the Mediterranean. But even if the thing was done simply out of dislike of the Jewish people, is it not true that even the Balfour Declaration expressed the dislike of the British Establishment who wished the Jews to stop 'being what they are', that is, as it considered them, 'negative'?

Be this as it may, the Pilsudsky junta agreed and actually started training the Irgun men. Arms caches were smuggled into Palestine. The evacuation plan might have been carried out except for the outbreak of the Second World War. Then came Jabotinsky's death and the holocaust, and once more the stream of history abruptly altered course.

Yair was doubtless thinking of this failed plan – in which he had participated personally – when he considered for a fatal moment the spurious 'Mussolini offer'. And then it was too late. Yair had signed his death warrant – although not that of the movement of Israeli national liberation.

The end came swiftly. In December 1942 Yair was living in a garret in the populous Mizrahi B Street of southern Tel-Aviv. From there his personal couriers – mostly very young girls – carried his orders to his lieutenants. He could not see his wife, Roni, who was followed everywhere by detectives. He spent all his time on conspiratorial work.

On 12 December 1942 a detachment of CID men, under the command of an officer called Morton, broke into Yair's garret. The underground leader was hiding in a wardrobe. He was dragged out, his hands were shackled, and three bullets were pumped into his temple. The CID published a jubilant communiqué: 'The gang chieftain and England's sworn enemy has been killed – the man who was designated as the Italian Quisling of his country, Abraham Stern.'*

*Quoted by a Lehy leader who survived, Yaakov Eliav, in a letter to *Haaretz*, 23 April 1970, and re-translated from the Hebrew by the author. Eliav himself had been caught two weeks previously in a room where two of his friends were coldly shot down by the CID men, who planted Italian guns and grenades as 'evidence' that the Lehy men were indeed Quislings.

6 The Underground Nationalist Movements, 1942–8

Never had a movement for national liberation been in a worse situation than that in which Lehy found itself after the assassination of Stern–Yair. Ninety-five per cent of its membership had been killed, jailed or deported to British prison camps in Eritrea and other far-away places. Indeed, only eighteen fighting men remained outside. At their head was an experienced fighter, Yehoshua Cohen,* then eighteen years old. This dangerous gang had for equipment five revolvers, none of which worked very well. They had no bases from which to attack the enemy and no allies, and they were surrounded by a wall of incomprehension. The Jewish population was against them to a man, as were the underground fighters of Haganah and Irgun, who had made a truce with the British in view of the worse devil, the Nazis, then busy murdering Jews in Europe by the million.

Lehy fought on. And the desperate fight of this small band of patriots – patriots of a homeland which was neither the birthplace of most of them nor yet a state – was directly responsible for a change of heart which gradually drew over the whole of Jewish Palestine to the ideal of an independent, strongly nationalistic nation of their own. Till 1944, when the Irgun broke its truce and 'declared war' on the British empire, this was not a conscious thing for most uninvolved people in the Jewish community; till then they were still busy with the last phases of the Zionist revolution – the settlement of the land, the idealistic creation of economic, agricultural and defence instruments. The fight of the

*After the creation of the state of Israel Cohen became a member of Sdeh Boker, Ben-Gurion's own Kibbutz, and an admirer of Israel's first Prime Minister, who had always been a sworn enemy of both Lehy and the Irgun.

Lehy 'extremists' or 'outsiders' was dissonant and bothersome for those patriots of Zionism who wanted only settlement, immigration and the right to help the British fight the Germans in Palestinian-Jewish military units. Yet it was the voice of Lehy – and of its guns – which started the Jewish population of Palestine on its long and arduous journey towards national independence and statehood.

There was, as we have seen, Yoshua Cohen with his eighteen years, his five guns, and his eighteen freedom-fighters. They hid in orange groves and fed more than once for weeks on end on fruit. But another young man was active in the revisionist movement. His name was Itzhak Yezernitzky and he was a broad-shouldered, bushy-browed accountant, of secretive and retiring disposition. It was Yezernitzky who took upon himself the task of reorganizing the Lehy *apparat*. Taking the humdrum *nom de guerre* Michael as his own, he helped manage a break-out of Lehy men from a prison camp. Twenty-two escaped. Among them was the fabled Gera – Nathan Yalin-Mor, who had already earned a place at the very top of the organization, immediately under the orders of Yair himself.

There ensued a period of confusion, not devoid of internecine fights and back-stabbing. The fear of agents and CID provocations took its bitter toll in men and mood. The renascent band of underground fighters had to become more secretive, more ruthless, more close-knit, in order to survive. More than one innocent paid for this state of affairs with his life.

After a while things sorted themselves out. A shadow started spreading over Palestine – the shadow of a company of men prepared to do anything to bring about the creation of the State of Israel and the end of the Mandate.

And anything – or everything – they did. They killed civilians, they kidnapped enemies, they executed traitors, they laid bombs, they assassinated the British Commissioner for the Middle East, Lord Moyne, in Cairo. In short, they carried out a ruthless form of warfare against the people they considered the invaders and the usurpers of power.

As will be shown in a later chapter, this was at a time when the illegal Communist Party was trying to ignore the fight for national liberation of the Jews in Palestine, and concentrating on the much weaker and by then hopeless fight of the Arabs in the Middle East. If the communist underground had been daring enough to revise its policy at that stage of the game, and had worked for a common movement of national liberation for both Arabs and Jews, matters might indeed have developed differently. But the communists were mostly dogmatic, tired men. They even refused to realize that their patron, the USSR, was not at all hostile to the organized freedom fight of the Jews in Palestine. (Lehy had branches in Czechoslovakia, Hungary and Romania, and published 'clandestine' newspapers in Prague, Budapest and Bucharest as late as 1949. The USSR, it must be remembered, was, with the US, among the first countries to recognize the new State of Israel in 1948. Moreover she was instrumental in its defence, giving the communist authorities of Czechoslovakia the green light to send vast quantities of arms, ammunition, and even pilots to help the Jews to fight for survival and independence – hoping thereby to keep the Middle East out of the Western zone of influence, after Great Britain evacuated Palestine.)

If Lehy had not been such a sectarian, secretive and close-knit underground, there is no doubt that the communists would have infiltrated it – possibly to the advantage of both, by a kind of cross-pollination. Lehy might perhaps have adopted a revolutionary position towards the Zionist authorities and establishment, and the communists might perhaps have made a bridge between the movements of freedom-fighters in both the Palestinian and pre-Israeli communities. But this was not to be. Separately they gravitated to their separate and equally ineffective political ends.

However, Lehy *was*, in a way, a force embodying the various political elements to be found on the front line of any revolution or freedom fight. Small as it was, Lehy was a fighting coalition, a group of partisans of all hues, with a common goal: the expulsion of British imperialism and the creation of a national Israeli state. In Lehy's ranks were religious zealots with long forelocks; former Revisionist Zionists; *émigrés* from the Communists;

Kibbutz members and Labour men; and many individuals who would never have dreamed of joining the other clandestine bodies.

Later, when a system of getting civilian help was developed, it became clear that Lehy evoked more sympathy both on the 'Left' and among unpolitical people than did the Irgun, which was mainly popular among the middle class, the private-enterprise bourgeoisie and the have-nots – those living in the slums of the Hatikva and Shapira districts of Tel-Aviv and the Yemenite slum on the seashore.

In 1942, however, Lehy was quite alone in its implacable fight for national liberation. It had an urgent need not only for military reorganization, but also for increased and effective propaganda; and – what is more important – for practical political leadership. The death of Yair created the most serious vacuum of all; an intellectual vacuum at the top. In an organization less dedicated to its almost abstract but certainly unpopular ideal, this would have meant the end. But Lehy, it seems, was a special historical case. Its needs dictated the final constitution of the Central Committee (note the terminology: this was no simple para-military organization). From the moment it was reborn, Lehy abandoned the ideas, feelings and ways of thought of the Revisionist Zionist movement and its secret army, the Irgun. Perhaps the fact that the really important leaders of this movement had been killed or died – Jabotinsky, Raziel, Yair – had something to do with the daring of the lonely secret fighters who chose to change their image and their soul.

It was in secret Central Committee meetings that the second formative stage of the national Israeli revolution was reached. There the liberal Zionist revolution, already supplanted by a prosperous Zionist Establishment, expired quietly and finally. And there – in spite of, or perhaps because of, the inner contradictions embodied in Lehy – the fight for nationhood, for *Israeli* as separate from *Jewish* nationhood, was born.

The Central Committee of Lehy, the Fighters for the Freedom of Israel, was composed of three men. All were of Polish-Jewish origin, all were former Revisionist Zionists. But the resemblance between Gera, Eldad and Michael went no further.

The chairman of the Central Committee was Yalin-Mor, or

Gera. A ruthless man of brilliant mind and undoubted idealism, Gera reformed the policies of Lehy. The *Principles of Liberation* attributed to Yair, whether real or false, he discarded. He worked out a foreign policy which was as remote as possible from fascist inspiration; it was, indeed, anti-Western as well as anti-Nazi. He demanded the complete and unqualified neutralization of the Middle East in the confrontation between the USSR on one side, and the British empire and emerging US imperialism on the other. For the early forties, Gera's anti-imperialist policy was undoubtedly one of the most 'progressive' of any contemporary revolutionary group. In spite of the unpleasant experience of being jailed for a time by the Russians before he escaped from a war-torn Poland, Gera was a cool-headed neutralist who wanted a hard line towards British imperialism. 'We do not fight the British Mandate,' he asserted again and again, in his publications, clandestine broadcasts and broadsheets. 'We fight imperialism which is directed equally against all the peoples of the Middle East.'

Then there was Eldad, the nickname of Dr Israel Scheib, a scholar, a Judaist, a religious if not practising Zealot and a fanatic. Eldad was responsible for the mystical firebrand style of some of Lehy's manifestoes. He had no say in the Central Committee's political decisions; his 'puzzled professor' character hardly gave him the right to speak on matters of organization and clandestine fighting; but his demagogic style, his Jewish adeptness at turning a phrase or a thought inside out, and his subconscious identification with the more irrational *Gestalten* of the tormented or superstitious popular mind made him invaluable to the small underground body, keen to wield an influence out of proportion to its actual size.

The last, and the odd man out, was Michael, whom we have already met. Michael was a pragmatist, a born fighter, a figure such as may be found in Hemingway's books or in partisan stories from the Russian steppes and forests of the Second World War. He had a genius for organization, a passion for anonymity, a taste for violence – and he was an excellent chief-of-staff for his commander-in-chief, Gera.

Gera was the planner. Michael was responsible for the fighting.

The propagandist and least important of the three was Eldad. Yet he was hunted down and jailed and he broke his back trying to escape by climbing down a pipe which gave away. Later he was freed by his men, who mounted a daring attack on the prison. But while he was out of circulation, his loss was not greatly felt in the underground. Politically, Gera was probably the most important. But Michael was the man on whose shoulders lay the efficiency and effectiveness of the clandestine fighting *maquis*. He did his work brilliantly. Indeed, the measure of his effectiveness can be judged from the fact that he was the only one who never got caught.

These three, with their conflicting views, created Israel's first true anti-imperialist movement for national liberation. Their lack of personal egoism, their complete political and private dedication to the goals at hand, brought one of the greatest changes of mind ever effected in a people. Their achievement was all the more astonishing, given the problematic national consciousness of the Palestinian Jews, who had been 'Zionist patriots' for years but had their doubts, then, about becoming patriots *tout court*.

Under the twin pressures of the White Paper and the Lehy's fight, the Irgun abandoned in 1944 its policy of cooperation with the British and followed suit, and by 1948 Haganah had reached its own point of no return. This was the culmination of three years of changing policy during which Haganah had worked much with the British CID and informed on a considerable number of Irgun men. But by 1948 the increase in its clandestine activity – mainly sabotage and illegal immigration – had obliged the Zionist leadership to abandon its pro-British stance and to start demanding some sort of independence. This was all the more necessary because the conflict had inflamed the bitter hostility of the Mandate Administration to the point where it was no more possible for polite masks of 'cooperation' (that is, mutual exploitation) to be worn.

The total dedication of Lehy can be demonstrated by the fact that at no time did the organization attempt to carry the struggle *inside* the Jewish Establishment – except to punish traitors. Not once did they act for personal political reasons.

They suffered for it. When independence came, in 1948, and the same old men of the syndicalist Labour consolidated their power and destroyed the Left's Palmach and the Right's Irgun, sinking the Irgun's ship, *Altalena* (which was brought to Tel-Aviv loaded with costly arms to help the nascent state preserve its independence), it was Lehy which was least prepared for what followed.

It tried to go on as before. When the pro-American United Nations Envoy, Count Folke Bernadotte, attempted to internationalize Jerusalem, Lehy – in the guise of a 'newly created' group called the Fatherland Front, or Hazit Hamoledet – assassinated him.

It was exactly the opportunity which David Ben-Gurion, leader of the Labour wing of Zionism and Israel's first Prime Minister, was waiting for. He disbanded Lehy, which had emerged from anonymity after the founding of the state, jailed most of its members, and put into effect against it a revised text of the British Mandate's Emergency Regulations, so often used in the past not only against Lehy and the Irgun but against Ben-Gurion's Haganah itself.

Even then Lehy refused to die. With Yalin-Mor in jail, the members of the organization still at liberty started an intensive campaign for his liberation. The first elections to the first Knesset were coming up. A party was created, Mifleget Halohamim, or 'Fighters' Party', which collected 14,000 votes, freed Yalin-Mor from prison and sent him directly to the Knesset to take his seat as a member of the Israeli Parliament's first legislative assembly.

All the same, Lehy's backbone had been broken. Bereft of its weapons and of daily conflict, the organization had no clear-cut goals, no definite hopes for the future, no cohesion, no unity. Most of its most capable and dedicated members were on the front lines, preparing to fight off the intended invasion of seven Arab armies, or taking over cities and villages from which the Palestinians had been chased or had fled in fright.

Lehy went on for a while. But not for long. Scheib-Eldad provoked a schism and created a small, mystical, fascist group which produced a monthly, *Sulam* ('Jacob's Ladder'), to publish its demands for turning Israel to totalitarianism, for the adoption of a Jewish-religious line in all fields of endeavour, for the conquest of the territory which 'God gave to the seed of Abraham – from the Nile to the Euphrates', for the identification of Jewishness with Israeliness.

In 1949 most Israelis considered such ideas fascist and totalitarian. To begin with, only a minority of Zealots and extremist Revisionist Zionists approved. Gradually this changed. During a period of clandestine, splinter-group activity, in which former Lehy men were jailed again and again, Scheib hedged nearer and nearer to the official positions of the Zionist Establishment. And, wonderful to see, the Establishment came to adopt clearly and unambiguously some of Scheib's outlandish ideas.

David Ben-Gurion himself, in the autocratic years of almost single-handed rule over docile Zionist governments which came and went, became a mystic, a believer in the religious destiny of Israel. He gave much thought and time to the study of the Old Testament, particularly the chapters devoted to the Conquest of Canaan. The Bible-study circle in which Ben-Gurion imbibed these ideas also included Dr Israel Scheib-Eldad. Twenty years later, in the early seventies, the ideas of Scheib-Eldad had triumphed in almost all the upper spheres of the Zionist Establishment. What a Zealot could not accomplish by clandestine agitation was accomplished by the necessities of the basic exclusiveness of the Zionist idea – once Zionism took power into its hands.

Oddly enough, it was Lehy's lack of ambition, its lack of thirst for personal power, which made a failure of it after its first, its principal goal had been reached. It seems that not only power, but also powerlessness. can at times corrupt: the group never had any ambition of taking over from the syndicalist rulers of the Jewish *Yishuv*.

As for the greater part of Lehy, now the Fighters' Party, it lived on, desultorily, for a few years, Two wings developed: a Marxist one, whose members left, one by one, to adhere to the Zionist 'Left' or to the Communist Party; and a Social-Democratic one, led by Yalin-Mor himself. But the shock of transition had been too great for this gifted leader. He spoke only rarely in the first Knesset. And in the end he gave away to the families of fallen Lehy men and to the disabled veterans of the organization all the funds still remaining in the party's till.*

Thus ended a chapter which had promised much but never rightly got off the ground. The upside-down state of affairs in the Jewish national movement of liberation was at fault. The 'Left' was 'capitalist', with vested interests in the *status quo* and in more Jewish immigration; while the 'Right' was with the nationalists, the have-nots. The contradiction of interests so created was too big for the revolutionaries to cope with at the time, whether they were Moscow-line communists or the independent freedom fighters of Lehy.

The independent growth of a non-Jewish Israeli nationalism – which could easily have included the Palestinian wish for freedom and dignity, or could at least have co-existed with it – never took place.†

*This was necessary. For many years the Zionist Establishment refused 'official' status to 'outsiders', the men of the Irgun and of Lehy, who died or were injured for the creation of the state.

†This short story of Lehy would be incomplete without a mention of what happened to its other two leaders. The fortunes of that astonishing man, Yalin-Mor, will be seen later. Michael, however, the partisan leader and anonymous freedom-fighter, went back to the fight. Without wishing to identify himself with either of the two ideologies of Lehy's splinters, Michael decided that his task was what it had always been – to fight for his country. He became one of the best and most secret agents of the Shin Beit, the Secret Services. Under the auspices of Issar Harel, the man who kidnapped Eichmann personally and directed Shin Beit for many years, Michael became one of those responsible for the 'executive' side of the Secret War. When Egyptian Intelligence in the Gaza Strip of the fifties created a centre for terrorism and infiltration into Israel, staffed by Palestinians, it was Michael who sent the booby-trap which killed the unit's organizer, one Commander Aly. He was responsible for many acts of secret retaliation. He also made sure that the perpetrators of the Bernadotte assassination (some of whom had fled abroad) should never be punished, although they were known to Issar Harel and Ben-Gurion. Indeed, this pardon was part of the price for the services of this disinterested fighter and killer, this most dangerous patriot. Today Itzhak ('Michael') Shamir, formerly Yezernitzky is retired, the owner of a prosperous garage in the Jewish centre of Jaffa.

7 Recognizing the Arabs: Canaanites, 'Pax Semitica' and Semitic Action

The Zionist revolution was the movement of a half-nation. It tried, strenuously enough, to convert the masses of Jewish individuals into an organic unity. It took the territory it needed to carry out its purpose – the conversion of the half-nation into a national entity, bound by its territory and conscious of its identity.

It failed in that purpose. But not because it was, at one and the same time, a liberal movement of national liberation and a colonizing movement. The poetic justice which forbids such roles to run in harness together exists only in the mind of textbook-spouting revolutionaries. In fact, the assertion of any new national entity – the United States of America, Algeria, Yugoslavia, Kongo-Kinshasa, the Sudan, the USSR – *always* dispossesses minorites, curtails the rights and privileges not only of former pressure groups and ruling classes but also of ethno-cultural units to which the executors of the national revolution do not belong.

The two main peculiarities of Palestine were that, first, this was a territory in which two 'majorities', that is two equally 'strong' groups, equally well protected by their ideological and cultural hinterlands, competed for a single piece of land; and second, the Zionist Revolution defeated its own purpose by clinging to the umbilical cord of its birth: the religious-cultural background inherited from the Diaspora days. Through this it lived, as it were, in suspended animation, in an artificial womb created by traditionalism on the one hand and alienation from the outside on the other.

By not imitating the Young Turks of Mustapha Kemal Pasha, by not cutting themselves completely loose from their religious-cultural background, the Zionists signed the death warrant for their chances of becoming the dominant factor in the Middle East. This, perhaps, is all to the good of the pan-Arab cause. But, along with all the other destructive efforts of the two mutually exclusive sides, it threatens to bring tragedy upon the whole zone. The fact is that Zionism became, in spite of the ascendancy of the Labour wing, a racialist movement of Jewish revival and conquest – and not a movement of Jewish conversion into something else. Religious mysticism and Bible-thumping really were the best alibis for the uneasy consciences of former Marxists in the Zionist camp; so 'return to Jewish roots' became the rage. It was indeed necessary for the perpetration of territorial conquest and the eradication of all 'non-Jewish' cultural factors throughout Israel and in whatever territories it gained.

Zionism's first phase was characterized by the search for national unity; the second – somewhat overlapping – brought with it the desire for national independence, coupled with a territorial refuge. Its object was not simply 'Jewish', it was independence in 'the Land of Israel', Eretz-Israel. However, the independence fighters were still part Jews, part Israelis. Their arguments were mixed and so were their feelings.

The third evolutionary step towards national emergence was made in a different direction. It came from within the 'Land of Israel'. It tried to do what its two forerunners had not been capable of doing: to cut itself loose from Judaism. Why it failed and how it failed constitute a story of particular interest.

In 1944, while Lehy was involved in its fight to the death with the British imperialist power, a stencilled document was circulated in the salons and cafes of Tel-Aviv, in the university halls of Jerusalem, and even in some British army camps where Jews served. It was entitled 'A MESSAGE TO THE FIGHTERS FOR THE FREEDOM OF ISRAEL'. In it a group, which in due course defined itself as the 'Young Hebrews', asked Lehy to abandon its Jewishness, and to fight for an independent Hebrew nation, now being reborn in the land which was called Canaan long before Joshua and his Jewish cohorts 'cleansed' it from the rule of the Canaanites, Edomites, Philistines and other ethnic groups and tribes. In fact the peculiar new ideology demanded a return to the cultural tradition of old Canaan. The land of Baal and Ashtoret, it said, should once more become the starting-point of a young, healthy, non-religious culture.

Everybody born in the country was to be considered Hebrew. Everybody born abroad was an immigrant, a foreigner. To begin with, the Young Hebrews said that the only true Hebrews were the Palestinian-born. But soon they amended this. New immigrants, who came as small children to the land of Canaan and grew up in its culture, could be absorbed in the nation. The Arabs too could become 'Hebrews' asserted the 'Canaanites', as the new group promptly became known. They would become assimilated into the dominant, reborn Canaanite nation, which would conquer – shades of Anton Saadat's neo-fascist party – the whole of the Fertile Crescent. They would have to learn Hebrew, of course. But, as the Canaanites pointed out, there was not a homogeneous population in the Fertile Crescent. People of all kinds, from many different ethnic roots, lived there.

Unable to analyse what makes nationalism grow, and what makes even small groups cling to their identity, the Canaanites presumed that the youngest, strongest, most dynamic entity would inevitably absorb all others, both culturally and politically. The youngest, strongest, most dynamic entity was, of course, the Hebrew one. By abandoning its 'foreign' Jewish roots it would force the others to abandon theirs.

Thus the way to cut free from the past was to make alliances with other minorities of the zone, such as the Shiite Moslems, the Alawys, the Druze population, the Maronite-Christians of the Lebanon and the Copts in Egypt. (In any case Egypt, the Canaanites declared, was not Middle Eastern at all, but an African interloper in Middle Eastern affairs.)

One can easily see how a natural instinct to cut free from decaying roots prompted a group of intellectuals to declare themselves 'non-Jewish Hebrews'. Unfortunately, the non-Jewish element did not go far enough. Being Diaspora-born themselves, they were still Jewish enough to believe the new nation must grow from their own beginnings – the Hebrew language, the Jewish-Palestinian community, and so on. Unable to acknowledge the positive role of the Zionist Revolution, or the equally positive role of the Arab national renaissance, these fugitives from Judaism still remained bound by some of their most sensitive Jewish roots and complexes.

The thought that something completely new, something neither Hebrew-Jewish nor Arab-Moslem, could be their foundation never occurred to them – for the simple reason that the two embryonic movements of national liberation, the pan-Arab and the Zionist, had not yet reached their (mutually contradictory) goals.

Most of the young Jewish-Palestinian intellectuals of the forties were influenced to some extent by the Canaanite ideology. While the group itself, which later took the peculiar name of 'Centre of Young Hebrews', never became a mass movement, its two or three leaders had the dubious satisfaction of seeing their brain-child beget progeny of its own. Some of Israel's more considerable works of art bear the 'Canaanite' imprint – such as the unforgettable statue of the god Tammuz by the famous sculptor Itzhak Danziger. As Jewish religion forbids the 'making of graven images', the Canaanites had a liberating influence on many artists, as well as on the evolution of the Hebrew language, which they enriched by going back to purely biblical and pre-biblical sources.

In politics, however, their influence was nil. None of the Canaanite ideologues was a proper politician: there was Yonathan Ratosh, a writer and poet of talent and thinker of no mean scope; Professor Adaya Horon, a historian; and Aharon Amir, a writer and publisher who was personal *aide de camp* to Ratosh but not himself a man of ideas. None of them contributed actively to the Israeli movement of national liberation.

Trying to justify the political failure of the Canaanite movement, its founder, Yonathan Ratosh, alias Uriel Shelah, once told me: 'They took away my demographic majority!' Ratosh was referring to the fact that up to 1948 the Jewish population grew slowly and in a well-integrated manner. This allowed the Israeli-born generation to take a dominant (though not uncontested) place in the scheme of things, and to liberate itself from the beliefs and ways of life of the 'old men of the Diaspora', the old-style Jews. After 1948, however, the immigrants came in succeeding waves, which flooded the country, destroyed the thin veneer of independent thought and territorial nationalism, and swung the Jewish population – now a majority – back to its Zionist ideas, Jewish beliefs and Diaspora usages. This, in the last analysis, changed for the worse the thought processes of the younger native Israelis as well. In other words, Ratosh and the other Canaanites claim that if the State of Israel had not assimilated so many immigrants in so short a time the Diaspora would not have assimilated Israel to its Zionist fold.

This analysis may be quite correct. But the Canaanites ignored the main stumbling-block in the path of their ideological revolution. In a country like Palestine, where two such potent national blocs exist, it is no use trying to build a new political structure on only one of them. The fact that the Canaanites were 'Young Hebrews' and not 'Young Hebro-Palestinians', speaking both languages or advocating some third one, was enough to prevent their upheaval from being more than an inner-cultural happening on the Jewish-Palestinian scene.

For similar reasons (but this time due to their Arab identity) there is, in the seventies, no chance at all that the Fatah, the Front of Popular Liberation of Palestine or the Democratic Front will ever wield any influence whatsoever on the Israeli population. Even those Israelis who disapprove of Zionism, who abhor the military occupation and hate the political annexionist tendencies of the Israeli leaders, bristle at the thought of a foreign, non-Israeli identity being the dominant one in their country. In fact, some Arabs did become quite sympathetic to the Canaanite ideas, if never active in the group. But sadly enough these were Palestinians already assimilated – mainly for economic reasons – to the Zionist-Jewish Establishment.

So much for the Canaanites who failed to become Zionism's alternative. But before we take leave of this minor but significant footnote to the history of Israel-Palestine's national liberation, it is worthwhile chronicling the development of the group.

From the late forties to 1953 the Centre of Young Hebrews had a fitful existence, issuing irregularly a publication called *Aleph** and creating waves of shocked criticism in the Zionist press. In due course the Canaanite writers, sculptors, painters and journalists won important positions in the Zionist Establishment and became less extreme in their views. The closed circle of military incidents and counter-incidents, reprisals and counter-reprisals, culminating in the Sinai campaign of 1956 which changed the psychological climate of Israel, contributed its part to the eclipse of Canaanite activity.

In 1967, however, after the Six Days War, the Canaanites resurfaced. They had changed! The cultural renaissance was almost discarded. What had once been a revolutionary idea was now being exploited to consolidate the military, economic and sociological conquests of the Israelis. Except for Ratosh himself, a genial but shunned and martyred man, the promoters of the Canaanite idea found this a very natural transition. Once they had been rebels and pariahs, now they were pillars of decorum and bourgeois success: such men as Binyamin Tammuz, literary editor of the biggest daily, *Haaretz*, and later Cultural Attaché at the Israeli Embassy in London; Itzhak Danziger, who accepted the Israel Prize for Art from the Zionist Establishment and, under pressure, withdrew his name from a declaration in defence of the Palestinians' rights; and Aharon Amir, who became a founder of one of the chauvinist movements for the annexation of the territories, and cooperated there with Jewish religious zealots: could play with annexionist ideas, but certainly could not afford to put themselves, once again, in opposition to the Establishment of which they had become part.

There was one encouraging aspect to the conquest-inspired Canaanite revival after 1967: the obvious sincerity of the new, younger generation of Canaanites who wanted to 'teach the Palestinians Hebrew and let them fight with us in the Israeli Army', while, avowedly, holding on to the Occupied Territories. It was, at least, a further step away from the racialist separatism

*First letter of the Hebrew alphabet and, from the very beginnings of Hebrew culture, symbol of a new start.

of the Zionists, but, it did not touch the crux of the problem: the Palestinians' and the Israelis' sense of separate identity.

*

In 1945 the lights went on in Palestine. Thousands of young men, still in British uniform, came back from reconquered Europe. The cafes opened once more, and in the heat of the *Khamseen*, the 'sirocco from Hell' which covers the Middle Eastern cities with sweat and sand, life looked interesting and full of promise.

The *Khamseen* was not the only wind that blew that year. After the defeat of Nazism, the young felt they could tackle anything. While some had fought far away, others younger still had studied for their exams and in their spare time conspired to overthrow the 'foreign bad men'. Things had not stood still.

Yes, they felt anything could happen. On the other hand, Palestinian Jewish society was as petrified and stratified as ever. The 'old men' ruled always and everywhere. And if somebody had the guts to protest, he was lost. No jobs for him in official or semi-official enterprises. No chance of publishing his articles, his short stories or his poetry in the party-controlled press. No way, in fact, of proving to himself that he was *alive*.

For a considerable minority the way out was in what Menahem Beigin, once leader of the Irgun and later minister in the Golda Meir 'Cabinet of National Unity', described as 'the rebellion'; what the anti-imperialist Yalin-Mor defined as 'freedom fighting'.

But there was another minority of thinking men who did not accept the Jewish-mystical slogans mixed up with the heroism and the blood-and-tears ideology of the two fighting undergrounds. For these thinking few the Canaanite philosophy had much to commend it. But it also had a flaw. They had just come through the traumatic experience of the Second World War without actually fighting in it – a war in which the ultimate enemy was racialism. The 'holier than thou' racial ideology of the Young Hebrews, keen to prove they were not Jews of the old kind, disappointed and revolted them.

Some of them drew the necessary conclusions. One of them was a young Germano-Jewish immigrant called Heldmut Osterman, who renamed himself, as is the usage in modern Israel, adopting the Hebrew name Ury Avnery.

Avnery was a particular kind of politician. He was a man wholly fascinated by himself and for this reason saw power as a means of expression. Although a genuine freedom-fighter and fervently aware of the injustices done to his fellow-men, Avnery was impressed from his earliest youth by the fact that power, lies, brute force, are able to sway the masses. He relates* how weak he felt himself, as a child, faced with the force of the Hitler Youth. Perhaps it was this trauma which gave him his ambivalent attitude to the power-rule of the individual.

In his early youth in Tel-Aviv, he wore jackboots and uniforms he designed himself. Later he gave up this childish expression of his concern with power, but the essence of his obsession remained. During his long and arduous career as an Opposition newspaper man, he tried to create the image of a Saviour who would come to redeem the State of Israel from its too-early decline. At different times he offered bizarre candidates for this task, suggesting the most unlikely men in adulatory articles in his weekly, *Haolam Hazeh*. They included the Labour leader Yigal Allon, Professor Yigael Yadin; world Zionism's leader Dr Nahum Goldmann; even at one point Moshe Dayan. And always, of course, Ury Avnery himself.

However, Avnery's 'king-making', and his disagreeable and somewhat self-defeating habit of putting himself forward in any situation, book, or political essay, were in the last analysis minor points against him. Avnery showed an enormous amount of good sense, journalistic acumen and creative analysis together with straightforward demagoguery in fighting for just goals: peace with the rest of the Middle East and democracy within Israel. In spite of distortions, retractions, fear of the consequences of going too far, and a profound dislike of any freedom-fighter not associated with himself, Ury Avnery consistently played a major role in the camp of peace fighters in Israel. In the confrontation between lunacy and sanity, Avnery has been one of the very few

* *Milhemet Hayom Hashviyi*, Tel-Aviv, 1969; published abroad as *Israel Without Zionists*.

standing almost always on the 'right' side of the fence. The only trouble is his refusal to let anyone stand beside him, far less above him.

The start of this remarkable man's political career was a brochure-like publication of which only four issues appeared. It was called *Bamaawak*, which means in Hebrew 'In the fight', but which might also be translated 'During the fight'. And this is exactly what it was: a document published by men who could not share in the underground fight against the foreign domination of their country but felt they had to do their bit, in their own way.

Avnery altered the Canaanite ideas. He kept the difference between Diaspora Jews and Israeli 'Hebrews' but (being himself born and grown up outside the country's borders) declared that an education in Palestine was enough to shape the citizens of the new commonwealth. It was a far more rational approach to a problem of national and cultural self-determination than the hereditary, or rather racialist, approach of the Canaanites. The fact that it also fitted like a glove Avnery's own case-history was just one of the lucky coincidences which have paved his path to this very day.

He made another, and crucial, alteration to the Canaanite ideology. The Canaanites retained the old Jewish self-centred conviction of 'You have chosen us from among all nations' (although without the Chooser). Avnery identified himself with a bigger force, outside the Jewish entity – the force of the Arab movement of liberation. He found a term to cover both his renaissance aims and his identification with this strong and – as he felt – just historical current. That term was 'Semitic'.

The Jews and the Arabs are of Semitic origin, Avnery said. Let us then create a commonwealth of Semitic peoples, have a *Pax Semitica* in the Middle East, and stand against all foreign rulers.

It was a beautiful solution. It could even have worked, except for one fact. Like his Canaanite predecessors, but precisely in the opposite direction, Avnery identified himself at that stage with an exclusivist revolution, that of Pan-Arabism, without taking into account the nationalist and individualist forces then being born in all the different Arab countries – and in Palestine.

And he did this, of course, without relinquishing his own particularised brand of Hebrew nationalism.

It was as if he were saying: 'We stay Hebrew, and help all the Arab countries to stay pan-Arab and to fight the foreigners.' His argument was based on a fallacy. The pan-Arab revolution, a neo-religious movement to give the feudal masses a militant, national-religious consciousness, could not and did not tolerate non-Arab independence in its midst. The Arabs had no reason to believe that a strong, nationalist 'Hebrew' nation would be preferable to a weak socialist Jewish community in Palestine; and Zionist penetration had understandably done nothing to persuade them otherwise. From its own point of view – that of an exclusive, conquering movement of renovation based on a popular but reactionary ideology – pan-Arabism quite rightly judged Zionism, or the creation of a Hebrew state, to stand in the way of its goals. There could be no *Pax Semitica*.

This did not worry the *Bamaawak* people. Where the Canaanite 'solved' the contradictions by 'assimilating' the Palestinians to the Young Hebrew nation in their minds, the *Bamaawak* ideology tried to 'incorporate' the Young Hebrews in a federal *Arab* framework.

Both solutions ignored the crucial fact: that inside Palestine, a country in which, although geography, economy and foreign rule had laid the foundations for a separate 'historical personality', two groups existed at *different* stages of their national formative process. No 'Hebrew' state could – or ever can – contain the Palestinians. No 'free secular Arab' Palestine could – or ever can – contain the Jews. What the emerging nationalism of the Middle East needed was separate, equal and converging development towards union. What they had was development in opposite directions – on the same piece of soil.

The obvious answer to the dilemma – namely the creation in Palestine of a completely new entity, cut off from both the Arab and Jewish spheres of influence – could not be even suggested in the 1940s, when *Bamaawak* was forming its ideology. Neither the Arabs nor the Jews had yet reached the first stage of their renewed national and territorial consciousness. The Palestinian

Jews were, in the late forties, at the stage of developing a separate consciousness of their own, basically a non-Jewish one. Favouring this development was the need to fight British domination in order to allow in as many as possible of the Jews abroad from Hitler's holocaust. The Jews of Palestine had begun, as a people, the slow collective change from a feeling of isolation to a feeling of belonging to a given place and a given set of circumstances. But in spite of this they still considered the Jews abroad as part of themselves.

The Palestinian Arabs, on the other hand, remained then and later a part of the 'Arab sea', as it has often been called; even in their isolation inside the Jewish state. Only after twenty years of bitter rejection, by both Israelis and other Arabs, did they reach, in 1967, the point where the Jews had started their journey towards a national consciousness able to survive even without the backing of the 'only true religion'.

The *Bamaawak* group published the four issues of their paper and one pamphlet written by Avnery himself: *War and Peace in the Semitic Area.* Meanwhile the 1948 war broke out, and the Arab armies tried to foil the creation of the Jewish state, but instead foiled finally the creation of the Palestinian Arab state which the United Nations' resolution of November 1947 had recommended. Fighting ensued, the Zionist leadership exploited – not for the first nor for the last time – the errors of the pan-Arab nationalists, and the Palestinians became the new 'Jews', the new dispossessed people of modern history. In this atmosphere of utter Palestinian despair, while the Jewish community exalted in the joy of their new own state, proving to itself, for the first time, that it was militarily more powerful than its rivals, the ideas of such men as the Canaanite Yonathan Ratosh and the Semite Ury Avnery were bound to have very little impact. In the wake of succeeding waves of immigration which brought to Israel two and a half million new Israeli Jews, these ideas seemed to lose what little importance they had. They dwindled to a sidelight on the scene, balefully outshone by the fires of war and destruction.

*

Shortly before the Suez campaign of 1956, a series of somewhat stealthy meetings took place in various cafes in Tel-Aviv, usually in the old Cafe Herlinger, founded by an immigrant from Vienna. The 'Herlinger Circle' or even 'Herlinger Underground', as these meetings came to be called in the hostile Zionist press, was a motley group of politicians and intellectuals who met once a fortnight. They set out, like the Encyclopedists before the French Revolution, to change their world simply by putting down exactly how it should look. The document first produced in September 1958, and issued in a revised form in July 1959, was no less revolutionary for Israel than the Great Encyclopedia, which the French King first sequestered and then censored, was for Europe. But it was of more modest scope.

The Hebrew Manifesto, as this document came to be called, stated for the first time, in unequivocal terms, the following about the new Israeli society:

> A new nation has been born in the Land of Israel.
>
> It is bound to the Jewish Diaspora only emotionally, by the personal, emotional and spiritual bonds between the Hebrews and the Jews.
>
> The Hebrew State of Israel is part and parcel of Eretz-Israel 'from the sea to the desert'. Eretz-Israel is part of the Semitic Area.
>
> The Land of Israel is the fatherland of two nations – Hebrew Israelis and Arab Palestinians. The Palestinians should become independent.
>
> A federative solution should be found to ensure the unity of Eretz-Israel-Palestine. The federation should be carried out gradually.
>
> The union of Eretz-Israel can only be carried out by a true partnership between 'the Hebrew nation and the Arab nation' in that country.*

This document, a real Magna Charta of the rights of both Israelis and Palestinians to their homeland, was a giant step in the right direction. It blended the best elements of the Canaanite, *Bamaawak* and Lehy ideas. It demanded for the first time the separation of the Israelis from the Jews. It gave the Palestinians that which was theirs – the right of return to the refugees, the

* *Haminshar Haivri* ('The Hebrew Manifesto'), The Central Committee of Semitic Action, second and complete edition, Tel-Aviv, July 1959.

right to create their own country in their own fatherland to the Arab-Palestinian masses.

It was not, however, followed by further steps on the logical journey towards complete identification with the need to unite the ethnic and political entities struggling in Palestine into a single nation, a single community of interests with a single destiny. So far even the political encyclopedists of Semitic Action – as this group called itself – would not go; or perhaps could not. Even this comparatively innocuous document, not revolutionary in essence, was greeted with cries of 'Treason!' So in Israel are greeted all efforts to arrive at a non-racialist, non-Jewish solution to the problems engendered by the duality of rights to the homeland.

The times were seething with conspiracy, intrigue, power-seeking. It was the era when the Shin Beit's use of political plotting and provocation was at its apogee, under the inspiration of a power-élite known to its enemies as the 'Black Hand Group' and to its admirers as 'David Ben-Gurion's young men'. These young men – the youngest well on the wrong side of forty – were, among others, Moshe Dayan, then Commander-in-Chief of the army; Shimon Peres, Deputy Minister of Defence; Teddy Kollek, who was an Ambassador and later Mayor of united Jerusalem; Issar ('the small one') Harel, boss of the Shin Beit.

People expected Semitic Action to be, like so many groups before it, revolutionary, activist, rabble-rousing, perhaps even bomb-throwing. At any rate, the undercover agents of Shin Beit had no difficulty in making it look like that. But the truth was rather different. The men who directed Semitic Action – indeed who *were* the movement, for it never got off the ground as a mass-organized body – were one and all respected, with their more violent years behind them. Some of them have already made an appearance in this book.

There was Nathan Yalin-Mor, former leader of Lehy, former member of parliament, now a prosperous journalist and businessman. There was Ury Avnery, former Independence-War soldier, former young revolutionary, now editor and owner of Israel's only Opposition weekly. There was Binyamin Omri, a Russian-born engineer, maybe the *doyen* of the group, who had fought with the left-wing radicals in the Labour movement of Palestine, but had become progressively disenchanted with Zionism. There was Shalom Cohen, the urbane, intelligent and effective deputy editor of Avnery's paper, and the only Oriental Jew in the group. There was Dr Yaakov Yerdor, a lawyer born in Romania, once the Paris Bureau chief of Lehy and the man who planned and almost brought off the bombing of London by a monoplane, piloted by an eccentric nationalist Rabbi, known only as 'Rabbi Korf'. And there were several more. Altogether some dozens of men cogitated over the drawing-up of the *Hebrew Manifesto*. But these five men were its main pivots.

The *Manifesto* and the ensuing well-planned publicity campaign provoked enormous indignation in Zionist circles, by challenging in hard-headed political terms the ideal of Jewish purity of the Israeli state. It also provoked widespread interest among Arabs abroad. But, in the last analysis, Semitic Action and its *Hebrew Manifesto* were a failure.

The men who formed this group were individualists. As almost always happens in Israeli politics, each considered himself an exclusive leader in his own right. Each was unwilling to give up too much of his personal dignity and renown for the sake of the common movement. Avnery was making headway with his weekly. Yalin-Mor was unenthusiastic about changing to mass-movement tactics: perhaps after his underground experience, he was unable to. Others were envious of these two king-pins.

So no 'professional revolutionaries' were fathered by Semitic Action. No *apparat* was created, and the enormously sympathetic response which the *Manifesto* awakened in the youth of Israel went to waste. The middle-aged encyclopedists had no place for young activists. For six years and more Yalin-Mor published a bi-weekly, *Etgar* ('Challenge'), to fight the increasingly 'hawkish' policies of the Israeli Establishment, while Avnery fought on with his sensationalist, mass-circulation paper which he himself described as 'a mixture of *Playboy* and *Foreign Affairs Quarterly*'.

There were some stirrings against all this hope and goodwill going to waste. A grass-roots group, calling itself Koah Yozem

('Initiating Force'), was founded in 1960 by a handful of young men who did not wish to stop short at the idea of a Hebrew nation and a Palestinian nation. They advocated a bi-national state, and indeed a bi-national community. They did something Semitic Action was afraid to do: for the first time in a non-communist movement in Israel they made Palestinians and Israelis fully equal within their activist group.

For this was the second and, in the last analysis, decisive flaw in the *Hebrew Manifesto*: it was *Hebrew*. It was, the Semitic men declared, 'the document of the new Israelis'. And they added: 'Let the new Arabs write a Palestinian Manifesto of their own.'

Some ten years later they did. By then the escalation of oppression and counter-terror had reached a point where this document was inevitably pan-Arab. It was called *The Covenant of the Palestine Movement of Liberation.*

But in the late fifties the Palestinian guerrillas were still muddled, half-hearted, and inflicted with a corrupt leader, Ahmed Shukeiry. Egypt was anxious to ensure her supremacy over all fighting Arab movements and for this reason backed Shukeiry. The Palestinians were isolated and politically immature. No voice answered the *Hebrew Manifesto* from outside Israel's borders. In the country itself, Semitic Action would not allow the intellectuals of Israel's big Palestinian community to adhere to its movement. And anyway Semitic Action's precepts were drafted in an exclusive Israeli form – 'Hebrew nation, Eretz-Israel . . .'

As for the Koah Yozem group, it had the right ideas but not the necessary standing. Nor had it any kind of charismatic leadership. After the gestation period, some of its members began to fear that the movement would attract, as one of them put it, 'hundreds of Arabs and only a handful of Jews'. The repeated, hapless efforts of the Communist Party of Israel had already proved how ineffective such a formula was. Koah Yozem therefore looked for allies. It found them in a splinter group of Israeli intellectuals who had broken away from the influence of the communists. In 1961 the two groups united to form the Israeli

New Left movement.* Its life was short. After a single year the New Left disintegrated because of intrigues, personal power seeking, and, above all, the former communists' now proto-Zionist fear of a 'non-Jewish essence'. (The same process was to be repeated later, on a bigger scale, when the Maki communists identified with the Israeli Establishment.)

This left the field to Semitic Action alone. It did nothing with it. The ball of Israeli-Palestinian liberation was left lying around, to be kicked desultorily and ineffectively by anyone disenchanted with the Zionist parties, or merely politically ambitious on his own account.

*Of which the author, a Koah Yozem member, became Secretary-General.

8 The Phenomenon of 'Haolam Hazeh' from 1950 on

In the years when Zionist ideology was losing ground among the younger generation, many Israelis found themselves fighting for Zionist goals – intertwined with the struggle for the existence of Israel – while shouting anti-Zionist slogans. During this period, roughly from the mid-fifties to the eve of the 1967 war, the very word *Tzionut* meant, in Hebrew slang, prattle, meaningless talk, nonsense. The reuniting of the territorial and mystic-Jewish goals in one masterful military operation briefly changed this. But the wariness of the average Israeli faced with party politics remained.

In this atmosphere developed an instrument of political propaganda and of civil rights struggle which was as far removed from stodginess as possible: the weekly *Haolam Hazeh*, edited and published by Ury Avnery and Shalom Cohen since 1950.

In the previous chapter we said something of Avnery's earlier career, in connection with the 'Semitic' movements. He met Cohen, an Iraqi-born and Egyptian-educated Jew, when they took part in the 1948 war. The paper they founded has had a deep influence on Israel, perhaps on the whole Middle East. They turned it into a racy sensationalist sheet, printed on thick, brownish paper, with lots of nudes as well as lots of political comment and social analysis. Above all, they printed revelations of what was going on behind the scenes of Israeli public life, and in the tills and bedrooms of the better-known Zionist bosses: the very antithesis of an Israeli Russian-type paper, florid, turgid, and full of Stakhanovite Zionist poems and exhortations.

More than once *Haolam Hazeh* found itself on the brink of bankruptcy. The army was forbidden to buy it for distribution in camp 'culture' rooms – a very serious drawback in a country where the average circulation of a prosperous weekly is between ten and twenty-five thousand and where the army alone may buy five to ten thousand copies a week. Moreover, government and Histadrut-sponsored publicity boycotted the paper. Considering that Histadrut controls so much of Israel's economy, either directly or indirectly, and considering in addition that much private enterprise is owned by men near to the Zionist leadership, these repeated blows were almost mortal.

When they failed in their purpose, other more tangible blows followed. In the early fifties Avnery and Cohen were attacked physically soon after an article criticizing the redoubtable Parachute Corps had appeared. They were beaten up; Avnery suffered cerebral contusion and one of his arms was broken. Shortly afterwards, a bomb was planted in the paper's printing works, injuring a journalist. Another bomb was planted at the offices of the paper. Later, in 1971, the newspaper's offices were destroyed by arson, shortly after Avnery unleashed a personal campaign against Moshe Dayan.

Several other efforts were made to destroy Avnery economically, or to dispose of him by putting him on trial. But his growing file of secret information pretty effectively prevented the maturing of these plans. In the years 1953–62, a whole series of weeklies was launched to break Avnery's hold on his fascinated public. One of these, *Rimon*, was almost certainly financed by the secret services.

The fact that only some leftover underground movement splinter-groups and *Haolam Hazeh* were 'outside the pale' of Zionist party life (for totally different reasons) allowed the government to accuse Avnery of terrorism. The allegations were proved untrue, but they left a mark. From these early years of struggle dates Avnery's almost superstitious fear of being identified with groups more extreme than himself, or whose ideas diverge from his. Along with this fear went his deep conviction that he, and he alone, was capable of changing things. All this made Avnery jealous of his partners, both journalists and politicians.

Avnery's purely political career started in 1957, when he helped the lawyer Shmuel Tamir uncover a direct connection between the leaders of the Zionist movement, Moshe Sharett, Ehud Avriel, Dr Chaim Weizmann, and others, and the fate during the Second World War of one million Hungarian Jews. By a conspiracy of silence, and by their cooperation with British Military Intelligence, the Zionist leaders of Palestine had foiled the Hungarian Jews' efforts to arrange their ransom and emigration to Palestine, Tamir charged.

Winston Churchill did not want trouble with the Arabs in a Palestine burdened with an extra million Jews. The Jewish official leadership did not want to lose to the Revisionist Zionists and their militant Irgun its ascendancy over the economy and society of emerging Jewish Palestine. Hence the plot.

The man responsible for contacts between the Jewish Community Committee in Hungary and the German S S and Gestapo (led in Budapest, at that time, by Adolf Eichmann) was a certain Dr Rudolph Azriel Kastner. Later in Israel, Kastner, by now a Labour leader, was accused of cooperation with the Nazis. He took his accuser, one Malchiel Grinvald, to court. Tamir defended Grinvald.*

Ury Avnery was swiftly aware of the explosive possibilities of the Kastner affair. Alone among the Israeli press, he supported Tamir unconditionally, built him up, and attacked Kastner and through him the whole Establishment. When Kastner was said by the judges to have 'sold his soul to the devil', and soon after was murdered by a former paid informer of the Shin Beit, Avnery and Tamir were already politically famous. But when Tamir launched a – short-lived – political party of his own, he disdained to associate a publisher of 'pornography' with his efforts. (Tamir has always been wrong in his political choices.)

*The whole affair has been tellingly, if biasedly, analysed in the late Ben Hecht's book, *Perfidy* (Julian Messner, New York, 1961). Hecht, a former Revisionist Zionist and an admirer of Jabotinsky, died of a broken heart over the Zionist leadership's perfidy. Tamir, also once a Revisionist, is a prosperous politician and lawyer, who meanwhile founded an ultranationalist group, Free Centre, which he represents in the Knesset and whose career is based on annexionist ideas.

Avnery turned against him, and in a series of poisonous attacks demolished the man he had helped to build up only a few months before. From then on Avnery was reluctant, for a while, to enter straightforward politics. But in the middle sixties the Israeli government lost patience with the Opposition press. Apart from ultra-religious and left-Zionist papers, it had dwindled to three main publications: the Communist daily *Kol Haam* ('Voice of the People'); Nathan Yalim-Mor's *Etgar* ('Challenge') and Ury Avnery's popular *Haolam Hazeh. Kol Haam* was estimated to have about five thousand readers, *Etgar* about two thousand, *Haolam Hazeh* no fewer than ninety to a hundred thousand. Obviously the 'scandal sheet' with a political message of peace was more serious an adversary than the ossified Marxist daily or the intellectual bi-weekly. Aware of this, the government decided to do something about freedom of expression. Ever since the creation of the state, censorship had been applied. But Israel's liberal-democratic heritage still ensured considerable room for free speech. Again and again, the Opposition managed to reveal unpleasant truths about the mismanagements, machinations, and downright oppression practised by the parties of the Establishment and led by the all-powerful Mapai Labour.

So, in 1965, a new Law of Defamation was proposed. Its one and only purpose was to forbid the use of 'information and innuendo' against persons and organizations. Avnery aptly called it the 'Law of the Gag'.

Under this slogan Avnery rallied his thirty thousand paper-buyers and their families – many of them too young to vote,* but others willing and able to do so – in a campaign to save his paper. 'If we are to keep the paper running,' Avnery and Cohen told their readers, 'you must put us in the Knesset. Only if we have parliamentary immunity can we go on publishing the whole truth.' And to this appeal the readers flocked. Other elements came too, such as the small Israeli Socialist Organization, better known as Matzpen ('Compass').

The election campaign was fought in the spirit of 'one against

*The vote is given in Israel at eighteen, when both men and women also become liable for service in the army.

the rest'. The basically generous nature of the Israelis responded to some extent to this line – which in spite of its arrogance and its holier-than-thou resonances had the truth behind it. With 1·2 per cent of the voters giving their ballots to the *Haolam Hazeh–Koah Hadash* list, Avnery won one sharply contested seat.

Three reasons, I believe, contributed to the change which took place at this point in Avnery. The first was the Israelis' mystique of war. Avnery has always been the kind of politician who, even in rebellion, manages to bet on the strong side, on the likely winner. This was why, to begin with, he identified himself with the Arab world, and this was also why, in the face of increasing Israeli strength, he acquired a taste for war and militarism. Israel is a country fascinated by military matters. From the strongly anti-militarist bias it inherited from the ruling Labour, it gradually became more sabre-rattling when Ben-Gurion took the reins of power, and was, in the 1960s and 1970s, drunk with the smell of steel. A newspaper, even an Opposition weekly, has to report on war and soldiers, on battles and reprisal raids, if it wants to keep its readership. Military matters and sex far more than political scandals and rumours became, in the sixties, the main selling-points for Israeli newspapers – as any professional Israeli newspaperman knows only too well.

A second reason for Ury Avnery's *embourgeoisement* was the fact that he came into daily, personal contact with the Establishment. This once most hated, most despised 'gutter journalist' was suddenly 'Most Honourable'. He had to talk to the men and women he had been attacking for fifteen years in the brown-yellow pages of his weekly. He had to meet them in the General Assembly, to sit with them in Committee, and above all to talk to them in the Knesset's restaurant, where most of the unofficial horsetrading is done.

Under the circumstances, he could not go on denouncing these quite nice oldish men in the extreme style he was accustomed to. And when new, more dynamic elements arose to initiate a frontal attack upon the Zionist Establishment, Avnery, who had always believed in his own effectiveness and in the impotence of nearly everybody else, was something less than pleased. In fact he was ruthless. He destroyed any chance of the various non-Zionist and non-religious political tendencies coming together to form a 'Popular Peace Movement'.

It took four years, the gradual worsening of the security situation in the occupied territories and the election of Shalom Cohen as the second Parliamentary Member of the party to ensure a partial return to the old savage, efficient style of criticism. And even then, the new weaknesses showed.

The third reason for the gradual change in Ury Avnery's policy is to be found in a simple biological fact: he was getting old. Israel, and before that the Jews of Palestine, had always been a community ruled by old men. This is a fact almost as important as the common Russo-Polish cultural and territorial background of so many of the 'ruling oldsters'. Avnery, on the other hand, started his career as a young man, a spokesman for the younger generation. 'All power to youth' was, in fact, the *Haolam Hazeh* slogan at one point. In sympathy with this slogan, the paper wrote about happenings in the Arab countries where, owing to the upheavals within it and to the periodic beheading of its power-élites, the leadership was, on the whole, young. But this policy of writing for the young left middle-aged Avnery still on the wrong side of the tracks, still outside the boundaries of the Establishment. His admission to the Knesset gave him the opportunity to join it.

Avnery made a discovery: the leaders of the Establishment were not as bad as they looked. Perhaps it was not without significance that these 'misguided fellows' had a monopoly of power in Israel, and that they kept the upper hand in three bouts against the combined strength of the Arab countries; or that they had bitten off chunk after chunk of territory and swallowed them.

For twenty years Avnery had been trying to make contact with Arab leaders. His 'open letters' to one or another of them were a recurring feature of his editorials. In addition he tried to get in touch with any number of minor Arab politicians through the intermediary of Western politicians and journalists, such as Eric Rouleau of Paris's *Le Monde* and Michael Adams of the

Council for the Advancement of Arab-British Understanding. When the 1967 conquests provided a new 'captive audience' of a million Palestinians, both Avnery and Cohen approached a whole series of Arab public figures there. Among these were the lawyer Aziz Shahade, who advocated the creation of a Palestinian state, even under Israel's vigilant protectorate; Anwar El Khatib, a former Jordanian Cabinet Minister who refused any kind of cooperation with the Israelis; and above all, the Mayor of Hebron, Ali El Jaabari.

Jaabari was widely regarded in the occupied territories as something of a Quisling. It must be said at once that he had no choice but to collaborate with the conquerors. In 1929, as we have seen, the Arab population slaughtered the Jewish minority of that biblical town. So when the Israeli tanks rumbled into Hebron in 1967, the Mayor and all his citizens hastened to hoist white flags, knowing some Israelis would be quick to take advantage of any resistance to wreak vengeance upon the whole community.

Jaabari understood this better than most. He gave the conquerors no opportunity to settle accounts. Hebron, he decided, would cooperate fully. It was the only town to do so, from the start. In the first eighteen months of occupation there was not a single serious incident or act of civil disobedience. While in Nablus and Gaza strikes and demonstrations were held, protests were organized, and bombs were thrown – bringing a response of wholesale destruction of homes and mass arrests – Hebron kept quiet.

Keeping quiet, however, solved nothing. But in spite of this Jaabari was the man Avnery repeatedly proposed as organizer of a peace conference to bring about the creation of a 'free Palestine', or Israeli protectorate. *If there had been no alternative*, this solution would no doubt have been preferable to the ongoing conflict. But for some Palestinians there was a fighting alternative. They found a way of organizing themselves in spite of the occupation, or rather thanks to it. The loss of the West Bank, which even under Jordanian rule was considered the Palestinians' 'province' of the Hashemite kingdom, united the Palestinians into a band with a common purpose – the struggle for independence and dignity – and with common interests.

Ury Avnery found himself in a quandary. On the one hand, he could not propose direct contact with the resistance organizations – the Fatah, the Popular Front, the Democratic Popular Front and the Syrian-inspired Saikka. This would have sounded the death-knell of his popularity with those people in Israel who saw in him the champion of a youthful and cleansing nationalism, in opposition to the decadent Zionist nationalism of the 'foreign-born oldsters'. On the other hand, *Haolam Hazeh* could not completely abandon its peace-seeking line. Apart from the pressures for ideological consistency, the occupation had created new opportunities for contact between Israeli and Palestinian peace-seekers. It was, once more, the differing timetables of the two national developments which strangled this opportunity at birth. The only thing Avnery could do was to look for allies in the captive audience. He found alarmingly few. Nonetheless, the desperateness of his position, dangerously poised on a cliff under which the nationalist passions of two opposing peoples slavered at each other, drove Avnery even further from the only revolutionary answer: the acknowledgement that the terrorism of El Fatah and the Popular Front was part and parcel of the freedom fight for the common homeland.

Ury Avnery was just not ready to throw away his career in the increasingly chauvinistic atmosphere after the conquests of 1967. Already he had got rid of the neo-Trotskyite Matzpen group, in spite of the contribution they had made to his first electoral campaign. Later he neutralized the pacifist efforts of the liberal vice-chairman of his organization, David Ehrenfeld, a prosperous diamond exporter who had been one of Avnery's main backers in the election. Ehrenfeld then gave up his active functions, leaving the *Haolam Hazeh* party 'cleansed' of its radicals, Marxists, pacifists, and militants – with the signal exception of the group's parliamentary secretary, Amnon Zichroni, a lawyer who had once served a jail sentence as a conscientious objector.

In 1967 Avnery voted in the Knesset for the 'irrevocable reunification of Jerusalem as part of the State of Israel' – a vote which is admittedly consistent with his ideological contention that Jerusalem must be the capital of both Palestine and Israel but which at a practical level means the direct unilateral annexation of the town's Arab city to Israel; this at a time when the camps were becoming clearly defined: Zionists and Israeli nationalists on one side, and Palestinians and defenders of a bi-national entity on the other.

Avnery vacillated; at worst he gave in to Zionist principles. As early as the imperialist war of 1956, when Israel, France and Great Britain invaded Egypt, *Haolam Hazeh* – which had been warning all along against just such an intervention – printed a delighted editorial endorsing the action and signed by Ury Avnery. Only when Nathan Yalin-Mor shook him back to his senses did Avnery understand the gravity of his action and the injustice of defending the imperialist invasion. In the following week another article signed by Ury Avnery appeared. This time he criticized the campaign and its effects.

In 1967 this was repeated. Avnery understood that in the current atmosphere of total *Gleichschaltung* under the National Unity Cabinet he was as good as lost if he did not swim with the stream. As always, the waters or political torrents carried this gifted man too far. In the daily news-sheet *Daf*, issued by *Haolam Hazeh* for two months during and after the war, Avnery signed, against the advice of his partner, Shalom Cohen, a leader entitled 'TO DAMASCUS!' He demanded that the conquest of Syrian territory should be continued. Later *Haolam Hazeh* advocated 'not stopping at Suez'.

Immediately the ceasefire agreements were decided on, Avnery retracted from his extreme warlike stance. Once more *Haolam Hazeh* began to publish warnings against 'losing the opportunity of making peace' with the Arabs. While no official leader saw fit then to talk to the captive Palestinians, Avnery was advocating such talks. He adhered to the Movement for an Israeli-Palestinian Federation – of which, more later. He published his Party's peace plan.

By March 1968, almost a year after the war, it was too late. The reorganized guerrillas had started their activities. The

Palestinians in the territories had rallied to partial passive resistance. At the Khartoum conference, the Arab states still refused (unbelievably, for the rank and file Israelis) to consider peace talks. The Zionist leadership was happy: in its short-sighted territorial cupidity, it thought that a state of 'neither peace nor war' could not be to Israel's detriment. The Arab leaders were equally convinced, but in their own interest, of a continuation of the *status quo*.

By now the waves had also carried Avnery too far downstream. The expelled Matzpen group jeeringly published his failings and shortcomings abroad, thus cutting *Haolam Hazeh* off from its former Arab contacts. The Palestinians remembered 'TO DAMASCUS' and similar material and became more and more wary. The Zionist Establishment, moreover, was growing increasingly fanatical and mystical. Even the comparatively weak dissent of Avnery came to be considered anathema. Threats were made against him and his collaborators.*

There, more or less, matters stood in the early seventies. Avnery's credit among left-wingers and Palestinians was at a low ebb. On the other hand, his was still the only group which fought consistently for an *entente* with the Palestinians. Thus, in the long hard struggle still confronting those who hope for peace, Avnery's organization cannot be ignored. It could still rally a biggish part of Israeli opinion behind it. In the 1969 elections it doubled its vote, and Shalom Cohen was elected together with Avnery, who retained his old seat. The votes for Cohen came mostly from the army: this could be ascertained because the army ballot-boxes have to be scrutinized a day later than the civilian ones.

It was after Cohen was elected to the Knesset, at Avnery's side, thus acquiring independence and staying in the limelight

*I was, at that time, Assistant Editor-in-Chief of the weekly. I was, myself, threatened with death three times, and once had to defend myself against right-wing hoodlums in a discotheque. Shalom Cohen was mobbed both by Jews and by Palestinian refugees when he visited a camp in the Gaza Strip. Only the utmost presence of mind saved him, the newspaper's photographer Uri Cogan, and the journalist Raffi Zichroni from being lynched.

on his own, that Avnery's quirk for quarrelling with his friends reached, after twenty-three years of partnership and struggle, Shalom Cohen himself. In the spring of 1970 the *Haolam Hazeh* partnership was dissolved, and the movement they had started together split. Subsequently, Cohen became a Black Panther's party-leader.

To sum up: in the early seventies, Ury Avnery's attitude, as that of his almost non-existent organization, is: Palestine-Israel is one common fatherland of two peoples. Two different states must exist within it. To make this possible, both states must sign a defence treaty forbidding any outside agreements harmful to the other. This would be a first step towards eventual integration.* This sounds a promising programme, but it is much less radical than would appear. The stronger and the more aggressive Israel gets, the better Avnery and the contributors to *Haolam Hazeh* like it. The man who was once, in a way, the most extreme ideologue of integration – an impossible dream even in 1947 – is now a Jewish nationalist of the post-Zionist kind. The Confederation of Israel and Palestine, as expounded by Avnery with the big Israeli brother influencing the Palestinians both militarily and politically, would bring about little more than an Israeli-controlled puppet state.

But Avnery still plays one of the most constructive roles in the camp of those who believe in peace with the Palestinians. Precisely because his ideas have lost most of their revolutionary content and have become no more than strongly reformist, even in the totally Zionized Israel of the seventies he has a quite large following which fights against injustices and insanity.

The 1971 split in Avnery's party, however, may be decisive. History may pass Avnery by. And this in spite of the long, arduous struggle which he and his friends have waged for more than twenty years: a struggle of a good man, with good ideas, who has been forced to sacrifice his convictions to expediency, and must pay the price. Yet the basic purpose of the man still shines through the rags of political expediency which cover the nakedness of his changing thoughts.

*'Project of Peace', presented by the *Haolam Hazeh* faction to the Knesset, March 1968.

9 The Israeli Communist Party

In order to examine an element in the situation which stands rather apart from the others, the Communist Party in Israel, we must go back some years. Israel's second and third official languages are French and Arabic. The lingua franca of all Israelis is English, an inheritance from the Mandate days. But the father-languages, the ones on which the culture of the founders of the Establishment is based, are Yiddish, Russian and Polish. Eastern Europe has for the Israeli of the waning generation all the love–hate attraction of a stern father who has rejected his son and been rejected by him in return. Russian absolutism, the Soviet Revolution, the individual as part of society and country long before he is allowed to think of himself as an independent agent – all these, deeply embedded in the Israeli consciousness, are direct descendants of the Russian complex of the founding fathers – people like Golda Meir, Israel Galili and Moshe Dayan's father.

No wonder then that the evolution of a hostile Russian policy towards Israel has been accompanied by a growing manifestation of the old mixuture of fear, love, apprehension and frustration which was the normal attitude of the early Zionists to Russia. Add to this the fact that the Zionist revolution came from the springs which fed the great Russian Revolution – the need to demolish the social context in which Jews, Russians and Polish citizens lived; add furthermore the continued existence of the biggest concentration of Jews anywhere, inside the borders of the USSR, and you get an extraordinarily potent and explosive mixture. Nevertheless this conflict of loyalties in fact influences the Zionist Establishment in favour of the West, and much more so than the 'affinity of interests between American imperialism and Zionism', so often denounced in Soviet and Arab propaganda.

The love–hate relationship also explains why the Communist Party has so little appeal for the Israeli worker – identified as he is with the interests of Zionist syndicalism – or the Israeli intellectual. And, indeed, where is the son who leaves his father's house and finds a home of his own, only to let his father equip it with his old, ugly furniture?

The beginnings of the Jewish-Palestinian communists coincide with the beginnings of Zionist colonization. In 1919, when the waves of 'leftist' immigrants started washing the downtrodden of Poland and Russia ashore in the Middle East, many among them had not lost their Marxist-Leninist faith.

In fact the role of the Jews in the Soviet Revolution has never been properly estimated. One forgets the Jewish Populist Movement, the 'Bund', which became a full-fledged associate of the big Russian Revolution before the takeover of the Bolsheviks. One forgets Pinhas Ruthenberg, one of the most stalwart Zionists, who later held the electrical concession for the greater part of Mandatory Palestine and who before that had been Minister of Police in Kerensky's short-lived government. Incidentally, Ruthenberg is reputed, as a revolutionary, to have been involved in plotting the assassination of a number of Tsarist officials and of the notorious police-spy and agitator, the priest Gapon.

In this atmosphere of Jewish involvement in the conspiracies of the Slav upheaval, and later in the Bolshevik revolution, it was not surprising that the more freedom-loving among them should fuse Marxism and Zionism. To weaken the Marxist element in the mixture by strengthening the Zionist element was, in fact one purpose of the Balfour Declaration.* Some blend of Marxism and Zionism was only to be expected from the ideological confrontation of the Jews in Slav countries with the upheaval on

*Christopher Sykes writes: '... in the last phase, before November 1917, it was believed that open British support of Zionism would detach Russian Jews from the Bolshevik party and so ensure that the Revolution would remain not only moderate but the belligerent ally of France and Britain. The last belief, although even less realistic than fears of [First World War] German Zionism, certainly accelerated the issue of the Declaration.' *Crossroads to Israel*, p. 22.

one hand and with their wish for a revolution of their own on the other. In the confrontation, the Eastern European Jews acquired a dynamism and grimness of purpose which went much further than the experimental socialist enterprise of the first Western Jewish immigrants to Palestine. The socialist Jews from Russia and Poland found themselves running the Zionist revolution – a utopian social revolution, with the exclusivist traits of any social movement which evolved in a narrow national framework alone.

But not all of them. As far back as 1919, when Palestine was still under the military occupation of the British OETA, a Marxist-Leninist minority broke away from the then left-wing Zionist Workers' Party (Poalei Zion Smol) and went on to found the Bolshevik-orientated Workers' Socialist Party, known by its Hebrew initials MPS (Mifleget Poalim Sotzialistit) and derisively nicknamed 'Mopsi' after a breed of little German lap-dogs. Mopsi was not yet clearly communist, but its members found it repugnant to be part of a purely Jewish, racialist, revolution. They had enough class-consciousness to see something which the sufferings of the Jews abroad obscured in the minds of the Zionists: the harm done to the indigenous population. Speaking Arabic as its feudal masters did, the indigenous population were beyond the sympathetic understanding of the Zionist revolutionaries, who had trouble enough replacing their native Yiddish, Polish and Russian with Hebrew. Their language barrier, together with a single-minded dedication to abolish the centuries-old injustice suffered by Jewish minorities, prevented the newly-established colonist-revolutionaries from seeing the plight of other men just beyond the fences of their settlements – even though this plight had been to some extent inflicted by the founding of these same utopian-communist settlements.

It seems that doing good, working with others hand in hand, helping men redeem themselves by work, are possible only within the narrowest range of identification. Anything beyond that range can be ignored or is considered hostile. In this ambiguous atmosphere Mopsi evolved, its members still under the spell of what they saw as the marvellous, violent socialist upheaval which had happened in Russia so shortly before. Lacking a basis for common action with the feudal-dominated Palestinian masses, and taking stock of the contradictions of the early Zionist Labour movement, they opted for the only 'logical' patron: the world-wide Bolshevik Revolution due to explode any day now across the countries of the globe. To this day the legend is passed on in ex-Mopsi circles of the personal involvement of Leon Trotsky, who used to receive the envoys sent by the group to keep contact between revolutionary Russia and the Middle East.

These were the days when Russia started to organize popular revolts in various parts of the imperialist-dominated Afro-Asian countries. In China Russian commissars fought (with André Malraux, among others) to liberate the people through the revolutionary action of the Kuomintang. It was only natural that a similar experiment should be attempted in the Middle East, a zone actually bordering southern Russia.

From the Russian viewpoint, there were no better agents for the task than the Marxist Jews, some of whom still had the confidence of the British Mandate. But these Marxists were too innocent to succeed. Copying the pattern which had emerged in China, they tried to launch yet another left-wing party in Palestine to exploit the nationalist stirrings of the Arabic-speaking area. It was a piece of simple-minded dogmatism such as the world has only too often seen. Although feudal in its own right, Chinese society was some thousands of years beyond the primary nationalist stage of its development. The Arab leaders, in contrast, were just beginning their attempt to create nationalist feeling among the downtrodden, hoping thereby to prop up a single autocratic Arab empire, or at worst several Arab kingdoms. A comprehensive national revolutionary pan-Arab movement was as yet something for the future. In the early seventies, the pan-Arab movement does qualify for an attempt at takeover by a foreign-based Communist Party. In the early twenties it did not. Integration in the pan-Arab movement meant only one thing for the communist revolutionaries: they had to support monarchist, feudal and totalitarian stirrings if they wished to manipulate civil dissent and disorder.

The communists supplied funds to the pan-Arab nationalist

movement – or rather to the *Effendis* who directed it. The fact that the suppliers, who were of course the heads of Mopsi and its successors, were Jews – usually Polish- or Russian-born – enormously reinforced the Judeo-Bolshevik legends then starting to circulate in Western countries, Great Britain not excepted.

But the Comintern did not stop at giving money. On May Day 1921 two things happened simultaneously. On the beach at Tel-Aviv the first open clash between the Zionist Workers and Mopsi occurred when two processions attacked each other; and in the nearby town of Jaffa Mopsi speakers harangued the crowd. This double event had unexpected and tragic results. Arab rioting started in Jaffa, where the inhabitants of a New Immigrants' Home were murdered, and spread to the rest of Palestine. Altogether there were 314 casualties, including forty-eight Arab and forty-seven Jewish deaths. The British Military Authorities, with the open connivance of the Zionist leadership, forbade the activities of Mopsi. The communists' first effort had proved to be both dangerous and self-defeating.

However, from the misfortune the Palestina Kommunistische Partei (PKP)* was born three years later, in 1924. This organization fulfilled its appointed task within the Moscow line – a line which at that time ignored Jewish Zionist nationalism and tried to graft the whole social revolution on the back of the pan-Arab and feudal-monarchist stirrings in the Middle East.

This Moscow *Diktat* caused deep concern to some of the Jewish communists, who rightly saw themselves as a marginal phenomenon in Palestine. Clearly the British authorities were on their way to implementing the Balfour Declaration and permitting the existence of a Jewish national home. And the Jews, with their higher culture, more advanced technology and further evolved national consciousness, were obviously the true promoters of change in Palestine, and through Palestine in the whole of the Middle East.

So there was another schism. The Yiddische Kommunistische

*The Jewish communists used German and Yiddish for their communications. Thus the name of the party was in German, which made it understandable to Yiddish speakers.

Partei, with a pro-Jewish slant, set itself up in opposition to the internationally-minded, Moscow-orientated PKP, which was ready to receive Arabs into its ranks. Both groups tried to establish some kind of official contact with the Comintern, by way of a former Zionist firebrand, the wife of the Austrian Bolshevik leader Hans Koplany, who had been a Poalei Zion Smol member before her marriage. The Comintern was ready to accept the two groups' candidature on one condition – the adherence of the Arab working masses.

The task of the PKP was to fight against British imperialism and the Jewish national home promised by the Balfour Declaration. Indirectly, it tried to widen the Soviet sphere of interest in the Middle East and to convert the Jewsektzia – the Jewish section of the Communist International – into an instrument of action inside the Arabic-speaking world.* Nonetheless PKP remained a Jewish head grafted on to a skeletal Arab body. It was by no means a bi-national entity, much less a harbinger of understanding and cooperation between two opposing but potentially complementary peoples. It was, rather, the bearer of a foreign standard in a battle where each side already had a passionate dedication to its own flag.

As late as 1923 the communists of Palestine were still at the stage where they boasted that *one* Arab comrade† had spoken at the inaugural conference of their group. But gradually the party's Jewish complexion changed: until the late twenties it was controlled by totally dedicated men such as 'The Professor', I. Mayerson; 'Red' Gershon Dua; Daniel Abu-Ziama (whose real name was Wolf Averbuch). But then a schism occurred in the 'Work Battalion' organized by the Zionists for the colonization of Palestine and the building of roads. Many volunteers left the battalion to return to the USSR. Some of these even founded a Jewish Kibbutz in Russia, the Vya Nova. Others joined the experiment of an autonomous community in Birobidjan. Many

*Throughout this chapter I am indebted to the scholarly articles of Haviv Knaan, *Haaretz*, of 16, 17, 19, and 24 April 1970.

†As can be seen in the minutes of the party's conference – Shmuel Mikunis' speech transcript.

others were killed, or jailed for uncounted years, when Stalin decided to 'purify' the international communist movement. A need for a new, if possible indigenous leadership arose in the Middle Eastern communist camp.

Henceforth the PKP became unconditionally a part of the Arab nationalist movement, hoping, as would any Communist Party in such a situation, to turn the movement from nationalism to social revolution. Thus the PKP put its hopes on the wrong nationalism. For in Palestine a separate nationalism was developing, quite independent from the rest of the Middle East, and this nationalism was Jewish.

If it had tried to unite the Arabs and the Jews of Palestine, the PKP might have brought about some kind of solidarity – or at least cooperation – between the communities. But Moscow was not interested in a Palestinian brand of Judeo-Arab nationalism. For one thing, Palestine was an artificially created country, and apart from Stalin's ideological requirements for what constituted a nation (a common language, territory, economy and culture: all of which the Palestinians shared with the rest of the Middle East), it was thought that an isolated communist success would be counter-productive. Moscow's own 'socialism in one country' was not favourably regarded, at that time, by the USSR outside its own borders.

So the fortunes of the Palestinian communists continued to depend on the framework they chose to work in: most of them, Jewish or Arab, identified themselves with the Arabic-speaking nationalist upheaval. From time to time, however, some Jews among them rebelled. Occasionally this was because they identified themselves with the suffering Jews of Europe, or those of Palestine. But sometimes it was because they made a Marxist-Leninist analysis of the situation, which demonstrated that the obvious nationalist movement to exploit was the Zionist one. For under the Zionists, capitalism or neo-capitalism already existed, whereas the Arab movement was still amorphous, pre-industrial, and feudal and had yet to experience the phase of autocratic nationalism which gripped Europe in the eighteenth and nineteenth centuries.

The ideological world of the Zionists (as of the Israelis later on) was the nationalism of the early nineteenth century. The Arabs, including the Palestinians, lived then in the early Middle Ages, and are today launched on their journey through the centuries of religious ideological backing for tyranny or regal absolutism.

Thus the story of the PKP and of the communists in Israel is a repeated tearing-asunder and precarious sewing-together again of the factions identifying themselves respectively with the pan-Arab and Jewish-Zionist nationalisms. In 1919 Mopsi was inside the pan-Arab framework. In 1921 the Arabs of Palestine, who were supposed to be Mopsi's backbone, revolted. From 1921 to 1923 there was the schism between the PKP and the pro-Jewish Yiddische Kommunistische Partei. In 1924 a united party was created under communist tutelage.

During the Arab upheavals of 1927–9, when many Jews were atrociously butchered, some Jewish communists became so disgusted with all the equivocations that they asked Arab nationalists to help them to emigrate back to Russia. They did emigrate, although without Arab help. The revolts, seen by international communism only as an anti-British phenomenon, finally established the need for an Arab leadership of PKP. The Jews were turned out of the Central Committee, until then almost exclusively Jewish, and sent to the lower ranks, and a Jaffa-born Arab from a Christian background, who as a stonemason had the correct proletarian extraction, was made secretary-general. Radjwan Hilou, a bright and efficient young man, started his task of activism and conciliation between the two, Arab and Jewish, tendencies.

Curiously, the PKP leaders, Arabs and Jews alike, made the same mistake and thus prepared the way to the tragedy of the Zionist and Palestinian communities. The Jewish leaders tended to see the problem in the context of the 'unity of the Jewish people throughout the world', and so overlooked the existence of a new – local – Jewish nationalism, growing up before their very eyes. And the Arab leaders failed to see the sociological effect this was having on Arabs born and living in Palestine. Indeed they refused to work in a national-Palestinian context, and remained pan-Arab. In this they were at a slight variance with the anti-Moslem policy of the Bolshevik government itself, particularly with the implications of the latter's policy inside Russia; but consistent with the line adopted by local communist groups in Moslem countries, including Far Eastern ones. At the fourth congress of the Comintern, in the twenties, the revolutionary leader Tan Malaka stated, for instance: 'pan-Islamism is . . . the struggle for national liberation, because for the Moslem Islam is everything. It is not only religion, it is the State, the country's economy, and all the rest . . . This is why pan-Islamism is now the brotherhood of all Moslem people, the struggle for national liberation not only of the Arab peoples but also of all Moslems oppressed . . . *

The communists' rejection of a Palestinian nationalism proved to be their undoing. They rejected a basic Marxist precept and tried to ignore or by-pass a historical phase: that of the development of religious-backed feudalism into autocratic, centralized capitalism, and into post-capitalist centralization of the economy.

In retrospect it seems almost absurd that the communists never tried to create a common anti-imperialist movement between *fighting* Palestinians, whether Jews or Arabs. But the fact is they did not. They preferred to dedicate their efforts to supporting Soviet policy and international scheming, to the emergence of the pan-Arab absolutist movement, and to opposing Zionist consolidation. And in opposing Zionism they did not attempt, as they might have done, to separate it from the normal nationalism of the *Tzabras*; instead they discounted its attributes, such as the Hebrew language, the newly indigenous habits and culture, and above all the Jewish underground's armed fight against British imperialism.

In fact, by one of the more scandalous ironies of history, the communists in Palestine had to be what Israeli slang calls 'vegetarian' – that is pacifist. They could not afford to encourage the armed struggle of the Jews against the British, because this

* Nathan Weinstock, *Le Mouvement révolutionnaire arabe*, Maspéro, Paris, 1970.

struggle was Zionist-nationalist. Nor could they altogether afford to encourage the armed struggle of the Palestinians, because this struggle was almost exclusively directed, at first, against those whom Yair's definition identified as the main enemy: 'those in control of your country'. And for the Arabs, this meant the Jews, the Zionists.

Since the pan-Arab rebellions of the 1920s and the 1930s flowed through primitive racialist and religious channels (reminiscent of late medieval religious warfare in Europe), they left a confusion in people's minds. The Zionists saw in them only an anti-Semitic pogrom. The Arab masses failed to see how their feudal leaders were exploiting the revolts for personal and class purposes. In the end the main victim was not the Zionist Establishment and the Jewish presence but rather the lives, fortunes and future of those Palestinians who spoke Arabic.

In the confrontation, the communists worked away with all the devoted wrongheadedness of alchemists. Instead of trying to discover the gold of modern nationalism – so susceptible to takeovers by absolutist ideologies – they tried to convert the raw lead of neo-religious and racialist pan-Arabism into modern nationalism. They failed. At least they have the bitter consolation of knowing they fell into the same trap as the British imperialists, bitten by the Lawrence bug.

The situation at this time is well summed up in an article published many years later (after he had become a Zionist) by Yossef Berger,* who was a member of the Comintern. He recalls:

> In 1925 the Comintern asked me to keep in close contact with Jamal Husseini, who was the right-hand lieutenant of the Mufti of Jerusalem, Haj Amin El-Husseini, the revered leader of the Palestinian Arabs. Jamal was the second most important man in the Palestinian National Movement. Before me it was Wolf Auerbach (shot in the courtyard of Moscow's Lubyanka Prison some years later) who kept in touch with

* *Haaretz* 19 April 1970. 'Barzilay' (his *nom de guerre*) was recalled to Moscow in the early thirties and in due course purged. He spent twenty-two years in Soviet prisons and slave camps until in the political thaw after Khrushchev's 20th Congress he was pardoned. He re-emigrated to Israel, where he has since published excellent books and articles on the plight and fight for liberation of the Soviet Jews.

the Arab Central Committee and the Syrian-Palestinian Committee. In the name of the Comintern we promised these Arab leaders organizational and financial help to consolidate the Arab national movement, and to unify the Arab people, which was under British rule in the Land of Israel and in Egypt, under French rule in Syria and the Lebanon. In those days our main aim was a *rapprochement* with the Arab national movement. Today it looks strange that PKP competed with ultra-religious Jews such as Dr De Haan and Rabbi Zonnenfeld in its endeavours to acquire the goodwill of the Arab nationalists against the Zionists.

We, the Jewish Communists of the Land of Israel, really believed then that, with the help of the Comintern, we would take our place in the Government of the Palestinian State where we would defend the rights of the Jewish minority.

We promised the Arab leaders that their National Movement would get the help of the Communist parties of the world, and we gave them money issued for that purpose by the Comintern paymasters. Several times I myself gave money to Jamal Husseini, in his own house in Sheikh Jarrah [in Eastern Jerusalem]. I believed in those days that the money would be used to strengthen the efforts of the National Movement fighting against imperialism, and only after several years did I understand that the money stayed in the pockets of the *Effendis*. Contact with the Arab leaders broke down in 1928, when Jamal Husseini and his friends expressed displeasure regarding the amounts we passed on to them, and which were, according to them, too small to help them in their endeavours. They did not hide from me that they expected bigger sums. Altogether I had passed on to them in three years several thousand pounds sterling.

The Arab nationalist leaders also threw into my face the fact that they now understood the Russians did not wish to intercede for them with all their might, and we on the other hand had to tell the Comintern that the Arabs were unable to carry on a dynamic political struggle.

Another source of disagreement was the 1929 upheavals. In Moscow, as we have seen, they were considered only anti-imperialist. In communist circles in Haifa and Tel-Aviv they were considered only anti-Jewish. This disagreement foreshadowed a more serious rift between Jewish and Arab Palestinian communists. It occurred during the more critical Arab revolt of 1936–9, when the Axis powers succeeded in alienating not a few communist Arabs – as well as huge masses of pan-nationalist religious Moslems who were anyway prone to racialism – from their former ally, the USSR.

During these years the PKP's political leadership – all Arabs now, although the organization's *cadre* of agitators and activists was still mostly Jewish – supported the Arab Revolt against both the British Mandate and the Jews as colonialists and individuals. (This revolt, as we have seen, gave the Haganah the opportunity to establish tighter cooperation with the British and to establish, with the help of the Mandate Administration, the basis of a paramilitary organization.) It also once more rent the communists asunder. The Jewish and Arab members of the party seldom met. Once again an outside intervention was necessary.

It came in the person of one of the leaders of the Comintern, an international agitator who was none other than the Italian *émigré* chief, Palmiro Togliatti. Togliatti sharply criticized the pan-Arabs' involvement with the Fascists, and particularly with Italian *Mare Nostrum* politics. Togliatti had the ear of Moscow, and of Joseph Stalin himself. Moscow gave the word, and the leadership of the PKP was obliged to include a Jew – Shmuel Mikunis, who later represented his party in the Israeli Knesset, and went on to join Dr Sneh as a 'Communist Zionist' when Rekah split from PKP's successor – the Maki Communist Party (see p. 150).

The co-dominion of Mikunis (a former actor) and the Arab Hilou (a former worker) was good for the party's unity, but it did not preclude the emergence of a 'Jewish faction' in the PKP led by the late Hanoch Bzoza, who took a highly critical view of the party's activists. At this point the Second World War broke out. After a time of great confusion, caused by the Molotov-Ribbentrop pact, the communists came to believe in the need for total cooperation between Jews and Arabs in Palestine. Till 1943, with Hilou and Mikunis still in control, all went well. Then, in a gesture of goodwill towards its new-found capitalist allies, Great Britain, Free France and the United States, Moscow dissolved the Comintern. And from the moment they were without an outside referee the Palestinian communists split. Once more it was on the question of nationality and nationalism. The PKP became all-Jewish for the first time. The Arab militants created the League for National Liberation.

In the league a totally new type of Palestinian leader made his appearance. Young men such as Emil Habibi, Emil Touma and Tawfik Toubi were an exhilarating mixture of Western-communist education, Levantine wisdom, and grass-roots contact with the Arabs working in the industrial and technological society created mainly by the Jews in Palestine. Together with men like Shalom Cohen in Israel, they were the most hopeful sign which had so far emerged on the Palestinian scene.

Their socialistic logic and political acumen persuaded them to abandon any thought of cooperating with the Axis powers for the sake of Arab independence. Like so many communists of the time, they saw in the USSR something wonderful, almost holy; and in Joseph Stalin the father of all communist fighters. But they also started thinking of the future of Palestine. Suddenly they understood that this country was fast becoming something in its own right. They realized that the creation of Iraq and Transjordan (later Jordan) by the Husseini dynasty of *Bedawi* origin forced them to work for the socialist revolution within the narrow framework of Jewish-Arab Palestine.

Too late. Already Palestinian nationalism was firmly established in an exclusively Zionist context. Arab nationalism, clinging to pan-Arab values and abruptly forcing Arabs to find themselves political strangers in their own land, was much to blame for this. But much more to blame were the communists of the PKP who had nourished the too ambitious and anachronistic dream of pan-Arabism, from outside, out of pure revolutionary dogmatism. The crest of the wave had thrown the party-men inside the cage of the Zionist Establishment.

Each of the communist splits had its own thesis. In the League this was that Palestine should be an Arab country with full minority rights for Jews. This thesis ignored the fact that the Jews had grown in number, that by right two – then – generations of *Tzabras* had some claim to be indigenous, and, most important, that the Jews had taken the nationalist initiative from the hands of the Arabs in Palestine.

The PKP men, on the other hand, rehearsed Stalin's list of requisites: language, economy, territory. The Jews, they claimed, were now, by these standards, an independent nation; and two nations in the Middle East obliged Palestine to become binational.

Too late again. The Jews were too far along the path to a purely Jewish state. In 1945 the Zionist leaders were already waiting for the moment when *their* state would be created. Such a situation obviously led to a narrowing of the chasm between the Zionist 'extreme Left', Mapam, and the PKP. None of the communists ever considered cooperating with the Zionist Establishment, and only a little breakaway sect was prepared to fight beside the anti-imperialist Lehy. This sect was the Hebrew Communist Party, which broke away in the forties and was led by a mixture of *Tzabras* (such as Simha Zabari) and Russian- and Polish-born intellectuals (such as Shmuel Ettinger, later Professor of Jewish History, and Shmuel Preminger, later a member of the syndicalist Labour).

Then the 1948 war came. The Palestinians disappeared for twenty years as an independent political force. The Arab leaders of the PKP – for the communists had reunited again – were either forced into exile or compelled to give a doubtful allegiance to the Jewish state. On 11 June 1949 the Conference of the Communist Party of Israel (Maki, thus renamed on the emergence of the new state) devoted its central speech to 'The Problems of Immigration, Colonization, and Territorial Consolidation of the Jewish People in its Homeland'.

It was in line with the Russian *Diktat*. Joseph Stalin, troubled by his own national minorities during the war, had been displeased with the pan-Arabs' sympathy towards the Axis powers. On the other hand, he had been impressed by the anti-imperialist fighters of Lehy and Irgun. In an earlier chapter we saw how Lehy was helped by the USSR and the socialist countries. David Ben-Gurion has often told how Russia helped the newly created State of Israel in May 1948: by giving its existence *de facto* acknowledgement, even before the Americans; by putting arms from Czechoslovakia at its disposal; and by sending pilots to help fly the new planes which the Israeli forces had got either by bribery from British army personnel or by courtesy of the USSR.

'It did not worry me that the Russians did this in order to get rid of the British,' Ben-Gurion reflected. 'We used the weapons.'

Thus the newly formed Maki was on the 'right' side of the Moscow fence. It was kept there by a man of extraordinary perspicacity and analytic power, who has the habit of betting on the right horse – but unfortunately always too early or too late. This man was Doctor (of medicine) Moshe Sneh. At one point Sneh was Commanding Officer of Haganah and a member of the General-Zionist Party's leadership, a party which was quite right-wing or bourgeois in the Zionist camp.* In the forties he left his exalted position and went over to the left, there adopting an extremely pro-Russian position.

For the first time Sneh had bet on the wrong horse in the right race. Like most left-wingers of his time he anticipated that the post-war world would be totally and immediately divided between the US and the USSR. Such a phenomenon as a 'third world' of 'non-aligned countries' was not foreseen by the communists and their friends. Sneh rightly decided that Great Britain's imperial power was waning in the Middle East, as it was waning in India and elsewhere. He decided wrongly that he must bet on the Russian camp.

This was particularly unfortunate for Sneh. He would undoubtedly have become a leader of the first magnitude in the Israeli government, the equal of, or perhaps superior to, Ben-Gurion himself, if he had not cast his lot with the forthcoming communist world future. He had the crystal-clear intelligence, the intolerance, the strength of character of the founder of Israel's first government; he also had a much deeper analytical capacity –

*It became, later, the Liberal Party and formed with Herut, the Irgun's successors, the Gahal block, represented in the Knesset by, among others, Menahem Beigin.

and a sense of humour. As a member of the rightist General-Zionists he could have been a counterbalancing co-regent, at least. But instead of the Middle East's immediate adherence to the Eastern camp which he expected came the American penetration of the area. His misjudgement cost Sneh his place in history.

For twenty years he fought – first in Mapam, then in a schismatic group called the Socialist Left, and finally in the ranks of Maki – for the pro-Russian line he had chosen. And always, of course, against the stream of history. He kept some indirect influence on what was going on in Israel by an alliance with Mapam's left wing. But as the Israeli State grew more and more rigid, more and more ideologically Jewish, more and more militaristic, Maki was left – like the small groups of Avnery, Semitic Action and Koah Yozem – outside the pale.

In 1965, with the Israeli leadership already well on its way to the 1967 policy of conquest and total Judaization of the state, and the Arabs talking openly of 'throwing the Jews into the sea', Sneh once more broke away from his past. Russia had become weaker, had lost its monopoly of leadership in the communist camp. To be pro-Russian was no longer a strong psychological card, even in radical Israeli circles. So Sneh declared his party to be against the Russian line – now, once again, pro-Arab as a result of developments in the Middle East. The party was split, the Sneh–Mikunis group keeping the name Maki while the pro-Arab section took the name of Rekah. (Reshima Kommunistit Hadashah, or 'New Communist List' – this meaning the list to the 1965 elections. Thus do fortuitous episodes name long-term political formations.)

In due time Moscow acknowledged Rekah as the only 'true' Communist Party, while Sneh's Maki went on to demand a 'Jewish International Movement', strangely resembling the international Zionist Organization which had become in the meantime an extension of the rulers of Israel.

In the Knesset Sneh abstained from voting against the war-cabinets of Levi Eshkol and Golda Meir, but kept his 'communist' identity for trips abroad, paid for by various Israeli funds, and aimed at influencing left-wingers in the West. It was, of course, a childish self-delusion: very soon Russian instructions to communists of her persuasion, and the propaganda of a newly-formed Israeli radical group which combed the New Left in Europe and the American continent, had disposed of Maki's ideological *saltos mortales*. Sneh himself died in 1972, after drafting a testament in which he expressed sorrow at having ever left the Zionist camp.

The new group which replaced the communists as a non-Zionist vanguard called itself the Israeli Socialist Organization but is better known by the name of its publication, *Matzpen* ('Compass'). Not split, at the time, as much as former Marxist bodies over the issue of the independent national identity of the country's inhabitants, it played, and still plays, an important role in the consolidation of just such an identity for Palestine-Israel.

10 Matzpen and Other New Left Groups

Numerically important though they are, the schisms from the Communist Party's ranks were not a decisive factor in the history of the two peoples of the land. Dr Sneh's first rebellion (resulting in the creation of Maki), for instance, made no basic change in communist ideology in Israel. After his second one (causing the Rekah split), Maki just became yet another extension of the Zionist Establishment, an extension using 'Jewish' instead of 'Zionist' slogans; while the recurring separations and reunions of the Arab and Jewish communists only emphasized the fact that even Marxists in the Middle East had to adapt themselves to the quirks of national identity and of belief.

However, one small group of communist rebels did cause a ripple in the texture of Israeli politics; and maybe, who knows, in the politics of the whole area. Moshe Machover was a young old-style communist who became a Party member after becoming disenchanted with the Zionist Left. In his boyhood he had been a member of the Hashomer Hatzair Youth Movement, which is affiliated to Mapam and destines its members to Kibbutz life. Like many other boys of wealthy upper-middle-class background, he had opted for the most 'radical' of Zionist youth groups. During his communist career he befriended another young man, Akiva Or, who has also come from the Mapam-affiliated group and who had joined the Communist Party with Sneh in the days before Sneh's return to the Zionist fold. Akiva Or was a very different proposition from the cold logical Machover. In fact, Or was that most prized of all communist possessions, a true proletarian activist. In the ranks of Israel's Merchant Navy he had helped lead the great seamen's strike of the 1950s, a truly social conflict which shattered the Zionist myth of 'class brotherhood in Israel'. Later he became a teacher in Jerusalem.

It can be conjectured that opposites met in Machover and Or precisely because they shared a concept of history and society but differed in background and feelings; for men above average, the other side of the psychological coin has often been an encouragement, a determining factor in one's own personality and imagination. Be that as it may, in 1962 these two published a book, *Peace, Peace But There Is No Peace*. They signed it 'A. Israeli', mostly to prevent their expulsion from the Communist Party. The ruse worked for a time, but ultimately they were forced to leave the party along with several others (among whom were Oded Pilawsky, brother of a senior Israeli army officer; Yeremiyahu Kaplan; and Moshe Sneh's ex-lieutenant, Elie Lobel, an economist who later served for two years, in the framework of French technical aid, as the virtual Minister of Economy in one of the francophone countries of Africa and who now lives in Paris.)

The new grouplet had doubts about its ideological orientation. To begin with, its members felt and thought as ex-communists do everywhere. But instead of taking Koestler's road of apostasy – the only one open to members of the Party who changed their mind during the thirties and forties – they tried to consolidate a 'separate but equal' class-attitude: separate, that is, from Soviet doctrine, but equal to it.

In 1962 the star of Red China was rising. For a while the group explored the Chinese brand of Marxist-Leninism, and several articles of their intermittent publication, *Matzpen*, gave proof of this investigation. But the four main activists – Machover, Lobel, Or and Pilawsky – had fallen out with the Communist Party precisely because of their repulsion from 'Stalinism' – that is, the more brutal and arbitrary side of the proletarian dictatorship. The Chinese Revolution, fighting off the encroachments of both Western and Soviet imperialism, and hidebound by the primarily agrarian character of its vast membership, had defiantly remained faithful to the image and ideas of Joseph Stalin – whose cities were then being renamed all over European communist countries, and whose statues had been pulled down from Prague to Moscow, though not in Eastern Germany, Albania or China.

Moreover, the Chinese version of the proletarian revolution, culminating in the Cultural Revolution of the Red Guards, was a bit hard to stomach for Israeli communists. Western communists, with no idea of what the extremes of totalitarism can be, could perhaps take it. An Israeli, even a *Tzabra*, knew too much; he lived among too many immigrants who had grown up under communist regimes. Thus the Chinese influence on Matzpen and the group's so-called 'Maoism', which was repeatedly exploited by the Israeli authorities and press for their own purposes, was never more than an instrument for breaking away from the Russian ideological noose.

For this reason, Matzpen's dissatisfaction with Mao sent it groping into what orthodox communism in 1962–3 still considered the worst kind of heresy: the work and thoughts of Leon Trotsky. In more than one way, this was fortunate. It introduced the members to the analyses of Zionism and the Jewish identity made by Trotsky himself and his biographer, Isaac Deutscher, and so gave them a class-oriented theory of the Jewish Question – something which had been bugging them since 'A. Israeli' analysed the Zionists' unwillingness to make peace. Secondly, it aligned the small new group with the up-and-coming political fashion of the West: the New Left.

It should be remembered that Trotskyism, so popular among Western youth in the late sixties and early seventies, was almost totally discredited during the long years when Soviet communism was the only permitted brand. With rare exceptions, such as the twice-successful Ceylonese Trotskyite Party, groups of this ideological character, united in the unwieldy, conspiratorial Fourth International, were then a very minor element on the political scene. All this changed with the 20th Congress of the Soviet Communist Party, when Nikita Khrushchev repudiated 'Stalin and his crimes'; with the ascendancy of China in the East; with the thirty-year war in South-East Asia; and with the rise of a rebel generation in the consumer societies of the West. All these factors contributed to make Soviet centralism a thing of the past, and Trotskyism more acceptable – if not by communist standards.

It would not be accurate to call Matzpen Maoist but nor is it true that it joined the 'Trotsky fashion' of the New Left. What it did was to try both suits of clothes for size – only to find one too restrictive and the other too old-fashioned. Some of its members were traditional Marxist-Leninists, but others broached the perilous – but intriguing – social *terra incognita* which lies between communist and anarcho-syndicalist domains.

At first the Israeli Establishment tended to see Matzpen as just another hapless splinter-group. Its flirtation with Semitic Action, at the time when this was led by Ury Avnery and Nathan Yalin-Mor, did nothing to change the Establishment's viewpoint. But gradually alarm grew at the violent diatribes against Zionism and the spirited defence of the downtrodden – the Israeli Palestinians but also the *Lumpenproletariat*, Oriental poor Jews, new immigrant non-professional workers and so on.

Just as in 1968, France – where the New Left had failed to find enough support in an industrial proletariat still faithful to the Soviet-communist trade union, the C G T – so the New Left of Israel, the Matzpen men, did not get much backing from Jewish industrial workers. And with good reason: this class was getting part of the economic benefits of the Establishment, in other words was part of the profiteering *people*. In accordance with proletarian revolutionary ideas, Matzpen nonetheless started agitation among the workers, industrial and sub-industrial; this was a failure. On the other hand, just as in Western Europe, the Israeli New Left did attract a modicum of attention among well-to-do or at least middle-class youths, *Tzabras* and soldiers, and even in some instances junior officers of the Israeli Defence Forces.

In Chaim Hanegbi, an Israeli Jew of mixed Oriental and Polish parentage, whose ancestors had lived in Hebron for countless generations, Matzpen found its first 'native-orientated' leader. Hanegbi was a lean, handsome, rather French-looking young man, whose somewhat wild appearance belied the good husband and efficient journalist he was. It was he who brought Matzpen into the first electoral campaign of Ury Avnery's *Haolam Hazeh* – Koah Hadash list. He had worked for several years on Avnery's paper and had friendship of its gifted if egocentric editor. But one may surmise that, in spite of the magnificent campaign work done by such professional Matzpen agitators as Oded Pilawsky, Avnery came to regret the link. At the 1967 conference of the Haolam Hazeh group – where as usual Avnery dominated his well-meaning troops and his lower-echelon careerists, riding roughshod over any opinions, ideological or practical, different from his own – the Matzpen men left, or were driven out. Avnery himself gave the reason for this in one of his periodic and choleric attacks on the Israeli New Leftists:

> ... You know well enough that no one among us will move from Israel's own frontiers. And I, who stand before you here, excluded from my party a great and important group called Matzpen because this group did not acknowledge Israel's 1947 frontiers ...*

Matzpen wanted a more radical attitude towards Zionism. They also wanted the retreat of Israel's armies from all the territories occupied during the Six Days War of 1967; a thing Avnery was, at first, not prepared to ask for. This, in fact, rather than the '1947 borders of Israel', may have been the cause of the disagreement between them.

Once they had cut their links with Avnery, the Matzpen men had to arrive at their own territorial, national and cultural definitions. These, by virtue of the members' communist past, became something quite outside the scope of nationalism, Israeli or Palestinian, or even Jewish or Arab. Akiva Or and Moshe Machover stated it thus:

> We reject the idea, upheld both by the leaders of Al Fatah and the leaders of Mapam, that the national struggle is prior to the revolutionary struggle for Socialism ... In our view there is only one struggle – the revolutionary struggle for a new society in the Middle East, including Israel. Only within the framework of such a revolution will it be possible to solve the main problems of the region, including the Israeli-Arab problem.†

Here the communist education of the Matzpen men clashed with their painful awareness of the injustices and sufferings borne by the Palestinians – and ultimately of the Israelis also, forced

*Ury Avnery, in a speech to the Knesset during the week 12–19 April 1970, as reported in his own weekly *Haolam Hazeh*, No. 1703.

†'Against the Zionist Left', *Israc*, No. 2, London and Paris, 1970.

into a useless and probably catastrophic 'Hundred Years War'. The solution they proposed was 'Revolutionary Struggle for a New Society in the Middle East'; the fact that there had never been a revolution without national characteristics was overlooked or ignored. The possibility that the Arab masses might adopt pan-Arab nationalism as the logical framework of social endeavour (as indeed they have done since the decline of the Ottoman empire, if not before) was not mentioned in the Matzpen programmes.

Although insensitive to the problem of identity, Matzpen showed much common sense in its appreciation of the narrow, national aspect of the Israeli-Arab conflict:

> ... One cannot ignore the clear fact that [the Israelis are] a national unit, differing both from world Jewry and from the Palestinian Arabs, with their own language, economic life and culture.
>
> The solution of the Palestinian problem must remove this group, or at least an important part of it, from Zionist influence and draw it into a common struggle with the revolutionary forces of the Arab world towards the national and social liberation of the whole area. It is clear that this cannot be done by ignoring its national character.*

Although in January 1970 Matzpen's numerical strength was well under 150 members, there was in wide circles of the younger generation a certain sympathy with these 'outsiders'. Partly this was due to Matzpen's campaign for justice; partly it was the responsibility of the Establishment's brainwashing which depicted Matzpen as the source of all evil not produced by the Rekah Communists.

Rekah, however, had at that point more influence than Matzpen on the Israeli Palestinians and Palestinians in the Occupied Territories. The Palestinians were sceptical of a group founded by Jews, and tended to consider the patronage of the USSR as more relevant to their struggle than the goodwill of the student's New Left abroad. As far as Red China was concerned, it began busying itself with Middle Eastern problems and provided quite a lot of direct aid to the Palestinian guerrillas. Thus the Palestinians

* M. Machover and A. Said (Jabbra Nicola), *Matzpen* No. 50, Tel-Aviv, August 1969.

of Israel and of the Occupied Territories had no use, in their overwhelming majority, for 'intermediaries'. Several, however, of quite uncommon stature, joined the Matzpen leadership.

One of these was an 'elder statesman' among Palestinian revolutionary leaders. Jabbra Nicola had been for many years one of the chiefs of the Palestina Kommunistische Partei. In the forties he was removed from the PKP leadership, although never officially expelled, when he developed a pronounced sympathy for Trotskyite ideas. Being an Arab and a Palestinian, doubts about fighting the social struggle from inside the womb of pan-Arab nationalism, which would one day give birth to the New Society of the Middle East, never entered his head; as they never entered the heads of the cultivated and extremely sincere leaders of the League for National Liberation, the Arab branch which broke away from the communists in the forties. On the other hand, as a man versed in Marxist theory, he acknowledged firmly, and at times at great personal risk, the right to 'self-determination of the Jewish minority'.

Pressure was applied to members of the group, of both Arab and Jewish origin. Chaim Hanegbi was summarily sacked by *Haolam Hazeh*. Dr Machover's contract with the Hebrew University was not renewed: he had to travel to England to find an academic job abroad. Or had to leave his position for similar reasons. Thus a Matzpen nucleus was created abroad, where the group, after founding a sister-organization, the Israeli Revolutionary Action Committee Abroad (ISRAC), concentrated, quite effectively, its anti-Zionist propaganda.

However, while helping the New Left of the West to understand some of the problems of the Zionist Establishment, the Matzpen group at home was left ideologically invalid. Its four best brains – Akiva Or, Moshe Machover, Jabbra Nicola, and Elie Lobel – were all out of Israel. Excellent organizers as they were, Oded Pilawsky and Hanegbi could never replace these four. The group stagnated, getting most of its ideological ammunition from Britain and France.

A young intellectual, Eilan Albert, had fought with the American Black Panthers and written a book about his experiences which was published in France and quite well received. Of mixed Turkish and Yemenite parentage, born and educated in Paris, Albert came to Israel after the 1967 war. He married there and eked out a living as a translator, as this was 'the only profession they cannot throw me out of'. For a while Albert, together with the gifted activists Hanegbi, Pilawsky and Bober, organized several cells of secondary-school and university students, and maintained contact with Palestinians, workers, new immigrants. Considering the immense amount of hatred and aggressiveness directed against them, as well as the systematic persecution by the authorities,* they did an extremely good job to drive a hard thin wedge between the country's Zionist leaders and the people – a job limited, perforce, by the atmosphere and conditions of immediately post-war Israel.

In the autumn of 1970, a double split occurred in the ranks of the tiny Matzpen, and two groups detached themselves from it: one 'proletarian', which carried Trotskyist orthodoxy to the point of advocating revolution through the industrial proletariat, which in Israel, as we have seen, is thoroughly identified with Zionism; and another 'Fanonist' group, advocating a variation of the old PKP formula of working only through the ranks of the Arab proletarian masses. With the latter group went Eilan Albert, bringing the intellectual decapitation of the home contingent of Matzpen to its logical conclusion. In 1971 a further split separated the Jerusalem branch, led by Arieh Bober and siding with the Trotskyite Fourth International, from the remnants of the movement.

Thus, the efforts of Matzpen and its sister-organization ISRAC had to be concentrated abroad. At times this brought quite startling results. For a while, an indirect influence was

*To give only two examples: the group was not allowed to publish an Arabic edition of their newspaper, even one reproducing verbatim the material already approved in Hebrew by Military Censorship – which anyway deletes about half the political material proposed to it by such groups.

Most Matzpen men of Arab origin are confined to the towns where they live, while the Jews in the organization are not allowed to enter the Occupied Territories.

wielded by the group on the extreme left wing of the Arab-Palestinian resistance movements. Nayef Hawatmeh, leader of the Democratic Popular Front (DFLP) stated, in an interview given to Beirut's *El Hourieh* in November 1969, that 'There is a serious dialogue between this guerrilla movement and the ISO.' The Matzpen men in Israel strenuously denied this, declaring it to be slander designed to weaken still further its almost non-existent influence on wider political life in Israel. Perhaps the explanation of the mystery is that ISRAC is not officially affiliated with ISO and alone carried out the dialogue with the DFLP.

Be this as it may: the fact was that the DFLP publications in Europe did reprint *Matzpen* articles and that the *Matzpen* journal of March 1970 reprinted a Hebrew translation of an article by Nayef Hawatmeh. (The printing of this piece was delayed. To begin with, the Military Censorship prohibited it, and gave way only on learning that it had already appeared in *Le Monde* and was circulating freely among French-speaking Israelis. In September 1970 *Matzpen* went even further and printed the DFLP programme in full.)

Inside Israel, however, the group made little headway. What was accepted as intelligent ideological thought in New Left circles abroad, and even among liberals, was complete nonsense to the average thinking Israeli. What was self-evident to the normal young man in Israel – as, for instance, that the army must be beyond criticism, being non-political, wholly beneficial, and absolutely essential to the country's survival 'in spite of any small defects it might have' – seemed an absurdity to many militants outside the Middle East. It was this confusion of terminology and of semantics which made so many New Left protests about the Israeli-Palestinian conflict wholly redundant, if not ridiculous, in Israeli eyes. Matzpen did not try to remedy this by acting as a 'translator'. This was its biggest fault, and in the final analysis the reason for its self-inflicted impotence in Israel.

The leaders of the Establishment were quick to understand how the Matzpen bogeyman could be useful to them. They inflated its importance, built up the people's hatred for these 'traitors' to Zionism, labelled any dissidence in Israel 'Matzpen-inspired' – exactly as the Colonels' Junta in Greece defined all opposition as 'communist'.

It is hard to estimate what importance Matzpen could now have inside Israel. It would seem clear that its real function is to establish some kind of bridge between the Marxist wing of the Palestine Resistance and the dissidents caged inside the Israeli Establishment.

*

Apart from the groups already mentioned there remain on the Israeli scene of the early seventies a few mini-formations fighting for peace and recognition of Arab claims. One of them, now reduced to a handful of intellectuals such as Dr Shimon Shereshewsky, was once the main flag-bearer of national co-existence of Jews and Arabs; Ichud ('Union'), founded by the late Professor Judah Magnes of the Jerusalem Campus and supported by the late Professor Martin Buber, was the first party to try to combine a humanitarian brand of Zionism with political bi-nationalism. It preached the return of the Jews to their homeland, to live in peace there with the Arabs. The humanitarian ideas of Buber and Magnes clashed with more traditional religious Jewishness and Zionist national renewal. The logic of history was in favour of the more extreme freedom-fighters, and, as is usual in turbulent, formative conditions, the more ethical and philosophical voices of the nation were muted and ill-heard. Today Ichud hardly exists as an organization. Even among the intellectuals who used to sympathize with its ideas – mainly in the Hebrew University of Jerusalem – it has no influence.

Instead, many of these intellectuals, as well as their friends in the University of Tel-Aviv, the Technical Institute of Haifa and the Weizmann Institute of Science in Rehovot, organized themselves – loosely, it is true – into a body called Shalom Ve'Bitahon or Peace and Security. This committee was formed shortly after the 1967 war to encourage the 'doveish' wing of Israeli politics supposedly represented by the Foreign Minister, Abba Eban. At his most daring, Eban remained covertly expansionist, fearlessly defending the annexation of at least huge lumps of what had already been taken from the Palestinians while piously urging that no more be taken. Even so limited a programme as his, involving the return of '*some* of the conquests against a peace treaty', was very badly received in Israel.

Shalom Ve'Bitahon tried to fight this hostility. It paid the penalty of leading a difficult and shadowy existence, unable to make any impression on the nationalists of the Israeli campus who wished that the professors would shut up and let the army do its job'. Then, in the first half of 1970, this movement gave birth to a group called Siah, incorporating also former members of Mapam and Maki disenchanted with the Zionism of their parties who, they said, were giving a 'cosmetic treatment to organic problems'. Siah soon evolved into two currents, geographically and politically different from each other. While the Tel-Aviv branch of Siah continued to look for ways to 'correct the errors of the national leadership', the Jerusalem and Haifa branches, benefiting from much deeper intellectual thought and formed by more aggressive men altogether, began to define itself as 'Marcusian' and to demand a 'total change of all institutions'. One of the main slogans of Siah-Jerusalem was a 'frontal attack against the Israeli Establishment', which found its first expression in a demonstration organized near the private villa of the prime minister, Golda Meir, when she refused to allow Dr Nahum Goldmann, the former Chairman of the World Zionist Organization, to visit Cairo and offer President Abd-El-Nasser his suggestions for peace.

Slowly but surely Siah-Jerusalem's discussions turned it into a theoretically revolutionary group. Nothing was sacred to its members. Everything was thoroughly dissected, including the most holy of all Israeli sacred cows, the army – although, apparently for tactical reasons, no criticism of the Israeli defence forces was voiced. Siah adopted the American students' slogan: 'Revolution comes before Ideology', thus conveniently avoiding for the time being the moment of truth of its confrontation with its Jewish problem.

On a non-party basis the League for Human and Civil Rights was founded, also in Jerusalem, by Dr Israel Shahak, a lecturer in micro-biology at the Hebrew University and a Warsaw Ghetto survivor, who was assisted in his efforts by Uri Davis. It fought for the rights of both Jews and Arabs in Israel and the territories.

Another group which struggled, logically enough but not very successfully, for a short time after the 1967 war was the movement for an Israeli-Palestinian Federation, founded by Nathan Yalin-Mor, the journalist Amos Kennane, and several Israeli intellectuals. It had no echo whatsoever among the masses. Ury Avnery, who had adhered at first, later abandoned it, fearing the movement might become a competitor.

In 1969, in the aftermath of war and at a time of increased guerrilla attacks on Israel's towns and borders, an election was fought. In such circumstances, the results could only be favourable to the majority (which, anyway, continued in full control of the state's economic means of existence) and to the annexionist policy which was at that time the majority Labour Party's official programme.

In these elections Matzpen played the extra-parliamentary game, well knowing that, prevented by the Emergency Regulations from working among the Israeli Palestinians, it had not the slightest chance of getting the ten thousand or so votes needed for one of the 120 seats in the Knesset. Even so, Matzpen members who helped actively in Rekah's electoral campaign were arrested and detained for a while – as also were most Arab militants of the communist group.

Very few Israeli parties fought for a liberal, truly anti-chauvinist policy. Rekah demanded that the United Nations Resolution 242 of 22 November 1967, asking for an Israeli withdrawal from the Occupied Territories, should be implemented. So did another small group, the Peace List, founded after the demise of the short-lived Movement for an Israeli-Palestinian Federation by Nathan Yalin-Mor and a university teacher from Tel-Aviv, the radical Zionist Gaddy Yatziv. (They later worked on in the framework of the Peace and Security lobby.)

The Peace List was sharply contested, not by the Right and the government but by Ury Avnery's own group. There was the usual smear-and-smut campaign. The Peace List lost, getting only 5,138 votes against Haolam Hazeh's 16,853, which, after some adjusting with the help of 'supplementary votes', gave Avnery and Cohen two seats in the Knesset.

Avnery had fought a wily battle, judiciously mixing nationalist slogans with his standard demand for a policy of peace and an agreement with the Palestinians. This mixture particularly appealed to the politically uneducated younger generation, who did not see the deeper issues but sympathized with Avnery's wish to 'get things moving towards peace'.

Maki, the communist-Zionist group of Moshe Sneh, fought on a platform indistinguishable from the left-wing opinions inside Mapam. Already Mapam was a willing part of the National Union government, whose policy was to keep the 1967 conquests. Maki got one seat, and thus was able to go on playing communist 'dissenter' for the benefit of the Israeli government.

So things stood when a new round of fighting, the 'attrition war', started along the Suez Canal and in the Lebanon in 1970. The issues argued over in the Knesset were not the vital issues of peace and a future settlement. The lop-sided Parliament became a travesty of itself, a place where the 'old boys' played and one or two dissidents raised their voice from time to time, while serious things were decided elsewhere. Fifty years of indoctrination with exclusively Zionist slogans had prevented the Israelis from thinking for themselves. They were bound to spout the feedback of racialist, 'purely' Jewish ideas and feelings with which they and their fathers had been indoctrinated. Meanwhile, absolute political control exercised through Arab straw-bosses, and economic pressures, prevented the Israeli Palestinians from voting outside the framework of the Zionist parties. The best they could do was to make a gesture against the Establishment by giving their vote to Rekah or Haolam Hazeh, but even this was dangerous in small villages where everyone knew everyone else's affairs and opinions.

Psychologically, the country was under the shadow of constant apprehension, caused by 'the danger from across the borders'. The twenty-odd-years-old state of emergency seemed more justified than ever. Not only on the body politic of Israel but also on its ideas there was a stranglehold.

11 Racialism in Israel

The failure to come to any understanding with the Arabs in Israel, which has been the theme of the preceding chapters, has had grave consequences for every aspect of life in the country. In this chapter we shall examine the growth of racialism and religious intolerance, in subsequent ones matters such as censorship, class inequalities, and their effect on typical institutions such as the Kibbutzim and the army.

Israel has gradually become a more and more openly racist country. Anyone not Jewish is at best second-class in Israel. The government has never acted according to the precepts of the country's Declaration of Independence. It is true that this declaration, solemnly signed by all the founders of the State of Israel, never did become 'law' and has certainly never had the status of a constitutional document. The Zionist governments which followed each other in Israel took good care that this should be so, and carefully avoided giving the state a proper constitution. Instead they created a whole series of 'Constitutional Laws', always adopted according to the political needs and personal wishes of the members of the reigning Cabinet – and, of course, propped up by the essentially repressive Emergency Regulations inherited from the British Mandate.

The Declaration of Independence – a statement of intent, not a law – promised that all citizens of the State of Israel, 'the Jewish State', now created, would be equal before the law, whatever their sex, religion, or affiliation. The promise was not kept. From the first, the diverse religious sects were kept separate and segregated by the prohibition of civil marriage. Thus if a girl born into the Jewish faith wished to marry a man whose family had been, say, Catholic, she would have to change her faith to his, or at least to marry in his church. Alternatively the man could become a Jew, get himself circumcised, and marry his bride in a synagogue. A third alternative would be for both to become Moslems and marry in a mosque. There were and are no magistrates or mayors empowered to marry non-religious Israelis – or foreigners who want to get married in Israel.

If members of different religions wished to marry they had but a dreary choice: emigrate, or go abroad just for the ceremony, whereupon their marriage would be recognized by the Israeli civilian authorities, never too keen to abolish International Law usages which guarantee reciprocity in matters of civil law.

So from the date of the creation of Israel, no real freedom has existed in matters of religion or race. However, since the first Ministers of the Interior were mild leftists – members of the Mapam party which at that time defended quite progressive opinions, such as the right of Kibbutz members to live in a legally recognized state of 'unmarried love' – chaos ensued. To complicate things, it had already been decreed that the identity card of every resident and citizen should carry mention of his *Leum*, or 'Nation'. It became the custom to write in the space provided 'Jew', 'Arab', or 'Christian', and the fact that nobody had heard of a Christian 'nation' did not deter the official mind.

There were exceptions. One such was the gifted writer and poet Yonathan Ratosh, alias Uriel Shelah, the leading spirit of the Canaanite movement.* Ratosh, who 'refused to be a Jew', managed to have his document inscribed 'Nation – Hebrew'. Here fate interfered and supplied comic relief. Ratosh lost his identity card, and since meanwhile a new Minister of the Interior had been appointed from among the members of the National Religious Movement's leadership, he was refused his old inscription on his new card. Ratosh therefore rejected the document – which must be carried, by law, in Israel. Later, due to a freak definition embodied in the Amendment to the Law of Return, 1970, the High Court forced the religious Minister of the Interior to grant him his 'Hebrew' identity card, without this affecting in any way his being, for identification or legal purposes, a 'Jew'.

*See Chapter 7.

But let us leave the poets and dreamers and turn to ordinary mortals. Once the Religious Movement understood the theological importance of the Ministry of the Interior, its leaders forced the majority Mapai (Labour) Party to give them this coveted plum in succeeding Cabinets. It served the Zionist-Religions zealots of Mafdal* not only as a means of distributing bounty to party followers but also as one to control who is and who is not a 'Jew'. In the State of Israel, officially defined as 'Jewish' just as Rhodesia's or South Africa's are 'white', this is a most important means of personal tyranny.

A Jew has inherent rights in Israel even if he is not born in the State. A Jew is considered an insider, while a 'Goy' (Gentile, non-Jew) always remains an outsider, even if born inside the country. He can become 'one of us' in Israel only if he publicly changes his faith. As many of the most ardent non-Jewish Zionists were irreligious, sometimes even Marxist, this was bound to cause some trouble and despondency among the 'semi-outsiders'. But on the whole the situation worked very well. A man's 'Jewish' identity was considered the better part, as it were, of Israeli nationality.

Thus a caste of Israelis was created, first by usage and then by written law, a caste which, being 'Jewish', had automatic rights and intrinsic qualities which made it the élite, the only true insiders. All others, by force of this evolution, were obliged to become second-class citizens. No wonder then that, in spite of an economic renaissance such as no other Arab community experienced in the last twenty-five years, the Arabs living as a minority in Israel still felt rejected, outsiders and second-class. To begin with they were only humiliated, but later there was an absolute decline in their rights and freedoms – except, as has been said by Geries, the 'Diaspora Jewish' right to make money and still more money.†

As Israel progressed towards its consecration as a 'pure Jewish' state, it found itself giving more and more power to those zealots

*Miflaga Datit Leumit, a grouping of the two main Zionist-Religious groups.

†Cf. *Les Arabes en Israel*, by Sabri Geries, Maspéro, Paris, 1969.

who held Zionist-Religious views. How the Religious Parties, at most sixteen per cent of the total Israeli population, acquired such an enormous influence over the people, the law and even the Army of Israel is worth further analysis. *Prima facie* it looks as if the Zionist-Religious parties (later uniting into Mafdal) had astutely become the determining parliamentary factor, the small minority which controlled a coalition Cabinet by throwing its weight on one or the other side. A more profound look at the political situation inside Israel tends, however, to dispel this illusion. The zealots' influence is born of deeper-seated and more disturbing elements.

Since the inception of the State – indeed, since the inception of the Zionist movement which fought for the State fifty years before its foundation – the so-called 'Left' social democratic party of Mapai has played the decisive role. This party, once Poalei Zion ('Toilers of Zion') and later Mifleget Poalei Israel ('Party of the Workers of Israel', or Mapai) controlled whatever happened in Israel and, indirectly, the powerful resources of the Zionist movement abroad. On its left stood only the Mapam Marxist-Zionists, and the outright communists; on its right, a plethora of parties of which the nationalist Herut (founded by the fighters of the underground Irgun) and the capitalist Liberals were the most important.

Now, in spite of many decades of effort, constant machination, and their joining together in the sixties in the United Block of Gahal parties, neither the Liberal Party nor Herut ever attained the prized prime ministership or won control of either the Zionist movement or, after its inception, of the State. For most of these seventy years Mapai kept its position in the Zionist leadership, and later in the Israeli parliament and cabinet, by playing the left-wing Mapam against the Religious Parties, and ultimately against the united religious Mafdal. Fearing the pro-Russian past of the Mapam Kibbutzniks, and drifting gradually nearer an American view of Middle Eastern affairs, the government based itself more on support from Mafdal than on support from the Marxist-Zionists. Only after the Mapam leaders ignominously capitulated were they readmitted under the thumb of the succeeding 'strong men' of Mapai: Ben-Gurion, Levy Eshkol, and Mrs Golda Meir (whose energy was such, incidentally, that even before her appointment as prime minister she was referred to in Israel as 'the only he-man in a government of old women').

Shortly before the outbreak of the 1967 war a 'Cabinet of National Unity' was finally formed, leaving outside only the communists and the party of Ury Avnery. The right-wingers of Gahal and the (Mussolini-style) national-syndicalists of Mapai started working together, for a while. In theory, little Mafdal was not needed any longer. And here, suddenly, the real power of the Zionist-Religious zealots was revealed. Laws became *more* religiously stringent, not less. Biblical echoes appeared in more and more official publications. The annexation of conquered territories was advocated by formerly rational ex-socialists who now invoked arguments on the lines of Israel being 'the Country Which The Lord Has Given To Abraham Our Father'.

What had happened? In the twenty-five years which had passed since the formative days which preceded the creation of the State, the half-conscious alibis of the majority, needing its old Jewish prop to justify its more negative policies, had allowed a small and astute minority to become not just another strong religious party but something the Jewish religion in the Diaspora had always and most fortunately lacked: a religious hierarchy, a church wielding the most outrageous temporal power, priests.

By rejecting a trend apparent in the beginnings of the new State, by which the Israeli Jews started evolving towards a new and partially separate national entity, the Israeli leadership allowed the darker aspects of religious belief to gather strength. The wilful identification of 'Jewish' with 'Israeli' reconstituted a state of affairs which had existed, for this people, only in the days of the Kingdom of David, in an epoch in which religion and nationality were, in all parts of the world, one and the same thing, the hoop holding people together, the mantle later to be supplanted by the common territorial, psychological and economic bonds of 'modern' nationalism.

The return to the Kingdom of David and the Temple of Israel was bound to bring about, as a corollary, the elimination of the 'heathen nations of Canaan' – or, in a modern context, of the Palestinians: for even the most sceptical or unbelieving citizen of a religious state will 'respect' the prevailing religious views and pressures, as these give him the *moral* pretext he needs to justify his social actions.

Expropriation and colonialism are not a logical corollary of a *laissez-faire* society. To justify *in one's own eyes* the exploitation of one's fellow-men, one has first to consider why 'we are better' or, at least why 'we are different'. For two thousand years the Jews, trying to remain a separate national entity without the characteristics of state, economy and territory, were persecuted, killed, tortured, and despoiled by Spaniards, Arabs, Crusaders, Cossacks, Ottomans, Nazis – all those zealots who wished to find an object 'different from themselves', that is, whose despoilation was 'morally justified'. Now, in the State of Israel, those who are tempted along the hallucinatory path of power and conquest have to justify their course by calling on the same devils who, in the Diaspora, were directed against themselves.

The mounting tide of these pressures was felt by all idealistic or simply upright Israeli citizens, who, unlike the politicians, knew themselves to be Israelis but not, in the old religious sense, Jews. They felt, without understanding their feelings, that such a definition accounted for their new pride, their lack of the old complexes and their force of character, unpropped by irrational belief; in short, that they possessed qualities sadly lacking in most Diaspora Jews.

An outsider would have said that on the basic psychological level they had found in their common territory, common fight and interdependence something real, something capable of eliminating the inferiority complexes of a people deprived of 'its own way of life'. Some of them, such as the Canaanites and Ury Avnery's early Bamaawak group*, pushed their discovery to the limits of ideological fancy. But most had no need of ideology. They just *felt* different from the Diaspora Jews, *were* different, *reacted* differently.

* See Chapter 7.

Confronted with a vicious circle of danger breeding action, harmful action breeding ideology, ideology breeding further harmful action, they tried to respond by opposing, each in his own way, the tide of racialism, of reaction, of the movement 'back to the sources'. Of course these healthy individuals had not a dog's chance. Israel's isolation, the fact that it was surrounded by another racialist ideology, separatist and pan-Moslem, forbade any possibility of rejecting the 'return to Jewishness'.

In this situation, the struggle of a reserve officer in the Israeli armed forces, Naval Commander Binyamin Shalit, had important consequences. According to the *Jerusalem Post*, Commander Shalit is of 'impeccable background', his father, a psychiatrist from Latvia, being firmly Zionist. By his own testimony, Shalit himself, born in 1935, grew up in a 'completely secular home' but one which did not allow him to forget his thorough Jewishness. He was educated at, among other places, Carmel College, the very Establishment, very high-class Jewish public school in England founded by the late Rabbi Kopul Rosen.

Later, at the University of Edinburgh, he met his non-Jewish wife, Anne, a Scotswoman who like him was studying psychology. Like many British Gentiles from an idealistic, Bible-inspired upper middle class, she was a convinced Zionist. Her grandfather was Sir Patrick Geddes, a distinguished Scots townplanner and sociologist who came to Palestine in 1918 at the invitation of the Zionist leadership. He was asked, among other things, to plan the future Hebrew University, and insisted it should be built in Jerusalem and not in Rehovot, on the coastal plain, where Professor Chaim Weizmann, who was to become Israel's first President, wanted it. Sir Patrick 'saw in Jerusalem the natural centre of the *new* Jewish culture'. In 1920 Palestinian Arab leaders protested to the British Mandatory authorities about 'that terrible Zionist, Sir Patrick Geddes, who has come to help the Jews'.

Anne Shalit's father, Dr Arthur Geddes of the Department of Geography at Edinburgh, was also a personality in his own right. His mother, *née* Réclus, was a direct descendant of the French nineteenth-century anarchist, Élisé Réclus. There was also Senegalese blood in the family. Anne admitted more than once that she was completely unreligious and felt out of place not only in Israel but also in 'Protestant Edinburgh'.

Such cosmopolitan links give a modern, intelligent and active man who has learned how to fight in one of the best armies of the world the necessary spirit to challenge the Establishment of Israel. Commander Shalit, the navy's first psychologist, now applied a little of his knowledge to the task he felt was most urgent: to determine whether Israelis of mixed 'racial' (that is, religious) background were still first-class citizens. He decided to find out in the most direct way he could who was a 'Jew' in the eyes of the Israeli courts and State. He had a vested interest in the answer: his two children. The Jewish Torah, the law of Mosaic religion, derives Jewishness from the mother. A child born to a Gentile father and a Jewish mother is, according to the Torah, a Jew. But a child born to a Jewish father and a Gentile mother can become a Jew only by conversion and, if he is male, by circumcision. Since 'mixed' marriages cannot be performed in Israel, and such mixed couples as arrive are barely tolerated, the status of their children is, to all practical purposes, little better than that of a bastard in other societies.

Commander Shalit asked the Israeli Supreme Court to rule that his children were Jewish, in spite of the religious definition and in spite of the law of the land. On 3 July 1969, in a split decision, the High Court did just that. This decision was rejected both by the Zionist-Religious zealots and by the government Labour Party, already hedging towards a more 'mystical' attitude to the Land of Israel and the God-given permission to hold all the territory it could get.

If it was to survive in power, the Labour party needed at that time the 'Government of National Unity'. It needed the zealots and it also needed the right-wing Gahal block which had long ago adopted the slogan: 'One country on both sides of the Jordan for the Jewish people in Israel.' Even before the elections of November 1969 a secret deal had been made between 'the two Shapiros' – Minister of Justice Yaakov Shimshon Shapiro, and the zealot Minister of the Interior, Chaim Moshe Shapiro, who died shortly after the close of the 'Shalit case'. In return for the zealots' support, the government agreed in due course to pass an amendment to the Law of Return (see below), ensuring that only Jews by religion would from now on be considered 'National' Jews, Israelis Thereafter the lay, national definition of 'Israeliness' would lose all significance.

On 11 March, 1970 the showdown finally came. The Government of National Unity – constituted by all rival Zionist tendencies to fight the Six Days' War – now fought another kind of battle. The Labour party with its socialists; the Gahal block of secular nationalist hue; and of course the zealots of Madfal marshalled 51 votes in the Knesset, out of 120 Members of Parliament, only 74 of whom were present.

It is interesting to note that the Mapam Marxist-Zionists abstained. They did *not* vote against the amendment. By their discreet absence they gave their blessing to the 'anti-Semitic measure in reverse' which was being adopted in a *soi-disant* free country. That night's betrayal by Mapam members is one of the unhappier chapters in the history of the Israeli labour movement: a movement whose democratic record is not among the most noble, in spite of the romantic appeal of utopian communes.

Against the shame of racialism in a Jewish state only fourteen men raised their hands. They were communists of the pro-Arab fraction; Ury Avnery and his comrade-in-arms, Shalom Cohen (who publicly tore up his identity card on the same impulse that made American war resisters burn their draft cards); and a few individualists from the ranks of the bigger parties.

The vote centred on a document called 'The Law of Return', which granted any Jew automatic Israeli nationality, the right to immigrate into Israel and a few additional minor privileges.*

*Non-Jews, including Palestinian-born Moslems and Christians, were automatically granted Israeli nationality only in three cases: (a) if they were registered as Israeli residents on 1 March 1952 in accordance with the Population Census Law of 1949; (b) if they were residents of Israel in April 1952; (c) if they lived in Israel from the State's creation on 15 May 1948 to 1 April 1952 or entered Israel legally in this period. Thus the return of Palestinian-born refugees was legally precluded after 1952.

Theoretically, this document only facilitated the main goal of Zionism: the concentration of the majority of the Jewish people in the Jewish State of Israel. But in practice it has become the *Magna Charta* of the Establishment, the gate barring non-Jews from adhering to it. Anyone recognized as an immigrant, an *Oleh* ('one who mounts'), is *ipso facto* part and parcel of the ruling majority of a non-equalitarian country. In South African terms one might say he had been 'classed white'.

On 11 March 1970 the Law of Return emerged, amended, from the Knesset's Law, Constitution and Justice Committee with the following basic features:

– Only a Jew had a right to Alyah or unconditional immigration into Israel.

– Immigrants' material rights – such as duty and tax-free periods, a period in which they did not need to serve in the army, and so on – would acrue to Jews; to the children and grandchildren of Jews; and (in a beautiful rush of generosity) to non-Jewish spouses of such children and grandchildren.

– Such rights would also accrue to former Jews 'who left the Jewish faith involuntarily'.

– The Civil Register of the Israeli Ministry of the Interior would in future include a compulsory entry under the heading 'Nation' in which people would be classified as 'Jew', 'Arab', 'Druze', and so on. Up to that date many variants were possible, according to the indecision of the registering clerk. From now on, racialism was to be guided by law.*

Now the amendment to the Law of Return provided that when differences arose over the 'Jewishness' of a would-be registrant it was the Chief Registration Officer and not the local clerk who would decide. One must add at this point that the Chief Registration Officer is invariably a party member of whatever party controls the Ministry of the Interior. For the last few years this Ministry has been in the hands of the zealot National Religious Movement, a member of the National Union Coalition which ruled Israel since the 1967 war, and of the smaller coalition which ruled from 1970 on.

*The High Court later somewhat modified this proviso.

The official *Jerusalem Post* of 11 March 1970, revelling in what amounts to an example of totalitarian enforcement, goes on to say that the Amendment determines 'that registration as a Jew by nationality or religion under the Population Registry Law will only be possible for persons born of a Jewish mother, or converted, and not members of another faith'.

The Law of Return grants special privileges to Jews in Israel, privileges which are essential to a citizen's well-being, and the question may reasonably be asked: Why make this difference? Why is it so important to be considered 'a Jew' in Israel, and why does this law take such trouble to ensure that 'a Jew' by State law should be the same thing as 'a Jew' by religious, or so-called *Halachic* measure?

The answer is very simple: during the twenty-three years which preceded the Amendment to the Law of Return, the Zionist Establishment did everything possible to equate citizenship and Israeli national consciousness with Jewishness. Someone who was not a Jew in Israel, but wanted to be a good Israeli, would create a disrupting, non-Zionist influence on the monolithic character of Israeli society which is, according to the Zionist leadership, essential to the existence of the present state.

The vote left unsolved many religious problems which had arisen after the High Court's decision. For instance, there is in the general stream of Jewry a strong current of reformism, particularly active and prosperous in the United States. As these American Jews, who often marry Gentiles, are part of the Zionist Establishment and provide much of the economic ammunition needed for the preservation of the Zionist State, a sop had to be given to them. The Amendment to the Law of Return therefore made it clear that spouses of Reform Jews, who had been converted by Reform Rabbis, not quite in accordance with *Halachic* law, were Jews too. It did not, on the other hand, allow for Reform conversions inside Israel's borders.

Even these limited concessions were unnerving for some of the most extreme zealots. One M P, the Agudat Israel member, Rabbi Menahem Porush, spat on a Reform prayerbook in the Knesset and publicly threw it from him. Agudat Israel – which is not even a Zionist party – was duly warned by the Speaker, but the warning did not prevent Rabbi Porush from declaring: 'In spite of this Amendment, there are now two kinds of Jews – those of the state, and religiously approved Jews.'*

*

Thus, from 1970 a situation has been created in which, as in the more obnoxious regimes of the Western world, Church, State and War are the three interlocking elements. It is a situation which ensures territorial conquest; the continuation of a small caste; the destruction of any worthwhile opposition; and the irremediable sweep into tragedy of a whole gifted, freedom-loving nation, which has even the advantage of a sense of humour.

When the Israeli identity card became a neo-religious document it was found necessary to re-class several kinds of non-Jews as Jews – by dint of pseudo-conversion – just as Maori sportsmen have been re-classed as white by the South African racialists to preserve the whiteness of New Zealand visitors. It should not be imagined that all Israel accepted the growing racialization of the country with good grace. There were demonstrations, dispersed by mounted police and water-hoses in the good old tradition of all disciplinarian regimes. The leading middle-of-the-road daily, *Haaretz*, went on record on 9 January 1970, when the Amendment was being drafted, with a leader captioned 'A TRAGEDY FOR ALL GENERATIONS TO COME', in which it bitterly attacked the government decision to steamroller the Amendment through the Knesset. On 1 February 1970 *Haaretz* carried a story about a Jerusalem schoolgirl, born of a non-Jewish mother and a Jewish Israeli father, who had run away from school because her classmates shouted at her again and again 'You're not a Jewess!' It was not an isolated case.

*By virtue of the High Court decision based on the law as it was *before* the passing of the Amendment, the children of Commander Shalit continued to be considered Jews, in spite of their Scottish mother, even after the Amendment was passed by the house – but they became by virtue of the law the *only* Jewish children born to a Gentile mother in Israel. A further child, born to the Shalits after the passing of the Amendment, is thus considered a Gentile.

On 2 February 1970 the Itim Newsagency (the official agency of the Israeli Newspaper's Association) reported that Yossef Klinghoffer, a non-practising Jew, had unsuccessfully tried to have his Christian fiancée converted to the Jewish faith so that he could marry her and ensure their children would enjoy first-class 'racial' rights. After the girl had spent many months receiving lessons from a Rabbi's wife, the Rabbinate still refused to allow them to celebrate their marriage. Klinghoffer rioted in the Rabbinate's offices, was arrested, fined one hundred Israeli pounds and given a forty days' suspended jail sentence. He subsequently married his bride in a Christian religious ceremony in a Protestant church in Haifa.

Another case was that of Hanan Frank, born of a Christian mother, who came to Israel from Holland in October 1968. He joined the outpost-Kibbutz Regavim, in the Negev desert, and was immediately co-opted into the Army's Nahal settler-soldier units. Serving in one of these units, his half-track struck a mine while pursuing terrorists, and Frank lost both his legs. He wrote to the Prime Minister, Mrs Golda Meir, asking why he was 'a hundred per cent Israeli, a hundred per cent invalid, but only fifty per cent Jewish'. The Prime Minister never answered.*

A third tragedy was that of a fifteen-year-old daughter of a Polish-Christian couple, who asked to become a Jewess and whose request was rejected by the District Court of Haifa 'as long as her mother did not convert first'. The mother herself had requested the Rabbinical court to allow this girl, living in Israel with her sister since 1962, to be converted. The Rabbinate, however, asked for a ruling by the District Court. Chief District Justice Moshe Etzioni ruled that a minor cannot be converted to a religion to which neither of her parents belonged and asked therefore for the mother's conversion first.†

Zealots in the Jewish Diaspora rallied, of course, to the government's restrictive definition of a 'Jew'. Rabbi Dr L. I. Rabinowitz, a former Chief Rabbi of the United Hebrew Congregations of Johannesburg, wrote for instance: 'The incalculable harm which

**Jerusalem Post Magazine*, 20 February 1970.

†*Jerusalem Post*, 13 February 1970.

might have resulted from the decision of the Supreme Court of Israel, granting the application of Commander Benyamin Shalit to have his children of a non-converted non-Jewish wife registered as being of Jewish nationality but of no religion, has been averted by the swift action of the Cabinet and the Knesset in confirming the (religious) position that only a person born of a Jewish mother and not adopting another religion or a person formally converted to Judaism can be registered as a Jew.'

There were many such opinions published. Reuven Gross, a religious immigrant from the United States, compared the amended Law of Return to the Nazi laws as 'it gives immigration privileges to anyone who is Jewish under the Nürenberg Laws' definition, i.e. having a Jewish grandparent'.* This, of course, is true; but Gross failed to mention that the 'purely religious' definition of a Jew is even more draconian, involving as it does, in male circumcision, a physiological change which not everybody wanting Israeli nationality and full first-class citizenship might contemplate with enthusiasm.

Thus, instead of the monolithic unity desired, a deep cleft was carved in the Israeli nation – a cleft best represented by Private Nachum Bashunik, who in April 1962 was serving with the Armoured Corps. Bashunik's mother was a Christian. He applied for his identity card to be marked 'Jewish' and when this was refused declared: 'Either I am a Gentile or I am a Jew. If I am a Jew, let them say so in black and white. If I am a Gentile, I don't want to serve in the Israeli army.' In fact, it is the usage, though not the written law, that Moslems and Christians are seldom drafted – except when they can be counted to serve faithfully in the 'Jewish army'.

The dilemma was encountered by no less a personality than the Minister of Defence, Moshe Dayan himself: 'All Israelis are equal,' he declared. 'There was a case of an Israeli born to a Gentile mother who fell in battle . . . He was brought to a Jewish grave like all his comrades in arms.' *Haolam Hazeh* weekly of Tel-Aviv investigated this assertion and found it to be true of a twenty-year-old captain who was killed on the Gaza strip. But

**Jerusalem Post*, 1 February 1970.

for another soldier who fell in battle, religious discrimination went as far as the grave.

Yaakov Markus was born in Berlin on 22 November 1927 to a non-Jewish mother named Mathilde Markus and to a Jewish father. He came to Israel and in the fifties was drafted to serve in the 1956 Sinai campaign. He was killed there and buried provisionally at the Shelah Military Cemetery. Later this cemetery was abolished and the dead were transferred to other, permanent graves. Yaakov Markus's bones were to be interred – as Jewish custom stipulates for Gentile dead – 'beyond the pale', that is, behind a small stone fence cordoning off a piece of the Haifa cemetery.

In this plot were buried other non-Jewish fighters, pilots and technicians who lost their lives helping Israel win her independence in 1948 and preserving it in the years which followed. Markus's parents did not accept the Rabbinate's ruling. They asked that their son be granted the same honour as the rest of his fallen friends – burial in the Military Cemetery. General Goren, the Chief Rabbi of the Israeli Army – a visionary racialist who wanted the conquest of both banks of the Jordan, advocated a religious state and tried to modernize religion for that purpose – was not in the country. The bereaved parents appealed directly to the then Prime Minister, David Ben-Gurion, who had to make a special ruling for them. Markus was finally buried in the same row as his fallen friends. But so that 'his bones should not mingle with theirs', as Meshulam Shlesinger, Director of the Military Cemetery, put it, his grave was set somewhat apart.

Meshulam Shlesinger officially stated that the corpse of Yaakov Markus had been circumcised after his death, to allow it to lie beside the Jewish fighters. This was later denied no less officially by the Ministry of Defence. But the grisly and macabre atmosphere surrounding the case has done much to deepen public concern.

12 Censorship

Freedom of speech is not only one of the most basic expressions of democracy. It is also one of the most evident. For a regime claiming that democratic life is its natural framework, the right to freedom of speech is both a psychological necessity and a means of propaganda. However, if such a regime evolves gradually towards an exclusive and racialist society, it is forced to try to limit freedom of speech. For the Zionist Establishment, then, the problem is how to control the expression of opinion without this control being too apparent.

By the early seventies, control had not been completely achieved. Nonetheless the surreptitious gagging of the apparently open mouth of the Israeli nation was well on its way.

Hebrew is the main and official language of Israel. At the beginning of 1972, thirteen daily newspapers appear in Hebrew. Of these one (*Davar*) is controlled by the majority party, the Labour Party, and one (*Al Hamishmar*), by Mapam, which is a partner of Labour in a so-called 'alignment', actually a federation of the two ruling parties. Two further dailies (*Hatzofe*, *Hamodia*), are published by religious parties either belonging to the coalition government or cooperating with it. Another (*Shaar*) is an economic information sheet, partially owned by the Dahaf Publicity Company, a majority of whose shares were in the hands of Labour Party activists who controlled *Dahaf* for the sake of their movement and by means of the Labour's funds. *Dahaf*, incidentally, runs public opinion polls: a very practical side-line for a party of an élite who not only need to know what the masses want, but at any given moment to tell them what they apparently want. A smaller financial daily, *Yom-Yom*, is independent.

Next there are the three most important dailies: two evening papers and a morning paper. Far the biggest paper in the country is the evening *Maariv*, a stodgy, privately-owned publication. Its main shareholder, Oved Ben-Amy, the Mayor of Nathanyah and one of the richest men in Israel, is irrevocably committed to an expansionist policy of annexing as much territory as possible and to an exclusivist Jewish society with religious roots. Most of the editors and senior staff consistently support whoever in the government calls for a policy of war. *Maariv* was instrumental in rallying the masses to Moshe Dayan on the eve of the 1967 war, and thereafter expounded, in a rather boring manner which appealed mainly to the middle classes, the theory of the Chosen People in its Promised Land.

The second biggest newspaper, also an evening paper, is *Yediot Aharonot*, which is directed *de jure* by one of the most rabid extremists in Israel: the elderly Dr Herzl Rosenblum, who advocated mass hangings of Palestinian resistance fighters, the censoring of books and plays passed by military censorship, and the gradual limitation of freedom of speech. However, this paper is in effect run by an astute journalist, Dov Yudkowsky, who manages to give one page in fifty to Opposition columnists. Without questioning the basic Zionist structure of society, they attack the signs of totalitarianism in Israel, while the rest of the paper's columnists are busy strengthening it.

There is one more daily paper – *Haaretz*, the oldest and most serious of the morning press. Directed by a millionaire born in Germany, Gershom Shocken, *Haaretz*, no less than other influential Israeli newspapers, is Zionist. But it is also liberal-minded. A fugitive from Hitler's Germany can really understand the dangers of totalitarianism. So, while assisting in the ascendancy of Dayan before the 1967 war, *Haaretz* thereafter consistently practised an 'open pages' policy, allowing opposition views to be presented side by side with those of the most extreme chauvinists. This policy, and some of its more lucid 'leaders', have earned *Haaretz* a not undeserved reputation as Israel's main daily bastion of free speech. However, on basic problems and on basic issues, this paper like all its brethren always opts for the exclusively Jewish interest – that is, it rejects basic democracy as far as the *whole* population of the state is concerned.

In addition to these there are also several small daily news-sheets, privately distributed; a typical one is called *Hakol.* It is not a newspaper in the proper sense. It is owned by a small extreme group of religious and non-Zionist zealots, and distributed almost exclusively among them.

So much for the Hebrew daily press: one hundred per cent Zionist, owned by many individuals and several subdivisions of a single ideology, apparently free but in fact working in concert on all basic issues and in moments of crisis.

Israel is a country where, as yet, half the population consists of first-generation immigrants. Many cannot read or write Hebrew, a difficult language for an adult to learn, with a script very different from Latin characters. As a result, many people employ their former tongues, and over the last fifty years a widespread press in these languages has developed. In the last decade, however, nine out of ten such daily newspapers have been in the hands of a single party – the Labour majority – and of its economic instrument, the Histadrut syndicate of labour. Under this absolute control are such sheets as *Renastera Noastra* (Romanian), *Uj Kelet* (Hungarian), *Letzte Nayes* (Yiddish), *Novini* (Polish), *Jerusalem Post* (English), *El Anba* (Arabic). The one exception is the German-language news-sheet, *Yediot Hadashot*, also called *Neuste Nachrichten*, and edited by journalists close to the Independent Liberal (Zionist) Party. This newspaper owed its existence to the formation of the Independent Liberal Party from the fusion of two political groups, one of which has been the political voice of the *Landsmannschaft*, the German Jews who emigrated to Israel after Hitler's rise to power.

After the 1967 war another Arabic daily, *El Kuds*, not belonging to the Zionist Establishment, was published in occupied Eastern Jerusalem. It was allowed a wide range of criticism against the Israeli occupation authorities, and so became a showcase of Israeli democracy and beneficent military rule. Of course it was not permitted to publish the harsher truths of the occupation. But neither were the Hebrew papers.

The 'free' Israeli press is controlled in two ways: firstly, by straightforward military censorship which deletes anything it objects to in connection with defence, security, economics, immigration, oil, the Occupied Territories, military law, legislation, official policy, cabinet meetings, diplomacy and so on; secondly, through the Voluntary Committee of Editors-in-Chief. Official bodies such as the Secret Services, the Ministry of Foreign Affairs, or the Office of the Prime Minister's Spokesman often convene this committee secretly and, strictly off the record, give full details of some affair, incident or development too delicate or scabrous for the democratic public to know about. The editors are then pledged not to print these revelations.

It must be emphasized that this Voluntary Editors' Committee is concerned with matters which the military censorship, in spite of its wide powers, cannot or does not wish to blue-pencil. It is a 'second line of trenches' in the battle against free speech. Only daily newspapers, however, are represented on it; weekly publications escape this control. So the editors of such weeklies are periodically invited to private meetings with the officials, who tell them secrets under the seal of a gentleman's agreement. The public is thus bamboozled by the very instruments of free speech which are supposed to open its eyes.

The broadcasting services of Israel are state-controlled. There are three radio services, two run by Kol Israel, the Voice of Israel, and one by Galei Tzahal, the Defence Army of Israel's broadcasting service. All three broadcast political comment, news, music and general programmes. One of the Kol Israel wave-bands also broadcasts commercial publicity. No advertising is accepted from political sources outside the Zionist Establishment.

The excellent staff of Kol Israel, and more particularly of its 'Newsreel' programme, once tried to keep a certain amount of independence, but in the late sixties political control was tightened. The fledgeling television services were also affected. Up to Ben-Gurion's final resignation from the premiership, no television existed: Ben-Gurion feared to spread an 'anti-image' – most of Israel's leaders being old and not very handsome men. Later a television state-monopoly was launched, staffed with foreign technicians and experts, who were replaced by party hacks as soon as this was feasible. In 1970 the Labour Party set up a political committee on television affairs – in addition to the checks already existing, and in addition to 'military', and practically political, censorship – not to speak of the fact that the TV directors were, all, trusted Zionist Establishment men. All these forbade even the mildest of mild anti-Zionism criticism. Even liberal views inside the Establishment were discriminated against.

So much for freedom of expression in the first section of Israel's population.

The second section – non-Jewish citizens who were not Arabs – being very small, had no publications except for a handful of thoroughly religious parish-periodicals, which were not widely read even by devout believers and were even less interesting from the civil liberties point of view. The third section, non-Zionist and anti-Zionist Jewish Israelis, had no daily newspapers. They were catered for by Hebrew weeklies, monthlies, and other less regular publications of limited effectiveness.

The Communist group, Maki, used to print a daily newspaper called *Kol Haam*. But when the group's leader, Dr Moshe Sneh, cut himself loose from Moscow and rejoined the Zionist Establishment* the funds which had sustained the paper ceased to flow into the party's coffers, and immediately after Maki's defeat in the 1969 elections† *Kol Haam* became a weekly.

Still Moscow-orientated, the second communist faction, Rekah, has an overwhelming majority of Arabs in its membership. For such a group, whose Jewish membership dwindled after the 1967 war, it was not worth while to publish a daily newspaper in Hebrew, not even a subsidized one. So its only Hebrew publication was the weekly *Zo Hadereh*, written in the stodgy, boring, long-winded style of all communist publications east of the Rhine. It was badly edited and its influence was extremely limited, although it was one of the few publications which consistently revealed military, civil, legal and economic repression, both in Israel and in the Occupied Territories.

*Chapter 9.

†See Chapter 10.

The biggest and by far the most influential of non-Zionist weeklies is *Haolam Hazeh*, edited by Ury Avnery, already discussed in Chapter 9. It is enough here to say that *Haolam Hazeh* carried out, almost single-handed, the fight for free – if often slanted – speech during the first twenty years of the State of Israel's existence. It was able to do so and survive because of the quirk in its editorial policy which we have already seen.

The Israeli press is, in general, not self-supporting. Except for the prosperous *Haaretz* and the two evening papers, financed by the private resources of their owners and by a sufficiently large volume of advertising, all newspapers are subsidized by the Zionist parties – which, in turn, are subsidized by the funds collected abroad from Western Jews and from other sources. In addition most parties organize private collections, but their main revenue comes from the 'split' or 'divide', as Hebrew slang terms the distribution of the funds from abroad. It is thanks to this 'divide' and other party help that most papers continue to exist in spite of their small readership. One additional trick is the exploitation of a captive audience of Kibbutz-members or of government employees who have to subscribe, for instance, to *Davar*, the main organ of the workers' syndicate, the Histadrut.

Anyone wishing to launch a new paper is at an enormous disadvantage. Without funds from the 'divide' he must build up a readership in the face of overwhelming competition. *Haolam Hazeh* did just this. Its method was the judicious use of erotic photographs and sensational news, published side by side with political comment. In the Israel of the fifties, still quite puritan in its outlook, Ury Avnery's newspaper caused a scandal which allowed it to compete – although at times precariously – with the captive press of the Establishment.

Haolam Hazeh has been censored times without number. Almost every week it appears with blank spaces where type has been taken out. This is a forbidden tactic, but since printing is timed to the last possible minute the editors can always claim they had no material to substitute for the items claimed by the censor. Thus they silently advertise the fact that once again they have been gagged.

Avnery is not a member of the Editors' Voluntary Committee, but since his election to the Knesset in 1965 he has been silenced in other, more amicable, ways. He was invited to 'consult personally' the Ministers responsible for facts which the Establishment wanted to keep hidden; and was promised a 'reasonable' answer. Thus, even in this most democratic of all Israeli publications, virtually the only outlet of truth in the country, items were often suppressed.

Non-commercial political organizations or individuals wishing to express dissident views resort to bi-weekly, monthly or other irregular periodicals, which are of course less expensive to produce. The Israeli Socialist Organization publishes *Matzpen*, which calls itself a 'monthly' although it appears only five or six times a year. This publication, like any organ challenging Zionist concepts, is thoroughly blue-pencilled, and the editors have often had to threaten the censors with an Order *nisi* from the High Court – the only recourse against military censorship, but one expensive both in lawyers' fees and in time, as it tends to disrupt the pitifully weak publishing schedules of such newspapers.

The Zionist Establishment has one further, and extremely effective, way of reducing the efficiency of non-Zionist publications. In all Israel there are only three or four newspaper distributors. An owner of a non-conformist publication wanting his paper to be distributed to kiosks throughout the small country has not only to pay a ruinously high forfeit-payment, but must also expect the distribution to be done with deliberate inefficiency and slowness. For the Zionist papers travel through the same channels, and the distributor is liable to threats if he handles opposition material with too much enthusiasm. If this should fail, a last-ditch tactic is to send hoodlums to selected kiosks whose owners forthwith decline to receive further copies of the 'trouble-maker' newspaper.

Small organizations such as the ISO try to remedy this by selling their publications by hand. But since 1967 and the war this has proved physically dangerous for the newspaper hawkers. To sell fifty copies of *Matzpen* in the Hebrew University,

ISO had to send, in 1968, a small army of perhaps a dozen members – something they are willing, at times, to do for propaganda purposes, but which, as a sales method, is not very efficient. And an individual with non-conformist ideas is in an even worse position than an organization. After 1968 even the sale of *Matzpen* by organized groups provoked lynch-like reactions on the cities' streets and on the campus.

In the wake of the 1967 war a group of non-conformist journalists tried an experiment in protest. A non-party 'free tribune' was launched called *Aheret*, or Otherwise. I was among its editors. Financed by a group of private individuals, the paper appeared irregularly. It encountered the usual response from the distributors: fewer than 200 copies left their warehouses. Therefore, more copies were sent through the mail to a list of possible subscribers, who were asked to send money back. Few bothered, and after four issues Israel's only free tribune passed out of existence.

Now for the fourth sector: the Palestinians of Israel. The first thing to be unequivocally understood is that no Palestinian in Israel has been allowed to publish a newspaper of his own which is not directed, or at least controlled, by Zionists. There have been several attempts to found an independent newspaper in Arabic, edited by non-Zionist Palestinians. All have failed. The best-known example was El Ard ('The Earth'), founded by a group of Palestinian nationalists and writers in 1960. The Israeli District Commissioner forbade its publication under the (British Mandatory) Emergency Regulations of 1945. The case was brought before the High Court, but since the Emergency Regulations had become part of Israeli Law the appeal came to nothing.

A few newspapers printed in Arabic exist in Israel. The two most official ones have already been mentioned, the dailies *El Anba* and the 'Jerusalem native', *El Kuds*. They are the 'tough cop' and the 'soft-hearted cop' of a conventional police team. *El Anba* is the official mouthpiece of the Zionist Establishment, while *El Kuds* is allowed a certain amount of criticism, and thus becomes an outlet for a good deal of accumulated grievance in the Occupied Territories. A controlled outlet for complaint was found expedient by officials in the Arab Affairs Bureau of the Prime Minister's Office, who feared that otherwise an underground press was bound to appear.

The Pro-Arab Communist Party Rekah publishes a bi-weekly, *Al Ittihad;* a very good literary and political monthly, *El Jadid*; a youth monthly, *El Ghad;* and an ideological journal which is issued irregularly, *El Darb*. These are the papers where nationalist and free-thinking Arabs print their works. All other publications are Zionist or at least Zionist-influenced.

Ury Avnery has an Arabic monthly, *Haza El Alum*, which consists mostly of articles reprinted and translated from his Hebrew weekly. He took care never to go too far, and his publication was tolerated by the Zionist authorities. It was even, at one point, printed in the Occupied Territories with their consent.

The Zionist-Marxist Mapam publishes an Arabic weekly, *El Mirsad*, which urges moderation, 'abstention from extremism' and so on. Contributors to this paper are mainly those Israeli Palestinians who want some kind of intellectual or professional future in the Israeli state but cannot stomach the more blatant stand of such Labour publications as *El Anba*. Until 1962 Mapam also published a literary monthly in Arabic, *El Fajr*, which ceased publication when its Arab editors refused to become Zionist propagandists.

The ISO has repeatedly been forbidden to publish an Arabic edition of its Hebrew *Matzpen*, and even this they were not allowed to distribute in various Arab-populated regions. They now print one page of this Hebrew organ in Arabic. One of the ISO's splinter groups publishes irregularly an Arabic journal.

An experiment was made by the late Dr Mordecai Stein of Tel-Aviv (a Trotskyist) to pass on to a group of Palestinian Israelis the permit he held for an Arabic review, as well as contributing his 'Jewish' editorship. For personal reasons the experiment failed, but the Israeli authorities agreed to the publication of the review, called the *Democratic Newspaper*, as long as the Jewish editor remained.

So Israel's 320,000 Arabic-speaking non-Jews and those more

numerous in the Occupied Territories subsisted on a meagre fare of books pirated from foreign editions and litho-printed (when and if censorship allowed), and on native ideological poetry and literature which was often issued with the typical blanks of military censorship. For them too, the distribution problem added insult to injury, as Arab distributing bureaux were extremely anxious not to get on the wrong side of the authorities. An Arab poet who wanted to sell his works of patriotism or protest had to take them by hand to the small, widely separated villages where most of the Arab population lives. And as most of the 'national minded' Palestinians in Israel were obliged by the Emergency Regulations to stay in their home-villages, they could not circulate their works by themselves. Here too a gag covers an apparently open mouth.

It is true, of course, that Arab poetry nowadays puts artistic values firmly in second place. First and foremost, poetry in the Middle East is a weapon of propaganda, used by the nationalists of all Arab countries and by the Palestinian Arabs both inside and outside Israel. It is also true that poetry can be incendiary at the level of the still undeveloped masses of this area. This was, then, the problem the Israeli censor faced. After some hesitation censorship decided to cut the evil at its root, and while the censors allowed the publication of militant Arab poetry in such left-wing publications as *El Mirsad* and the communist *Al Ittihad*, they often forbade the reprinting of these same poems in separate books, which might get the authors a wider, non-party public.

Fawzy El Assmar is an Israeli Arab poet and journalist, first editor of *El Fajr*, the Marxist-Zionist Mapam monthly, and later assistant editor of Ury Avnery's Arabic monthly, *Haza El Alam*. A radical left-wing socialist, Assmar was one of the founders of the Palestinian pan-Arab and nationalistic publication, *El Ard*, which was banned by the authorities together with the political movement it was trying to establish. After the Six Days War, since the Shin Beit has to decide whether an Israeli Arab may be employed in any public position, Assmar was forced to live from hand to mouth.

He also blotted his record by writing poetry, which like all

Arabic poetry in Israel had to be submitted to military censorship. His first book appeared with blank pages where poems had been cut out, although they had earlier appeared in the Arabic weekly of the Communist Party and even in that of Mapam; other poems had single words and phrases deleted. In spite of all this, the book was a success and was widely circulated.

In the second week of August 1969, Assmar was arrested by the secret police and held incommunicado. After two weeks, he was brought before a magistrate's court, where the officer in charge swore that his department had proof of Assmar being in contact with El Fatah terrorists, and he was remanded in jail. A few weeks later he was given, without a hearing, six months' administrative imprisonment simply on the signature of an officer of police. This six months was later renewed twice. Assmar was in jail, without trial, altogether some fifteen months.

In the summer of 1970 the organizers of the British Harrogate Poetry Festival wanted to invite two Israeli poets to read their works: a Jew and a Palestinian. The Jewish Israeli chosen was Nathan Zach, a well-known non-political poet and lecturer at the University of Tel-Aviv, then in England writing his doctorate. Zach submitted the name of El Assmar for the second invitation and the gaoled poet was invited. In spite of this opportunity for an honourable way out, the authorities renewed Assmar's detention once again. Three months later he was suddenly released without a word of explanation, but was confined to Lod and forced to remain indoors from sunset to sunrise. He finally left to study in the US.

Imprisonment upon a police officer's signature is permitted by Israeli law, which has integrated into the judicial system the Emergency Regulations of 1945, passed by the British Mandate to suppress first the Arab rebels and later the Jewish fighters for independence. The Minister of Justice, Moshe Shapiro, a member of the Mafdal and a well-known barrister, was responsible for applying these regulations – after their ratification by the Knesset. Not so long ago, in the forties, Shapiro was one of the more vociferous advocates for their abolition – by the British. At that time he declared the emergency regulations to be 'inhuman'. Now he became the main instrument for their use, but, up to 1970 at any rate, mostly against Arabs. As long as no violence was done to Jews, the Israeli population was content to believe that democracy still ruled their country. But in such a situation, Hebrew letters and art also decayed; the more abstract styles and forms in the plastic arts, literature and theatre were gradually relegated to obscurity by a society which was busy surviving as an organism consciously wishing to safeguard a given cultural or ethnic character, to the exclusion of all others.

Under a state of war, the sciences, political thought, the apotheosis of fighting and mistrust of all are who not 'on our side' supply good substitutes for poetry, imaginative literature, associative literature, non-realistic interpretation of natural history, deviation from state-controlled beliefs (religious or other), and so on. A short glance at this list shows that this is what happens both in Israel and in the neighbouring Arab countries, as it happened before in South Africa and later in Rhodesia. 'Modernism' and imaginative 'decadent art' were anathema in the more totalitarian countries of socialist Eastern Europe. They were capital sins during the Stalin era and are to this day. And they were, of course, burned in Nazi Germany.

Despite a certain intolerance towards 'deviant' artistic values, abstract and imaginative art forms and so on, there is in Israel no proscription of the modern Jewish creative trends; just an almost total lack of a remunerative market for such trends, which together with the prevailing political climate prevents effectively the evolution of a contemporary literature devoid of strong religious or patriotic context. Such 'modern' Israeli letters had a start, as a matter of fact, in the fifties; but the Suez war of 1956 did much to cancel out this trend and in the early seventies Israeli writing was back on the path of political realism and neo-Jewish mysticism. Hebrew poetry and literature became, on the whole, an instrument of the Zionist Establishment.

Up to September 1970 the control of Arab letters was direct, through use of the apparatus of military censorship. The Assmar case, and the administrative arrest or banning of several other Arab political poets, caused the Lebanese writers' association to complain before the International PEN club, and the Israeli League for the Rights of Man to protest publicly abroad. Shortly thereafter, in October 1970, military censorship regulations were somewhat relaxed, as far as Arab poetry was concerned. The Arab-Israeli poets were no longer required to submit their works to the censor; nevertheless, the President of the Association of Hebrew Writers, Abba Kovner, deemed it necessary to declare upon informing the Association of the new regulations: 'Military censorship had been instituted because of the inflammatory nature of the writing – especially poetry – produced by Arab writers since the Establishment of the State.' Moreover, Abba Kovner noted, *all* writers, Jewish or Arab, are still 'responsible before the law for the contents of their work'.

13 Behind the Scenes

Not long before the Bolshevik revolution, the Russian Tsarina expressed a wish to visit a zone of 'popular development' which was under the direct control of Count Potiemkin, of sad memory. In fact Potiemkin had not developed the zone at all. Peasants subsisted there, as from time immemorial, in run-down villages where the pigsties were indistinguishable from the villagers' homes.

To satisfy the curiosity of Her Imperial Majesty, Count Potiemkin gave orders. In febrile haste theatre sets were erected along the road the Tsarina was to travel. Since she never alighted to inspect the development, she went away convinced that all was well. A few years later some of the peasants living behind the camouflage sets were among her executioners.

In Israel, development of the Jewish part of the country (and, to a lesser extent, of the Arab part) is genuine enough. Israeli democracy, on the other hand, strongly resembles Potiemkin's villages. The State of Israel is presented, both at home and abroad, as the embodiment of social democracy, a mixture of all that is good in capitalism and in socialism, the original, the archetypal Welfare State. This suggestion is of course, a lie.

A welfare state is one where a kind of balance has been achieved between the classes. While in a 'pure' capitalist society (which is rare indeed) the means of production and financing are exclusively in the hands of the owners – which affects the degree of advantages and services non-owning workers of all kinds enjoy – a welfare state is one where the workers and producers can put a stranglehold on the means of production and, through periodic use of their force, make the government and the owning classes grant them more rights, advantages, power and income.

The degree of centralization in any welfare state also influences the will of the workers to obtain extra power. A bureaucratic class develops which, not being part of the capitalist establishment, creates an establishment of its own and strives to conquer what the British Labour Left has called 'the commanding heights of the economy'. This, however, is as far as the struggle for the means of production goes. And, above all, it must be remembered that in a welfare state the bureaucracy of the trade unions has a particular kind of power and privilege which the capitalist classes have not got. This being so, there is a kind of 'democratic stabilization' through the tug-of-war of two power groups. As long as the capitalists and the bureaucrats do not identify their separate interests, there is a polarization of interests which ensures the continuation of democracy. When these two classes do merge – often because of an overriding common enemy, belief, patriotism or ideology – then a fascist-type 'national syndicalist' society appears.

In Israel this has happened. Society, as we have seen, is divided into various national, or racial-ideological, groups. Israeli society is basically a settlers' society. It does not primarily concern itself with the 'Indians' or 'Niggers' of the land. Its first priority is the creation of a united economic establishment for the Jewish Israelis. Only then does it concern itself (almost as an afterthought) with the captive Palestinians. Since 1967, when the West Bank of the Jordan, the Golan Heights, the Gaza Strip and the Sinai Peninsula came under Israeli rule, the same priority has operated in the Occupied Territories; but here more 'logically': these territories were taken by open force of war, so it was not 'unnatural' that they should be arbitrarily administered by military rule; whereas during the first twenty years of Israel's existence, precisely similar military methods had been used on the Palestinians of Israel without any justification whatsoever.

This military rule, then, is what is hidden by the Potiemkin institutions of Israel. It is not unduly cruel. It is not irrational or sadistic. It does not advocate the systematic use of cruelty for 'practical purposes'. On the contrary, it can be beneficial for the neo-feudal society of the Palestinian villagers in Israel and the Occupied Territories, and particularly for the people in the *Bedawi*, or Bedouin, nomad camps. For the first time these people are given medical aid, veterinary services, education, agricultural instruction, gynaecological care and even lessons in the use of modern rifles.

The trouble is that all these benefits are incidental. The true purpose of the military rule is the containment of the Palestinian *outside* the power structure of Jewish Israel and, by the use of both force and psychological repression, the creation of conditions by which the Palestinians will be incapable of challenging Zionist majority rule. Another, but less important, goal of military rule is agricultural expropriation.

Though the pretext for military rule is to keep the Israeli Arabs (and, since 1967, the Arabs of the Occupied Territories) quiescent, and let the Jews pursue their 'return to their land' in an orderly fashion, the historical result of this policy has been to impede the development of a bi-national society which, in spite of the creation of the 'Jewish State' in 1948, would certainly have evolved in Israel because of the higher Palestinian birth-rate* and the difficulties of attracting more Jewish immigrants from abroad, once the first waves of Hitler's victims were saved from the European mainland between 1945 and 1952.

The desire for a 'purely Jewish' society is freely admitted by the Zionist leadership, which always adds as a rider that Arabs in Israel are given 'equal but separate' opportunities for development and live in good conditions; in peace and in freedom. Unfortunately, the rigours of military rule – to all practical purposes the law of the land, as far as Arabic-speaking Israelis, both Moslem and Christian, are concerned – have repeatedly shown this rider to be untrue.

Military rule covered directly extremely large areas of Israel: the whole of the southern (Negev) area where *Bedawi* tribes roam; almost all northern Israel, or Galilee; and the central

*The birth-rate of Arabic-speaking Israelis is three times as high as that of the Hebrew-speaking majority.

area, called the 'Big and Small Triangles', which mostly consists of Arab villages. Broadly speaking only Jerusalem, Beer Sheba and the densely populated coastal and central areas of Israel, which include Tel-Aviv, Haifa, and Natanyah, are outside the control of direct military rule.

A Palestinian Israeli living in an area of military rule may be subjected to curfew. For fourteen years tens of thousands of citizens in the central area who had, according to Zionist propaganda, 'full civil and democratic rights' were forced to enter their homes by ninc o'clock in the evening and not allowed to leave them before five o'clock next morning. At times the rules were changed: the curfew ended at four in the morning but it began at 8 p.m. One can imagine the psychological effect on someone who for the first fourteen years of his life is forced to stay indoors at night, as a persecuted criminal is forced back to his cell from the exercise yard. The curfew was not abolished until the spirit of the central area villagers had apparently been totally broken, and they had become what in Israel is euphemistically termed 'non-political'.*

In Israel there has been a good deal of discussion about military rule, and a lot of opposition to it. At one point in 1964 the decision to end it was almost taken; but by one vote the renewal of the British Emergency Regulations was approved.

If he wanted to leave a military area, an Arab had to get a permit; in theory this applied to the Jews too, but nobody ever asks a Jew to produce one. However, a Jew entering such an area might be asked to show his permit, and if he was known to be a non-Zionist opponent of the regime he might be turned back. Thus, these Bantustans are visible, or rather transparent. Now you see them (when you are stamping out opposition) and now you don't (and can declare democracy to reign supreme).

The law was enforced in the invisible Bantustans through three channels: (a) the 'village elders' or *Muhtars* and the religious leaders, both Moslem *Kadis* and Christian priests; (b) the structures of military rule, assisted by an intricate net of informers

*In the Gaza Strip, occupied in 1967, a night curfew was still being imposed as late as March 1972.

and stool-pigeons who enjoy hidden or open benefits;* and (c) economic rewards and sanctions, such as remission of taxes, agricultural loans, minor public posts. It is through this last channel that most of the relatively modest economic development of the 'Arab sector' in Israel has happened. Arab village society being neo-feudal, even in Israel, it is enough to help the bigger landowners, the rich and religious men quaintly called 'Notables', to ensure the obedience of most, if not all, of their villagers.

In the twenty-odd years of Israel's history, the Palestinians have never been allowed to create an independent political movement. Whenever such a movement has appeared the huge weight of military rule has been directed against it. When the group centred on the *El Ard*, publication was established in the sixties with a clearly Arab nationalist programme, it was simply proscribed by the courts.

Any Arab who became politically active, either in the ranks of the Communist Rekah Party or as an individual defending his civil rights, was blacklisted by the military government and the Security Service (Shin Beit), which secretly control development of the non-Jewish sector – partly through the Department of Arab Affairs of the Prime Minister's Bureau; partly through the so-called Special Branch of the police; and partly through parallel organisms planted in the various civil services such as the Ministry of Posts and Communications, the Ministry of Agriculture, the Ministry of the Interior, the Ministry of Culture and Education and the Histadrut. This overall checking is systematic, regulated, and consistent with the Zionist Establishment's policy of allowing the Arabs controlled development in separate, limited and sharply delineated areas.

When elections to the Knesset are approaching, additional pressure is put on the 'doubtful' elements among the 'controlled' Arabs. The authorities let it be known that their jobs are in danger, their property may be in jeopardy, their future as students

*In Lod, for instance, a 'stool-pigeon quarter' was built, exclusively inhabited by Arabs who served the military government and other hush-hush organizations. These were the only Israeli Palestinians known to have been granted permits to carry hand-guns.

is uncertain, if they get out of line. Up to 1969 this policy had the hoped-for effect of breaking the Palestinians' spirit: no independent Arab list of candidates for the Knesset not aligned with one of the Zionist groups was ever formed between the 1948 and 1969 elections.

Controlling Israeli-Palestinians in non-rural areas is a bit more difficult. There are in Israel two biggish Arab towns: Nazareth and Acre. In both, 'parallel Jewish quarters' have been created to neutralize a possible majority of Palestinian voters who might elect municipal representatives of their own, either on a nationalist or personal basis, or through the Rekah party. Nonetheless Nazareth at least twice elected a Rekah majority. Gerrymandering and the buying-off of municipal council members and officials with political advantages solved this problem. The authorities now hoped to prevent such further crises by the redrafting of the Nazareth electoral area through the inclusion of the voters of the *Kiryat Nazareth* (or upper town of Nazareth) constructed on the slopes of the hills above the old town and inhabited by Jews.

Incidentally, the building of new housing developments is usually the joint responsibility of the Ministry of Absorption (of Jewish Immigrants) and the Ministry of Public Works, which are assisted with money supplied from other sources. The building of 'Upper Nazareth' was however, pushed through with funds from the Ministry of Defence, whose areas of responsibility are officially war and security.

In despair, aware that they have no political outlet, either democratic or revolutionary, some Israeli Arabs tried to find a way out of their predicament in the old way of the Middle East: by religious conversion. Judaism, however, is not a proselitizing religion like Christianity or Islam. Procedural and administrative difficulties are heaped in the path of would-be converts by religious Jewish authorities, charged with examining the candidates for circumcision or – if women – conversion by ritual cleansing.

Politics, racialism and irrational beliefs are now mixed and indistinguishable. This may be the reason why the Shin Beit vetted the Arabs who wanted to become first-class Israelis, or Jews. In answer to a Parliamentary Question,* Israel's Minister for Religious Affairs declared: (a) It was true that the security services examined the records of the candidates for conversion, as the police did – the first in order to establish that the prospective new Jew is not a 'security risk' and the second to see that he has no criminal record; (b) that this procedure had been adopted at the request of 'security sources'; (c) that some candidates had been refused conversion to Judaism because of a negative security check and that there did exist instructions to the Rabbinate to act thus, in case of a negative security check; (d) that this was 'only natural, as when we go about a conversion the first question is always if the candidate is a honest man; and if one can take seriously his honest wish to take upon himself the faith of Israel. If he is a criminal or has a criminal record, the question arises if one should not consider this or believe what he says.' As a result of the outcry which followed the Question, and as usually happens in such cases, the official open regulations were changed and the security checks were 'abolished'. In point of fact, the Shin Beit's control of who was to be converted and who was not went on.

Under such circumstances, law and order can have no sympathy for young love. The romance of Jewish Ofra Zazal and Arab Edmund Hadad is both an example and a warning. In 1965 Ofra Zazal was almost fourteen years old – and well developed, as are all Oriental-born Jewesses. Her neighbour in the townlet of Lod, not far from Israel's main airport, was an Arab, Edmund, then nineteen years old. They fell in love, and Ofra became pregnant.

In Israel, as in many Western countries, seducing a minor is considered as statutory rape. Edmund knew that as an Arab who had 'seduced' a Jewish girl under age he had small hope for mercy. The two were truly in love. At first, they decided to elope. But Israel is a small country; there was no escape for them inside its borders. Ofra's parents refused to hear of marriage with an

* Dr Zerah Warhaftig, answering M. K. Ury Avnery's Question No. 1343 in the final week of November 1970.

Arab. So Edmund tried to commit suicide. He was saved, just in time, and Ofra then told him she wanted him to stay alive and well, at her side, in spite of all.

There was no choice for the young couple. One moonless night they eloped, crossed the barbed-wire lines and mine-fields and went to the Gaza strip, then under Egyptian administration. From Gaza, after a period in an Egyptian jail, they were allowed to go to Egypt itself, where Ofra was converted to the Greek Orthodox faith – Edmund Hadad's own church. Then they were duly and properly married at a Christian religious ceremony.

Meanwhile the 1967 war broke out. The young couple was regarded with some suspicion by the Egyptian Security Services, and had to live isolated in their new harsh country. Finally Edmund had had enough. He decided they should go on. Egypt's security men, keen to use the couple for propaganda purposes of its own, promised to supply the two of them with exit visas – provided Edmund would sign a document stating that the Israelis had tortured him because he had dared to love a Jewish girl. This was a plain falsehood, but Edmund signed, and the two travelled to Switzerland.

That country proved even colder and more alien than Egypt for the youngsters. Ofra, nineteen by now, pined away. Edmund, of no known profession, did not find his way in Europe. They wrote to Israel, throwing themselves upon the mercy of the Israeli Security Services. The Israelis, like the Egyptians before them, jumped upon the propaganda-value of the young couple. For them it was a question of showing their captive Arabs that 'crime does not pay'. They allowed the return of the two and promised lenience.

Edmund and Ofra Hadad came back. Their marriage and Ofra's conversion were cancelled by an Israeli court. Edmund was sent to jail for one year; he got nine months for crossing illegally the border into enemy territory and another three months for having had sexual relations with a minor, as well as a suspended sentence of another nine months for the same offence.

There was no way out for Ofra and Edmund's love. There is

no way out – short of exile – for an Israeli Arab, who wants to enjoy full rights and the full citizenship of 'democratic' Israel.

*

As Israel is, in the early seventies, a developing country with a shortage of workers, the existence of an Arabic-speaking, underdeveloped proletariat is desirable; all the more so as the wages of Palestinian Israelis are often lower (if unofficially so) than those of Hebrew-speaking Israelis. The influx of Arab workers from the countryside into the towns is therefore encouraged; but it is also controlled. In the past, permits to move outside their home-zones were granted only to 'good' Arabs, not to the uppity 'political trouble-makers'. Then on the eve of the 1967 war, and following much criticism of military rule by liberal Jewish circles in Israel, the reverse system was put into practice. Henceforth the 'good' variety of Arab could circulate freely – subject to road-searches, security checks, political bosses and informers – and positive restrictions were imposed only on trouble-makers. Some were not allowed to leave the town or village where they lived; others had to obey a sunset-to-sunrise curfew; the most 'dangerous' were exiled from their native town or village, often at the cost of their livelihood. Obviously, an extensive list of the trouble-makers was kept by the Shin Beit and freely consulted by Jewish employers.

This meant that no Arab agricultural worker, no artisan, no shopkeeper, no student, no accountant or lawyer or physician could afford to fall foul of the whim of military rule. Only somebody bent on economic suicide or a truly desperate man would brave the gale of Zionist displeasure in such a climate. The great mass of Arabic-speaking citizens did not want to commit such economic suicide: they were also simply glad to obtain better-paid jobs than their former agricultural occupation. Once again the mixture of the economic carrot and the stick of straightforward repression – which had already broken the spirit of the Israeli Palestinians before this phase – was put to work. Most Arabs were prepared to put up with the situation as long as they were left in peace.

The 'fringe benefits' thrown by the Hebrew-speaking Israelis, from their generally more advanced technological level, to the Arabic-speaking Palestinians really did improve their standard of living. One measure of this improvement was the rise in their numbers. Before 1948 the Arabs were the majority group throughout the total area of Palestine (that is, excluding Trans-jordan but including the Gaza Strip and the West Bank). When in 1948 the Arab countries' attack and the Zionist riposte drove some 600,000 refugees out of Israel only 108,000 Palestinians were left inside Israel. But in March 1968 an official publication of the Ministry of Foreign Affairs gave their total number as 313,000 – some 11·8 per cent of the population of Israel, excluding the West Bank and the Gaza Strip. This rise was partly due to their higher birth-rate, even in times of stress, and partly to the relatively high standards of living they enjoyed: four times higher than any Arab community elsewhere.

Israel as a whole developed much faster than the surrounding regimes. Mortality among Israeli Palestinians fell from 20 per thousand in 1948 to 6·1 per thousand in 1965: this, in spite of the fact that the Zionist policy of discrimination still left many Arab villages, particularly in the north, without physicians or pharma-cists, whereas the smallest and most isolated Jewish outpost had a well-stocked clinic, a doctor or at least a trained nurse, and an ambulance or other means of medical transport. In some Arab villages not even vaccination against smallpox was enforced. In December 1970 the Minister of Labour promised that seventeen Arab villages would get access-roads – in some three years' time. Many of these villages had no telephone connection to emergency services, although again, not a single Jewish point of colonization was without contact with the rest of the country, having either a telephone service or a wireless transmitter. All of which leads one to think how much worse things must be in the sur-rounding Arab countries for such a situation to be praised as an improvement.

Schooling in Arabic is provided for the inhabitants of the in-visible Bantustans, but efforts are made to prevent Arab children from identifying themselves too much with the Arab culture and history of the Middle East. On the other hand they are taught the history of Zionism and of the Jewish people throughout the world.

In Israel, as in the Arab countries, children are indoctrinated from the kindergarten. Although the Israeli educational authorities never went so far as the Egyptian educators in the Gaza Strip, who between 1948 and 1966 taught under-five-year-old children anti-Semitic slogans and inculcated blood-curdling sentiments of hate, the principles of indoctrination and educational falsification do exist. Teaching posts in the Arab schools cannot be filled without the approval of the Shin Beit.

Behind all this is the attitude: 'We have no choice, having been saddled with these unwanted Arabs'. But since the Israeli, and the Jewish culture he has inherited, are basically generous and committed to liberalism and humanism, a strange mixture of oppression and unwilling help is extended to the almost 12 per cent strong minority of non-Jews. Yet the prevailing feeling is, as a humorist once put it: 'Why don't the Palestinians go back to the place from which they didn't come?'

Fewer than one per cent of all Arabs in Israel pursue higher education. Even these – numbered by the Foreign Ministry in 1968 as 350 – are obliged to go to such 'Jewish' towns as Tel-Aviv and Rehovot, or 'mixed' towns such as Haifa and Jerusalem, to complete their studies. Only in these towns do colleges exist. By the spring of 1971 nothing had come out of a proposal to establish, in the occupied territories, an Arab university under Israeli auspices. In the Jewish ones, it is very easy to prevent non-Jewish students from taking part in political organizations, or forming an efficient students' union.

Arab workers are just as effectively controlled. For many years the main trade-union organization, the Histadrut, was officially 'The General Organization of the Hebrew Workers of the Land of Israel'. But this was changed later, when the Histadrut found it expedient to extend its influence. In fact, Histadrut has become one of the main instruments of control over Arabic-speaking minorities, as it already was over the Hebrew-speaking majority. Histadrut activities, such as organizing leisure, distributing work, educational programmes and so on, as well as directing industry, have become a further channel for the ubiquitous agents of the Shin Beit.

Histadrut also exerts influence in another way. In Israel there was no socialized medicine till 1970. Instead there were a number of 'sickness funds', medical insurance organizations affiliated to the different political parties and economic Zionist bodies. That of the Histadrut, simply called *Kupat Holim*, or 'Sickness Fund', is the biggest by far, covering some sixty per cent of the inhabitants of the country. Every worker or employee, Jewish or Arab, who pays dues to the Histadrut, automatically pays part of them for Medical Sick Fund services. Many villages in the Arab sector, however, have no *Kupat Holim* clinic. In January 1971 a law introducing compulsory sickness insurance through the existing sick funds was introduced. It gave an absolute majority to the Histadrut on the board of the Health Insurance services and thus created further pressure on Arab and Jewish workers to join the majority *Kupat Holim*. There was, of course, no independent Arab sickness fund.

14 The Class-Structure and the Economy

Even a superficial examination of the conditions of the Israeli Arabs shows that if their stomachs were full and their homes equipped with TV sets they were still less well-fed than most working Jewish Israelis. This is natural enough: if a group of men is allowed only partial development, they will tend to get less well remunerated posts. Moreover, if the society which ordains this is psychologically closed, giving preferential treatment to one ethnic, or rather ideologio-religious, group and discriminating against all others, those others must do whatever work they can find – or emigrate.

And indeed one hundred thousand Arabs did emigrate from Israel in the twenty years between the creation of the State in 1948 and the Six Days War. If the background of those partly willing emigrants were investigated, it would show that most of them belonged to the higher income groups and were students, graduates, tradesmen and so on. They are in demand elsewhere, but not in Israel.

Labourers, on the other hand, are a commodity which Israeli society is increasingly in need of. This need is the consequence of the evolution from an idealistic socialist economy, supported from the outside, to a capitalist microcosm with welfare and national-syndicalist features (still, however, supported from abroad). While the Israeli economy develops new and individual patterns, proper to the settler's society which has evolved in the Jewish State of the Middle East, ever bigger reserves are required. The Arabic-speaking contingent supplies them. This is an organic development, due to three differing causes.

First Israeli society is still in the course of expropriating the physical land of Israel from its erstwhile owners or labourers.

Though encouraged whenever possible, the expropriation is not yet quite complete, but since 1958, with the whole-hearted co-operation of most Israelis, the authorities have put into effect a policy which involves cutting off Arab villagers from the basically agricultural society in which they lived, as will be seen in Chapter 15.*

This, though desirable, was not, however, sufficient reason for converting the Israeli Arabs and the inhabitants of the Occupied Territories into a class of privileged helots. There was a second reason, the shortage in Jewish manpower, already referred to. Mass-immigration from underdeveloped countries had ceased for all practical purposes by 1970, educated Moroccan and Tunisian Jews preferring to go to France, for instance, where they could raise their standard of living to that of the French industrial proletariat; in Israel most of them would have had to spend from four to ten years in one of the isolated Moshavs, or settlers' non-cooperative villages. Such immigration as still existed in 1970 was from prosperous middle-class Jewish communities in the U S, France, South America, Britain – and to a smaller extent from the U S S R.

The third reason which caused the Arabs to become Israel's *Lumpenproletariat* was the cheapness of refugee-labour. The conquest of the Occupied Territories in 1967 created a need to employ huge numbers of new Palestinians, most of them potential trouble-makers, vegetating in their camps. At the same time, the newly accelerating growth of the Israeli war-economy brought about an urgent need for new construction and fortification works, and gave impetus to the military-industrial complex of Israel. Likewise, part of the Jewish manpower was taken away by increased mobilization (three years regular service) and longer call-up periods for reserve duty. A private now had to serve, after being released from the army, some forty days reserve duty a year; an officer and N C O as much as ninety days a year.

The military-industrial complex found itself in the unique

* For a more extensive documentation see *Les Arabes En Israel* by Sabri Geries, Maspéro, Paris, 1969.

situation in which it had both a demand for manpower and a huge reservoir of workers who would accept far lower wages and work longer hours. This enabled more and more Jewish Israelis to climb the socio-economic ladder and join the middle and petty-bourgeois classes, leaving big gaps at the bottom of the ladder. These gaps were often filled by the dispossessed of the Gaza refugee camps, or the workers of Nablus and Jenin. Thus the common interest of all Israelis, which is due to ideological causes and to enjoyment of external sources of capital, acquired further reinforcements and became, *de facto*, a classes-complex, the expression of both long-range beliefs and immediate economic interests.

A monolithic society preferring cultural, religious and ideological identity to social and class allegiance now found itself with an insufficient unskilled Jewish working class – precisely in the decade (the 1960s) when the old utopian socialist values were finally laid aside by the ruling 'left-wing' establishment, together with the remnants of proletarian internationalism and solidarity.

At the same time the patterns of power in the State of Israel evolved from a mild brand of socialism, which tolerated a capitalist minority, to national-syndicalism on the Italian Fascist model, with a few variations: close cooperation with foreign capitalism, as well as with the native brand. The main initiator of this new trend, from socialism to national-syndicalism, was the government Labour party, which controlled, through the Histadrut and other bodies, at least seventy per cent of the country's means of production. This included the army's vast self-supporting industrial complex, which in 1969 exported more than forty million U S dollars'-worth of weapons and ammunition; the Histadrut industrial complex, which put in the hands of the trade-union bosses not only Koor, the biggest diversified industrial concern in the state, but also Solel Boneh, a huge building and engineering firm, with widespread activities both in Israel and in such countries as Brazil, Turkey and Iran; all the country's mines; almost all land development, through the Keren Kayemet organization; bridge building, road laying and public works; the Palestine Electric Corporation; most of the state's agriculture, through control of and help extended to the various party-based Kibbutz-movements; and many others. In fact, the government and the Histadrut are by far the biggest capitalists and employers in Israel, although the number of 'private' millionaires has multiplied.

The country kept on growing and developing. It was in need of more and more workers. It trained more and more people in the technical skills – a thing good in itself for the further development of industry, but which left a gap in building, agriculture and public works. It was to these fields that the 'suddenly discovered' Arab workers were directed; they were inexpensive, the overwhelming majority were not trained for anything more skilled, and to get industrial jobs most of them abandoned their traditional hold on the land of their fathers which could now be put more easily under Jewish rule, and become incorporated into the (purely Jewish) development schemes. As for the Occupied Territories' Arabs – they only had to leave behind them their refugee camps and their dreams of a return to the earth on which they were born. Particular help was extended to those Arabs from the Gaza Strip who were willing to abandon the area – avowedly due for incorporation into the Israeli State – in order to move to the West Bank where work was readily found for them.

In a way, all this was a curious inversion of the dictum that 'each people gets the government it deserves'. Here a government got the proletariat it needed, as soon as it evolved from theoretical socialism into an oppressive regime.

Thus a peculiar class-structure has evolved in the Israeli national-syndicalist state. At the top, controlling the pyramid of power, rules a bureaucratic class, the *Bitzuistim*, as they are called in everyday slang, or 'doers'. They include the higher military echelons, the Histadrut bosses, the Jewish Agency bosses, senior public servants, police and security administrators. In their allotted fields their word is law and their rule absolute.

Below them there is a wide-flung, and ever-expanding, capitalist class, often fed from above by the *Bitzuist*. The capitalists of Israel are the owners of private industrial works, commercial firms and privately owned services, often discriminated against by the national-syndicalists, who use the power of their tame labour-union forces to compete with private industry. The expansion of the Israeli economy and the end of the Era of Idealism have put an end to the period of 'socialist exploitation' of these capitalists, who were underprivileged by the bureaucrats and suffered greatly at their hands till the middle 1950s. At that time serious economic crises forced the bureaucrats to contemplate foreign investment of all kinds. Up to that date, there had arisen difficulties due to the fact that foreign capital, mostly American and Jewish, was not always willing to associate itself with State-owned and 'public'-owned enterprises. After the capitalists of both Israel and abroad were allowed to become active partners, rather than competitors of the national-syndicalist bosses, came a period in which Israeli capitalism was reborn and started flourishing to a degree till then unknown in the Jewish community of Palestine and in Israel. Some rich Arabs – though not very many of them – adhered to this Israeli capitalist class.

Below it there are the 'Centurions', an armed class which fulfils – in accordance with the pattern of militarised society throughout the world – the duties and gains the benefits which are proper to the upper middle classes elsewhere. These are the 'military bureaucrats', the middle and lower executive echelons of the professional army, political organizers of all Zionist parties, union leaders, operators in the security services, teachers exerting mind-control through indoctrination in both the Jewish and the Arab sectors, and so on.

Then there are the lower middle classes, including both the industrial and other skilled workers – who have lost, long ago, all their 'proletarian' characteristics; the Kibbutz rank and file; the shopkeepers, white-collar workers, etc; also, once they have finished their integration time (often many years), many of the new Jewish immigrants. The lower middle classes of all kinds enjoy some of the benefits of the Zionist Establishment but have no power whatsoever.

Immediately below them are the Jewish new immigrants – until 1967 the biggest contingent of the proletariat, but also that part which gets preferential treatment over the Israeli Arab workers; mainly in housing, loans, aid, transportation, health benefits and other services, rather than through higher wages. After 1967 a marked difference in wages divided the unskilled Jewish from the Arab-Palestinian workers.

At the bottom of the pyramid are to be found the Arab workers, the mass of the underprivileged. They are neither entitled to benefits nor allowed a place in Israeli society. Such skills as they have are discarded or underpaid, and their religious-ideological personality keeps them separate, a caste of people who cannot integrate into society.

In a highly cohesive and industrialized society the unskilled worker is a minority. By dividing *all* workers and employees into variously powerful and variously prosperous groups, with divided class allegiances and common ideological-religious beliefs, a proletarian consciousness is totally by-passed. In its stead appears a somewhat desperate national consciousness, particularly powerful among the very weak and the very strong of Israel. In any case, there is no community of interests for the Jewish and Arab workers. The Establishment makes sure that the separation of interests is not only ideological but practical, as well as economic: the Jewish worker not only is apprehensive of all Arab labourers, whom he considers his economic competitors and ideological enemies; he also earns more than they do – if not always enough – as long as he supports the Zionist ideals of racial separateness.

What strikes one, when considering this national-syndicalist pattern, is its similarity – in spite of obvious variations – to some patterns of Soviet economy; to some features of the U S military-industrial complex; and even to the largely similar, if under-developed, arrangements in Egypt and Algeria. It seems that as far as basic psycho-economic patterns are concerned the 'only democracy in the Middle East' is similar to both its enemies and allies, in the area and elsewhere. In fact, not such a one-time, seven-day wonder as Zionism makes it out to be.

While the usual confrontation of a capitalist class and its exploited masses is given impetus by both greed and want, the confrontation between the oppressed and exploited of Israel and their bureaucratic or national-syndicalist bosses has been held off by both belief and fear.

We might say that the greater the element of belief in a society's past, the greater amount of power will be concentrated into a smaller segment of society; and the more explosive that society's relationship will be with 'non-believers' from outside its framework. In Israel's believers' society, the ruling bosses are clearly entrenched not only behind their age-old separatism but also behind age-old fears, cleverly used. As matters stand in the early seventies, there is no chance whatever for a popular, mass-revolt of today's believers against those who rule them in the name of their belief.

*

For many hundreds of years there lived in Jerusalem some hundreds of law-observing religious Jews who had come to the Holy Land in accordance with the age-old precepts of their religion. They dedicated their lives to prayer and good works; and even when they tried to make a living as shopkeepers and artisans, the harsh realities of the Arab and Ottoman regimes and the poverty of the country obliged them to subsist on very meagre fare.

The rich and prosperous Jewish communities of the world – in Russia, Poland, Turkey, Egypt, Germany and elsewhere – felt a responsibility towards these fulfillers of the *Mitzwah*, the religious good deed of coming to the Holy Land. So they sent sums of money which were divided up among the Jews of Palestine, and as a result communities grew up in Jerusalem, Hebron, Safat, and other places.

The money thus distributed was called *Halukah*, 'the divide'; the Zionist revolution adopted the practice of *Halukah*, using the money sent from abroad to maintain first the villages launched by Baron Hirsch and Baron de Rothschild, and later the utopian-cooperative Kibbutzim.

The principle of collecting money from Jewish communities in other countries developed with the growth of the Zionist movement. It became one of the main ways of acquiring land from the *Effendis*, the Arab landowners. And for Zionist Jews abroad, who felt guilty for not leaving their riches and status to live as 'practising Zionist' pioneers in Palestine, it served as conscience money. For some of the richer Jewish-European capitalists it was also a way to invest capital and acquire political power.

After the creation of the State of Israel, a state at first founded on the premise that *all* Jews should be gathered into the old-new homeland, this system became even more comprehensive. Under the regime of David Ben-Gurion, rich men were not favoured as new immigrants: it was thought they would threaten the 'socialist', that is national-syndicalist, nature of the country's economy. The policy was, as one wag put it, 'to bring money without Jews and Jews without money'. This policy did permit the ruling Left to stay in control of the economy; but it also deflected the economy's evolution. By its ties with investment capital from abroad (mostly from the US) and by the Israeli leaders' stubborn insistence on having a tightly sealed-off state, without any economic relations whatever with surrounding Arab countries, the Israeli economy was finally forced into a pseudo-capitalist pattern.

All this left the country unhealthily incapable of supporting itself. Its main natural resources were phosphates, an expensive but modern agriculture, the somewhat problematic possibility of discovering wide reserves of oil, and a steady stream of tourists. The State of Israel was confronted with a choice.

It could decide to create a self-contained economy, for which purpose it would have to develop an industrial life based on the advantages it did have, such as a rich vein of technologically advanced manpower. Possible directions for such an industrial life to take were the makings of electronic precision instruments, or watch-making. In fact, some efforts were made in this direction by the diamond-polishing industry, which exploited its relations with this eminently Jewish *métier*, abroad. The exigences of war, however, later directed this wealth of talent and know-how towards the consolidation of a weapons and military aircraft industry – a destructive slant for a sound economic idea, no doubt channelled that way by the growth of the Zionist garrison-state, the attacks of pan-Arab nationalists and the hesitation of the big powers, prepared only to be Israel's arms-providers, not her economic liberators.

The alternative would have been to use existing and new economic and technological resources in cooperation with the Arab countries. For instance, although within its limits brilliantly successful, the piecemeal development of agriculture in the Kibbutzim and Moshavim of Israel was irrelevant. What could have happened was the nationalization and industrialization of the agriculture of the whole Middle East, under the auspices of Israeli technology. This would have been fruitful to all the peoples of the area, as would have been the cooperation between the merging Arab proletariat and Israeli technological expertise. Together, these two elements could have taken on and beaten the established industrialized agriculture of Europe and America.

For this, however, some kind of common ideological ground would have been needed, or at least a belief on both sides that co-existence was possible. The Jews and the Arabs were too busy fighting each other to gather the potential fruits of their co-existence.

As a result, any development of Israeli industrial power was, at best, collateral to the main economic activity of the country, which was and is called 'investment'. American industries, the completely 'Gentile' as well as those partly owned by Jews, need to expand. They need not only markets but also spheres of development. Israel was, reasonably enough, such a sphere. Hence investment became a normal part of the economic life of the state. So did other, less 'productive' sources of income – those from the new *Halukah*, the new 'divide'.

It worked two ways. First, there were the Jewish Diaspora organizations and individuals, who gave to Israeli charities and got income-tax reductions in their own countries. All Zionist colonization organisms were considered to be such charities. By the early seventies, any *local* charity was likewise coupled to the raising of funds for Israel. For the more commercial-minded, campaigns were organized by the United Israel Appeal (registered in the US as a foreign agency), the British United Palestine Appeal and the United Jewish Appeal for the sale of Israel Bonds. The

United States Treasury, for once, allowed these sales, technically in contravention of American financial regulations, because it suited the American policy of helping Israel and directing as far as possible its political development.

There were a few other, more transient sources of funds, such as the West German Reparations, paid to the State of Israel to the tune of 140 million marks a year, to compensate 'the Jews' for the economic persecution suffered under the Third Reich.

All these funds, as well as US aid and loans made with American blessing by the World Bank, were fed into the Israeli economy according to the pattern of distribution established by the 'divide'. Each Zionist party got a share of the money, according to its numerical strength or the influence it was able to exert on what was happening in Israel and among the Jews of the world; and these parties passed the money on to their 'own' Kibbutzim and Moshavim, to their 'own' sick funds, to their 'own' industrial developments and housing schemes. A feudal-industrial economy was thus created, based not on its natural reserves and ability to produce, but on money distributed from abroad; and in this economy, the Zionist parties were 'robber barons' of a new kind. Moreover, economic patterns tended to petrify: whoever had economic power tended to develop political power. In the first years of the State's existence the big problems were housing, agriculture, health, employment, and industrialization. The Zionist parties, and they alone, controlled all these fields and became the 'natural' and perennial carriers of the country's wealth.

The political structure of the parties became, as a result of this, also petrified to some extent and basically non-democratic. The leadership of the biggest, the Labour Party, for instance, is automatically co-optional by the present leadership, as far as 25 per cent of the 968 members of the Party's Assembly are concerned. The rest of the – elective – delegates are mostly small-fry. Among the non-elective 25 per cent one finds Israel's Prime Minister, the totality of the Labour Cabinet members, the Party's Knesset Members, Histadrut bosses and General Secretary, and the complete political committee and secretariat of the party itself.

Political sinecures, particularly ministries in the government, were distributed rather differently. They were shared out among the parties (a) according to the needs of the national-syndicalist economy and (b) according to the election's results. Since people voted almost automatically for whoever was providing them already with food, work and homes, or for whoever controlled, for instance, their own Kibbutz, it came to the same thing in the end.

Obviously the Arab minority got no control of any ministry. It benefited only indirectly from the 'divide' either by joining one of the Zionist parties' schemes (as teachers of Arabic, for instance, under the control of whatever party held the Ministry for Culture and Education) or as commissars in the lower ranks of the Arab Department of the Histadrut. The Arabs could not decently be denied, for instance, medical services and hygiene; nor did the majority of Israelis wish to deny them these things, guided as they were by liberal-humanitarian conceptions and a European consciousness of their duty as 'rulers' or 'owners' of the country. There was, however, a lot of discrimination. The main task of the State was the bringing in and the 'absorption' of the exiles, the Jews. The 'absorption' of the Palestinians was never part of official philosophy. It was at best a necessary nuisance, to be dealt with when and if the burning problems of the Jewish immigrants were solved.

In the fifties a serious economic and housing crisis exploded. There were even riots among lower-class, Oriental-origin Jews; and the Palestinians, no more than defeated enemies, had to take a back seat.

The Israeli Palestinians were 'politically controlled', as well as being put outside the scheme of normal Israeli life. There was no way for them to acquire independent democratic representation in the Knesset. The representatives who appeared in Parliament represented Zionism on the whole. Some space was allowed for non-Zionists, such as communists – perhaps on the assumption that they would be unable to seize power because they did not benefit from the 'divide'; perhaps from a wish to keep the formal or external manifestations of democracy, above all parliamentary representation.

Under the circumstances, it was not surprising that urban

Palestinian nationalists, Arabs who did not live in politically controlled villages or who did live in such places but had independent means, as well as the merely foolhardy, joined the Communist Party. Much later, other non-Zionist organizations developed.

In the 1969-elected Knesset there were 115 Zionists to five non-Zionists. The population of Israel was then some two and a half million, of whom 350,000 were Palestinian Israelis, i.e. certainly non-Zionist. About another 350,000 Jewish Israelis would have claimed to be non-Zionist if asked. Nonetheless, most of them voted in accordance with existing patterns. The five non-Zionists were: two Haolam Hazeh, three Relakh communists. To those might be added as possible opposition members, one Maki delegate, two Poalei Agudat Israel delegates, and four delegates of the Cooperation and Brotherhood and the Progress and Development lists. But this latter opposition was more apparent than real. Maki is the 'Jewish' Communist Party which actively supports Zionism in its international propaganda; Poalei Agudat Israel is a religious zealots' group which rejects Zionism on doctrinal grounds but cooperates with it and also participates in the 'divide' system. As for the last two, they are Arab puppet or quisling groups, led by Palestinian 'Notables' indirectly affiliated to the Zionist Labour Party and acting as wholesale suppliers of Arab votes.

Moreover, their representation in the Knesset did not mean the non-Zionist parties had the full benefits of parliamentary democracy, much less of the economic set-up. For instance, the General Assembly of the seventh (1969) Knesset had, in addition to the Speaker, no fewer than eight deputy speakers. All nine were members of the coalition government then ruling. No such polite considerations as fair play to the small non-Zionist opposition were in evidence. They were denied membership in all the important and powerful house committees, such as the finance, foreign policy and state defence ones.

The twin desires to keep the establishment as monolithic as possible and to whitewash the external facade of Israeli democracy made it extremely difficult for a non-Zionist force to get even one representative elected to the Knesset. Once this had been achieved, however, it was less difficult to keep him there: in accordance with the 'divide' system, a law enables any party already in the Knesset to obtain funds – in proportion to its parliamentary representation – for the next electoral campaign. The bigger the party in the Knesset and in the Zionist Establishment, the greater its benefits and even rights. Speaking time in parliament, for instance, was allotted according to the number of delegates a party had. A small party would get five minutes in a debate; a big one, such as the Labour Party, could speak for hours on end. The same principle governed the time allotted on radio and television during election campaigns, and even so broadcasts could be cut according to the political whims of the military censor.

The 'divide' had fatal consequences for democracy in Israel. But it was equally harmful to the independence of Israel and to its chances of finding a lasting peace with its neighbours.

For years it was argued that Israel's dependence upon Jewish communities abroad guaranteed there would be no absolute break with democratic principles. Quite apart from the fact that this argument overlooked the undemocratic attitude of the majority towards the Palestinian minority, the assumption on which it was based was doubly disproved by the Six Days War. First, there was the 'undeclared putsch' of part of the Israeli Higher Command. It happened in 1967, when the late Prime Minister, Levi Eshkol, was still hesitating about preparing the country for total war – not from pacifism, but from fear of his political rivals, and principally of General Moshe Dayan, who was then leader of the Rafi faction and known to want the post of Minister of Defence in any forthcoming Cabinet of National Unity. Some of the higher officers of the army went to Golda Meir, then the 'fixer' of the Labour Alignment, and threatened a putsch if Dayan was not given the Defence portfolio. Eshkol, never a strong personality, capitulated and the National Unity (and War) Government was formed.*

*Compare, among others, Jon Kimche, *The Second Arab Awakening*, London, 1970.

The second proof that the 'dependence is freedom' theory was a fallacy came in the reaction of world Jewry to the new situation in Israel: a most undemocratic reaction, and naturally so. It is natural for Jews, who identify themselves with the State of Israel, to be uncritical of its policies, particularly in a crisis; even more so when the policies are apparently successful; disastrously so when the successes are military victories, so dear to the minds of civilians, so encouraging for Jews who have no collective experience of military triumphs.

Moreover, the wars of 1956 and 1967 brought about a recrudescence of the Jewish character of Israel. The gradual fading of the blood-and-culture ties between Israelis and Jews abroad was violently replaced by a renewal of the post-religious, semi-mystical ideology of 'conquering the Land of Abraham'. This was, no doubt, pleasing to the Jews abroad, who had never understood what an independent, territorial Israeli nationalism could be.

Finally, the growth of the Middle East crisis meant that Israel needed still more aid from the 'divide', from abroad. As an American Zionist said: 'When blood flows, money flows.'*

The Israelis grew more dependent upon the Jews of America and elsewhere, and the latter grew more committed to Israel. A non-combatant always has greater expectations of victory than the men who fight. In their wish for additional territorial conquest, for more repression of Palestinian resistance, for a military rather than a political settlement, the Jews abroad were more extreme than their Israeli cousins, even those in ruling positions in the Zionist Establishment.

What guarantee was there that a rational Jewish consensus might hold off the gradual but certain deterioration of Israeli civil rights before the totalitarian point of no return? How could such a consensus stand up to the enormous pressure which the leaders of the Zionist Establishment in Israel might apply indirectly to Jews abroad by the simple expedient of opening fire, even locally, on one of the borders? This, in fact, has been done

* Quoted by the *Jewish Observer*, London, and *Haolam Hazeh*, Tel-Aviv, July 1970.

several times before with excellent results. The sound of gunfire is a sure way to silence the voices of prudence and caution.

Israel's very dependence on outside sources of capitalization led to the degeneration of its internal life. There is no doubt that this continued dependence, coupled to a state of emergency and war, can also bring about an identification of world Judaism with Zionism, which, if exploited by anti-Semites, and by anti-Zionists of the more illogical kind, may yet bring disaster to more than one Diaspora community.

More and more of the means of production and land controlled by the government have simply been handed over to private control. After the Six Days War it was found advisable to liquidate part of the 'socialist' industrial economy. There were two reasons for this: from a financial viewpoint it was not worthwhile; and because actual control of the political and economic set-up had clearly moved elsewhere – to the bureaucratic spheres which had been running 'emergency politics' and an 'emergency economy' throughout Israel's existence.

A Millionaires' Conference was called in Jerusalem after the 1967 war and scores of Jewish and some non-Jewish businessmen took part. On the agenda were: (a) to find investments for the development of Israel's dynamic war industries; (b) to find investors in other fields of economic endeavour; and (c) to ensure that those who took over bits of nationalized industries (and paid handsomely for the privilege) would not acquire the political power which usually accompanies economic power. This last object could not, of course, altogether succeed. The development of an investment society where local nationalized industries had existed before was bound to strengthen to some degree the right-wing Gahal block. Gahal had all the necessary elements – the free enterprise ideas, the Zionist expansionism, always the mark of the Herut party (one of the two components of Gahal), and the basically religious mysticism which could give an alibi of acting 'for the right purpose' to the worst forms of economic and social exploitation.

After the Six Days War a kind of 'normalization' started in the complex syndicalist-capitalist economy of Israel. Nevertheless, within the changing economic power structure real control still remained in the hands of the bureaucrats and war lords of Zionism, the men obliged by the 'emergency situation in which Israel is fighting for her life' to reject the economically sound solutions (from a capitalist viewpoint) inspired by the rapacity of the rising new bourgeoisie. The social pattern made familiar in Spain, Italy and Germany in the thirties, before the war, once more appeared – in Israel, of all places: the capitalists helped the bureaucrats and the war lords, but the bureaucrats and centurions did not respond by abdicating even part of their power or by straightforwardly serving the capitalists; on the contrary, the capitalists found themselves assisting an absolutist class which controlled the people by means of common beliefs and economic power; and controlled capital by means of economic profit. The pattern was all the éasier to achieve in Israel because the bureaucrats began by having power in their hands, thanks to a socially motivated ideology which had put them in the ruling position, at the beginning. So their giving away a part of their economic control and profits was really a matter of expediency, not the result of a defeat by a rising bourgeois class.

One must, therefore, profoundly distrust the capitalist 'normalization' of the Israeli economy. It must be considered in the socio-political context of the Middle East, where military dictatorships, protected by a hinterland of privileges and profit, grant rewards now to this class, now to another. In Egypt the war-lords control all other classes; in Israel the bureaucrats still have a precarious hold on the war lords and, in the early seventies, started to intermingle with them, as more and more generals and colonels went over to the managerial class.

One of the architects of the 'normalization' was the Minister of Finance, Pinhas Saphir. Excluding State-owned land, which had overriding emotional importance, he estimated the value of State-owned industries in 1970 at three billion US dollars, maybe more. The total annual income from this tremendous concentration of hardware was on average, however, only fifty-seven million US dollars – not enough to justify its being kept under State ownership. So Saphir founded the Hevra Leisrael, the Israeli Company Ltd, shares in which were to be held by private concerns and individuals, not necessarily Jewish. Thought was given to selling the public electricity company and the Red Sea phosphate works. But the prices offered by foreign investors for the latter were not enough to cover losses incurred by the inefficient company in the previous few years.*

The Israeli Jewish worker was faced with a constant decrease in the buying power of his income. For many years the Histadrut, which is controlled by the government, agreed to close its eyes to shameless falsifications of the cost of living index, according to which wages were supposed to be negotiated. Prices and pay were juggled with times without end, but even this was not enough, and in the last months of 1969 – shortly before the Knesset elections – the system was scrapped in fact if not in word and replaced by a so-called 'package deal' which regulated income tax, payments for defence purposes and net incomes in one and the same operation. The result was that in the year when the civil budget was at its smallest the military budget at its highest, and living standards at their worst, an average salaried worker or employee was paid *less* than before the signing of the package deal by the government-backed 'workers' representatives' of the Histadrut.

On 4 May 1970 the Labour-controlled *Jerusalem Post* had to state the bitter truth: under the headline '4% Up But More Down – Dip in Take-home Pay for Most This Month', the daily wrote:

Salaries for April, the first month of the new fiscal year ... will be smaller in take-home pay for most wage earners ... Choosing a workplace that contributes 16 per cent of wages into a pensions fund: a man (with a wife and two children) earning I£600 a month before April 1 suffered a deduction of I£98.80 for income tax, national insurance, voluntary Defence Loan and pension fund, leaving a take-home pay of I£501.20.

Today his gross pay is increased to I£624, but his net is reduced very slightly (by I£1.50) to I£499.70. Assuming he did not contribute to the Defence Loan last year, then his take-home pay at that time was

* *Haolam Hazeh*, February 1970.

I£526.70, and is now I£27 less. If compulsory loans are seen as part of net income, the earner does better, receiving I£534.50 after tax, national insurance and pension fund, or I£8.30 more than previously.

The following table shows the same calculation for salaries of I£1,000 and I£1,500 a month (in I£s):

	Last month	*Now*
Gross salary	1,000	1,040
Income tax	143.70	164.80
National insurance	13.30	33
Defence Loan	42	40.10
Compulsory savings (after tax)	—	27
Pension fund	43	40
Total Deductions	242	304.90
Net Salary	758	735.10
Gross salary	1,500	1,560
Income tax	378.20	425.10
National insurance	13.30	49.50
Defence Loan	62	76.40
Compulsory savings (after tax)	—	28.10
Pension fund	68	60
Total Deductions	518.50	639.10
Net salary	981.50	920.90

A man previously earning I£1,000 a month finds his take-home pay reduced by I£22.90. If he did not contribute to the Defence Loan last year, his net wage was I£800, so he gets I£64.90 less. On the other hand, if the compulsory loan and savings are seen as part of his net income, then his receipts are up very slightly, by I£2.20.

The person previously earning I£1,500 a month draws I£60.60 less. If he did not contribute to the voluntary Defence Loan, the fall in his take-home pay amounts to I£122.60. If the compulsory loan and savings are seen as part of his net income, he remains worse off all the same (net of taxes, national insurance and pension fund) – though by only I£18.10.

The employer also has to pay out more. In the case of a worker earning I£1,000 a month, he previously paid an extra I£173 in fringe benefits (to national insurance, the Histadrut sick fund, and pensions), or a total of I£1,173. Now the worker earns (gross) I£1,040, and fringe benefits total I£227, so the employer's bill comes to I£1,267, an increase of I£94, or eight per cent.

For a member of the staff earning I£1,500 a month, the employer previously paid another I£242 in fringe benefits, making I£1,742 in all. Today gross pay is I£1,560 and fringe benefits I£341, so the employer's total outlay comes to I£1,901, an increase of I£159, or nine per cent.

When this juggling was completed, taxes and the cost of living continued to climb.

A few facts may make this financial information less formidable and more comprehensible: in 1970 the average minimum wage was, I£600; in free exchange, about four Israeli pounds equal one U S dollar, about nine Israeli pounds equal one pound sterling. Practically all Israelis are obliged to buy National Defence Loan certificates; to the deductions listed by the *Jerusalem Post* chart, one should add the substantial Histadrut dues and sick-fund tax, which is obligatory in most private industrial and commercial enterprises and, of course, in all official ones. Moreover, at the same time as making these deductions, the government raised taxes by some I£100 million – this being only the latest in a long series of such increases. The *Israel Digest*, published by the Zionist Federation's Jewish Agency, promised prospective immigrants that 'Other indirect taxes will not be raised', but within months this had proved false.

A glance at the percentage of the tax-burden carried by salaried workers and employees showed that the former utopian socialist society was fast becoming just another theatre of social repression – behind the beautiful and enthusiasm-arousing curtains of a patriotic, racialist and messianic ideal. For instance, *Haaretz* reported in 1969 that income-tax files for 27,500 self-employed people showed that in 1968 (the year following the Six Days War) their average income increased by 17 per cent, whereas in 1967 (the year of the war itself) the average income of the self-employed had risen by only one per cent.

Yediot Aharonot, not one of the most liberal Israeli newspapers, nevertheless printed on 11 July 1969 an article by Itzhak Tischler in which he said quite openly that it was lucky the State's emergency situation left no room for social revolt. But he admitted it was not so lucky for the lower classes, whose income was getting smaller compared to the incomes of other classes while their characteristics – national extraction, lower education and so on – remained the same.

In other words: the 'monolithic' society of Israel had by 1969 disappeared. The gathering-in of the exiles, once a social and humanitarian task, had become a pretext for social exploitation and political rule. The quite genuine threat of Arab attacks and the ideological propaganda propped up by the latest victories still allowed the ruling bureaucrats to hold off any real social unrest.

Tischler also gave some facts established by an official census of the government-sponsored Central Statistics Bureau, an institution belonging to the Prime Minister's Office: in 1965 the average annual income of an urban Jewish family, whose breadwinner was an employee, was I£7,773; two years later, in spite of catastrophic increases in prices and taxes, it had risen to only I£9,377. Some individuals were much worse off. Real want often ruled the lives of some families, mostly of Oriental Jewish extraction, who had by no means been assimilated to the European-bred Establishment. 'As far as differences of income are concerned, the inequality of those who have lived in the country since 1950 further deteriorated in 1965 and 1966,' the Central Statistics Bureau reported. 'In 1967 and 1968, however, the inequality became considerably greater . . .'

In absolute numbers, in 1967 eleven per cent of the Jewish families investigated earned less than I£3000 per annum – less than US $750 or £333! Twenty-five per cent of the population earned less than I£5000 (US $1250 or £555) per annum. And since they were mostly Oriental immigrants, some of the families had as many as eight or ten children. These figures gain added significance from another statistic reported by Tischler and the Central Statistics Bureau: in the ten years ending in 1965, Oriental Jewish families earned an average 75 per cent of the income of a Western Jewish family – not bad at all, considering their lower educational level. In 1967, however, they earned only about

61 per cent of their Western cousins' income. As Tischler said, the poor were getting poorer.

In 1968–9 some 32·2 per cent of the country's social budget went to benefit the poorest fifth of the population. In 1969 their share had dropped to 28·7 per cent.

One tenth of the families in the country had a total income of I£1,700 (U S $425 or £188) in 1969, representing 1·8 per cent of the national income. Another tenth of the families in the country earned I£25,000 (U S $6,250 or £2,777), representing 26·9 per cent of the national income.

*

In 1970 Labour Relations Courts were set up, which of course were based on the assumption that the rulers (and the leaders) of the Histadrut were the natural defenders of the workers, whereas private enterprise could be presumed to be on the other, hostile side of the fence. In fact, the public prosecutor, the defence attorney and the judge combined against the workers' interests with a single aim in mind: to eliminate 'wild-cat' strikes, of which Israel has never known so many as in the late sixties and early seventies.

In 1969 the Zionist parties voted in a 'party tax' which most workers paid through their union dues to sustain further the cadres and institutions of the parties participating in the control of the Histadrut syndicate, or represented in it. At first the Zionists tried to exclude Rekah, the communist faction, from a share in this booty, but later had reluctantly to allow them two per cent of the income thus obtained, in proportion to their percentage in the 1969 Knesset elections. It should be added that the workers disliked contributing to the communist cadres quite as much as, if not more than, to the all-powerful Labour Party, or the so-called Zionist socialist Mapam party; but they bowed finally to their commissars' pressure.

In 1970 the government removed the interest-ceiling on borrowed money, until then officially 11 per cent. Also in 1970 the government decided to allow the gradual relaxation of the Rent Control Law, thus forcing tenants who might have lived for years in old buildings to pay more or get out. In Israel there are four types of dwellings in urban areas: rented flats, for which as much as I£600 per month for a three-room dwelling is paid; public housing sold to new Jewish immigrants or specially privileged bureaucrats on a mortgage paid monthly over twenty or thirty years; housing sold outright for huge sums in cash, usually involving disastrous interest for loans; and private accommodation rented on payment of 'key money'. 'Key money' was officially sanctioned in the early sixties, and thus became a kind of investment. The new law not only forced small-income tenants to pay more rent, but also deprived them of their hard-earned investment, because no landlord in his right mind would now sell them the flats they lived in for a moderate sum. Obviously only people of meagre means used the disadvantageous key money system. Thus the abolition of the Rent Control Law was a direct blow to the poorer citizens.

In 1969 and in 1970 the travelling tax – a financial trick unique to Israel – was twice raised. A low-priced steamer ticket from Haifa to Marseilles cost, for instance, some I£300; but any Israeli resident planning to use it had to pay approximately I£500 extra in travelling tax. Higher-priced tickets entailed higher taxes. A smaller source of potential irritation to socialists was the decision of Israel Railways to create a first class in its hitherto egalitarian wagons.

Kupat Holim, the sick fund of the Histadrut (to which 1,100,000 of Israel's population of three million were affiliated), decided that same year to charge for the medicaments it provided. Hitherto these had been free, thanks to the high Histadrut dues – which members went on paying.

From the late sixties, May Day, once observed as a holiday by Histadrut, became a working day – but not a paid one: members had to donate this day's wages to front-line settlements.

The economic decline of the working classes coincided with Israel's achievement in 1968 and 1969 of a world productivity record of 26.1 per cent, as stated by David Horowitz, then Governor of the Bank of Israel, who added that there were people living in the country 'below the poverty line' – a fact not sufficiently appreciated in Israel, where propaganda is so powerful.

The Governor went on to say that their income could be brought up to the 'minimum of subsistence' with an outlay of I£70 million to I£100 million – 'which is not much, provided it comes at the expense of consumption in all other classes of society': a socialist declaration from the chief capitalist-bureaucrat of the country who at least was not as hypocritical about the state of affairs in Israel as his 'worker-protecting' colleagues of the Histadrut were.

The official budget's contribution to defence for 1970–71 was 25 per cent; but even official sources said some forty-nine to fifty-one per cent went for direct and indirect security and defence needs altogether. This trend started in 1968–9, the year after the victory which brought 'peace and quiet' to Israel and the conquered territories and supposedly brought the possibility of a better life. In that year Israel earmarked I£1,407,000 billion for security purposes. On the other hand, only I£123 million were earmarked for public health; I£351 million for education (as compared with I£467 million in 1967–8); I£45.7 million for welfare (I£61 million); I£42.2 million for social security (I£61.5 million).

Some ministries improved their lot. The Ministry of Police and Jail affairs got I£119 millions, instead of only I£104 million in 1967–8. It is true that after the conquests many more jails had to be operated.

It is hardly necessary to say that the same thing happened in the tax years 1969–70 and 1970–71. Only it was worse. Israel had a declared war economy. Budget planning for the years up to 1975 reflected the same tendency, which may be indicative of the war and foreign policy of the Zionist leadership of Israel in the future.

15 The Takeover of the Land

The fact that Jewish nationalism and consciousness have survived for some two thousand years without any physical link to a homeland created one of the strongest possible feelings about the possession of tracts of earth. *Geulat Haadamah*, the Liberation of the Land, was for the early Jewish settlers a messianic goal and a means of self-redemption. The bearded visionary and prophet, A. D. Gordon, proclaimed the 'Religion of the Earth' as an atheistic replacement for the old Jewish religion; and the purifying influence of land-labourers and pioneers was to cleanse the Diaspora Jews from their somewhat pitiful economic past as entrepreneurs, shopkeepers, moneylenders and so on.

With the creation of the first communal settlements, the value of physical work became absolute, and the value of the land on which the communes were built became doubly so. Self-righteous virtue in land-possession, a feeling to which all settler-communities are prone, was compounded in this case by a legacy of religious myths, social rootlessness and physical isolation from 'natural' life. Jean-Jacques Rousseau, Moses, Joshua the Conqueror of Canaan, Marx and Gordon were mixed in the minds of the early settlers into an amalgam with all the force of a Molotov cocktail.

The consolidation of the State of Israel did not lead to the abatement of this feeling. Old-fashioned nationalism and nineteenth-century imperialism said nothing in favour of sharing land and property with the former owners. The emotions of the colonizers, the urgent need to resettle, later, the remnants of Hitler's holocaust, and the continued aggressive opposition of the Middle East Arabs, all did their bit to heighten possessiveness.

The land of Israel, indeed the whole of Palestine, is a comparatively small tract of country. There is much to be said for its development according to modern methods in a spirit of idealism and brotherhood. All this and more was done by the Zionist movement. The trouble was it was done on an old-fashioned chauvinistic basis – for Jews alone. The Palestinians became the victims of the Liberation of the Land.

Moshe Dayan once said, 'There is not a single Jewish village in the land which was not built on the site of an Arab dwelling place. Nahalal took the place of Mahloul . . .'* This much-quoted phrase, used almost daily by Arab League propagandists as an illustration of Zionist expansionism, is in the final analysis a rare example of lucidity in the dense mist which pervades Israeli thinking whenever the problem of the 'ownership of Palestine' is raised. An honest Israeli, challenged on the question, will retort to the challenger, 'If you are so noble, why do you stay? Either this is our country and nothing else matters; or we are conquerors and interlopers and have no right to be here.'

Thus the problem is kept, by Israeli and Palestinian alike, on a merely emotional and moral level. If the historical past is a criterion, the truth of the matter is, of course, that Jewish links to the country of Palestine did exist before the Zionist revolution began; but that this revolution was misdirected along settler lines, supplanting the actual, present inhabitants of the land. If the basis of Jewish colonization had only been a non-exclusive, non-racialist emigration to a land in which others lived too, a common effort to develop the land could have been worked out.

As it happened, the racialism of Zionism and the racialism of pan-Arab neo-feudalism met head-on. And the results were disaster for the people of Palestine.

These people were by no means homogeneous. As multifarious as the Jews themselves in their ethnic, national and cultural backgrounds, the peoples of Palestine fell into three main social categories: foreign rulers and administrators of the Ottoman and before that Arab varieties; landowners (some of them living, in fact, in the pleasure-cities of Cairo and Beirut); and the

*Talk to the students of Haifa's Technical Institute, quoted by *Haaretz* 4 April 1969. Nahalal was Dayan's birth-place.

dispossessed, property-less serfs who actually worked the land but did not own it.

In the Arab and mixed Arab-Jewish towns of Palestine the situation was somewhat different. A city dweller generally was better off than a peasant. He usually had his own house or had lived for years, perhaps generations, in a house for which he paid some kind of rent. He too, however, suffered from the Zionist Liberation of the land.

The first phase of that Liberation was the buying-up of vast tracts of land by bodies such as the Jewish National Fund and the *Keren Hayessod* fund. The land was bought from the *Effendis*, often at surprisingly low prices, and the agricultural workers who had lived there had to move. They migrated to other Middle Eastern countries, or to other Palestinian villages. Some went to swell the working force of the urban areas – although the Zionist movement was at the same time actively preventing the use of Arab workers by Jewish capitalists and communal organizations.

This, however, was not enough for the Liberation of the Land. In 1947, at the end of the Mandate, Jewish ownership of lands in Palestine amounted to no more than 5·7 per cent of the country.

The policy of 'buying another *dunam* of land and another goat' was opposed by the extreme right-wing Revisionist Zionist movement which demanded more forceful measures. The opportunity for such measures came with the Israeli War of Independence of 1948. Even now it is impossible to judge how far ideological and political factors contributed to the policy leading to the exodus of the Palestinians; or to what extent all other needs were subordinated to the wish to consolidate a 'purely Jewish' state within 'safe borders'.*

*The desire for such safe borders runs obsessively through the whole history of Jewish colonization of Palestine; by the end of the Six Days War of 1967 it had become one of the main bricks of Israeli policy. Again and again such apparently dissimilar politicians as the doveish Foreign Minister Abba Eban, and the hawkish ex-Irgun leader and later Minister without Portfolio, Menahem Beigin, agreed in stating that Israel must defend itself from within safe, that is new, borders.

The fact that far fewer Israelis had died and that peace was indeed much nearer in the years 1949 to 1956, when the frontiers of Israel seemed par-

One cannot underrate the emotional, cultural, and in fact religious influence of legends, prayers, promises – or the effect of the desperate insecurity experienced by the Jews of the world over the last twenty centuries. The longing for safety through ownership of land became consuming, fanatical, a way of life, even when this ownership avowedly did not bring about safety. The superstitious fear of 'mingling with the Gentile' prevented the holding of this land in common with the Palestinians who lived on some of it and left much more arid, bare and open to colonization.

These two interacting elements – the craving for land and the fear of mixing with Gentiles – set the basic pattern which in course of time, and due to the hostility of the Palestinians, changed subtly to become a fear of the Gentile who wanted to keep the Jews out of their promised land.

The culmination came in the war of 1948, when the Arab countries – Syria, Jordan, Egypt, Iraq, Lebanon and Saudi Arabia – attempted to destroy the Jewish community and 'throw the Jews into the sea'. As a result of this conflict, the first wave of Palestinian refugees billowed out of Palestine.

The question must be asked: was the damage done to Arabic-speaking Palestine an inevitable side-effect of the Israeli war of independence, or did the Israelis exploit the attack by the Arab armies and Palestinian irregulars to 'liquidate the Palestinian problem'? Unhappily, the second alternative is the correct one. This can be proved. Among other facts, one stands out: in 1948 and 1949 250 Palestinian villages were demolished, after the expulsion of some of their inhabitants and the exodus of the others – often no farther than to an adjoining village. By 1959 official Israeli sources could state: 'Village property belonging to Arab absentees, whether they are outside the country or living

ticularly vulnerable to attack, did nothing to change this position, held by the population as a whole. Nor did it change when it became known that from the end of the hostilities in June 1967 to October 1970 – that is three years and four months – there had been 738 Israelis killed, 2,728 Israelis injured and 1,778 'Arab terrorists' killed. In 1970 *alone* there had been 8,081 acts of terror, armed incidents and clashes along the borders, in the Occupied Territories and inside Israel itself.

in Israel, and acquired by the [Israeli] Custodian of Absentees' Property, includes some 300 abandoned and semi-abandoned villages with a total area of 3·5 million *dunams.** The agricultural property includes 80,000 *dunams* of orange groves and more than 200,000 *dunams* of orchards . . . Property in the towns includes 25,416 buildings, consisting of 57,497 residential apartments and 10,729 shops and light industry workshops . . .'† There was, then, considerable wealth in land and buildings taken over from the displaced Palestinian inhabitants. What happened to it?

Most of the property came under the administration of the Custodian of Absentees' Property. Given wide powers by a specially drafted law, adopted by the Knesset, this body could not only administer, rebuild, collect rent; but also destroy buildings, sell both buildings and land, and generally do as it thought fit with the property it controlled. From the late fifties the Custodian's policy was to sell buildings to Jewish tenants in, among other places, the town of Jaffa, which had seen a particularly large exodus in 1948 when Palestinian Jaffa fought it out with Zionist Tel-Aviv.

I myself, as a member of the Haganah, the Military-Defence organization, participated in the defence of Tel-Aviv and the subsequent conquest of Jaffa. After some six months of borderline firing we broke through after a series of pitched battles, initiated by the extremist Irgun men. Meanwhile the panic-stricken Palestinians were spreading rumours of the blood-letting that was to come. After all, this had always been the pattern when Egyptians, Chaldeans, Babylonians, Crusaders, the armies of Napoleon, the Ottomans, the Mamelukes and sundry other came to conquer them. So in time-honoured Oriental fashion the people of Jaffa took to boats to go to Acre, Gaza or Beirut; or streamed along the roads to neighbouring villages or the Arab-governed countries till the storm blew over.

We marched into a ghost-town in which less than a tenth of its former Palestinian population remained. They were concentrated

* Four *dunams* are roughly equivalent to one acre.

† *Israel Government Yearbook*, 1959, pp. 74–5, quoted by Sabri Geries, *The Arabs in Israel*, p. 61.

by the Israeli military authorities into a series of blocks in the Ajami district, code-named by the Haganah and Irgun 'the Arab Ghetto'. At first barbed-wire was put round this part of the town and no Palestinian was allowed to leave. Later the barricades came down. Nonetheless, many a citizen of Jaffa who had not left was unable to return to his former home, sometimes only a few hundred metres from his new appointed living quarters in the 'Ghetto'. The Custodian took control of all the houses and their contents and at once started allotting them to new Jewish immigrants, families of military personnel and so on. Jaffa rapidly became a Jewish town. It happened that at that particular time there was a wave of Jewish immigration from Bulgaria. To this day Jaffa is the capital of Bulgarian Jews throughout the world.

Some Arabs tried to return to their homes, from neighbouring houses or from other villages and places. To begin with, they were not allowed to. Although they were paying rent to the Custodian for wherever they lived in Israel, they got not a single penny for their former homes – in which Jews were now living. The Jews did pay rent – often only a nominal sum – but they paid it into the Custodian's treasury, which kept careful records for the 'absentee' landlords, often living in misery near by. The newly-adopted law forbade direct payment to the former owners.

This is surely one of the most shameful responsibilities of the Israeli citizen towards his Palestinian co-nationals. It is understandable that at a time of massive influx of Jews any and every opportunity of lodging the new immigrants should be taken, including the homes of people displaced by the misfortunes of war. It can never be explained away why my country refused from the start to compensate at least those householders who were still living in the country.

The Law of Acquisition of Absentees' Property, modelled on the Emergency Regulations of the British Mandate and passed by the Knesset in 1950,* is nothing less than a Law of Expropriation. It defines the 'legal status' of the 'absentees' who had left the country either *permanently or temporarily*. Whoeve

* Sabri Geries. op. cit., p. 59, quoting the actual text of the law.

left his 'place of residence in the Land of Israel' between 29 November 1948 and the abrogation of that particular Emergency Law 'shall be regarded as an absentee if he left the country during the above period to (a) a place outside the Land of Israel before the 1.9.48; (b) a place inside the Land of Israel at that time occupied by forces that wished to prevent the establishment of the State of Israel or fought it after its establishment'.*

In other words, and without the legal gobbledygook: many thousands of Palestinians who had sought refuge outside the borders or outside the Israeli-controlled territories in the storm of war were now deprived of their possessions for the duration of the state of emergency. So far, the state of emergency has lasted for twenty-odd years. Moreover, many innocent villagers who visited neighbouring countries as a matter of course were thus despoiled because they did what they had always done – not knowing, obviously, that this time a law would be passed against such behaviour before they could go back. But worse: the thousands of refugees who moved from countryside to village, from village to town, from hamlet to neighbouring hamlet, trying to escape death, were also despoiled and left without compensation. They remained in the State of Israel – as third-class citizens.

In all fairness, it must be stated that the Israeli authorities did allow for the return of a small minority of the 'absentees' – mainly in the framework of 'uniting separated families' or in the case of 'Notables' who cooperated with the Israeli Military Government. The Law was applied jointly by the Custodian and by the military authorities in the occupied zones. Not surprisingly it became an instrument of oppression and blackmail, not only robbing most of the Palestinian minority of their land and houses, but also ensuring the political neutralization of the Arabic-speaking citizens. For twenty years, till the 1967 war gave a new traumatic shock to the Israeli Palestinians, this policy of repression and blackmail worked extremely well. The Israeli Arabs grew servile, lazy and prosperous. What was more important to the Zionist Establishment, they

* ibid.

also became totally incapable of widespread political activity.

In Israel the High Court does not have jurisdiction over military matters, nor the last word in anything. Whenever there is a conflict between it and the Knesset, this lopsided Parliament merely 'amends' the law, and everything goes on as before. Such is the state of a country without the safeguards of a democratic constitution. In juridical cases brought by the Palestinians – mainly from the 'Triangle' area of central Israel, where quantities of land were taken from Arab villagers still living there – the High Court pronounced itself incompetent; the law governing these cases was the result of an armistice agreement between sovereign states, not an internal matter.

One kind of property expropriated proved particularly troublesome to the Israeli authorities – the WAFK property which in 1936 represented one sixth of the total area of Palestine, and which belonged to the religious Islamic community, who administered it 'in the name of God'. When the Acquisition Law was applied to it, Sabri Geries observed, 'Islamic WAFK property has been transferred to the Custodian of Absentees' Property on the assumption, perhaps, that God is an absentee ...' It may be argued that even a joint Jewish-Arab socialist revolution or one of the Atatürk-type, engendering reforms, would have expropriated feudal-religious institutions like the WAFK. But it would not have done so on a racial or religious basis. These enormous riches would have been given to the State for the good of the whole population, Jews and Arabs alike. In fact, the transfer of ownership was racially motivated, the WAFK being an Islamic, i.e. Arab, institution. Protected discussion and much haggling went on in the administration and the Knesset over the final status of WAFK property. The outcome of all this palaver was, however, that in spite of some compensation paid to the Arabs, Jewish Israelis administered this property mainly for the benefit of Jewish Israelis.

Expropriation was not the only tactic. Article 125 of the Emergency Regulations empowered the military authorities to forbid people to go, or return, to 'specifically closed areas'. In practice, villagers who had fled during the war and its aftermath were not allowed to return to such an area; or if they had stayed they were often thrown out. Some were compensated to some extent. Others were not.

The reasons given for 'closing' an area varied. One security-inspired reason was the creation of defence zones along the frontiers. Another official reason was the *Yehud Hagalil*, the Judaization of the Province of Galilee. In Galilee in the middle sixties, the Jewish settlers were still a minority. Steps were taken to change this situation, among which was the closing of areas, at first on thc grounds of crcating 'military shooting rangcs', later for the purpose of making Galilee Jewish. The town of Carmiel, for instance, was built for this purpose on Arab land, without any military justification. A writers' and intellectuals' quarter was created in Carmiel, and many Israeli writers were invited to take up a second home there. Some agreed. Others, to their credit, refused with repugnance.* On another occasion a series of protest marches was organized by Israeli intellectuals against the dispossession of Arabs living in *Shetah 6* or what had become all of a sudden 'Military Zone No. 6'. A young civil rights campaigner, Ury Davies, was jailed for not leaving this territory when asked to do so by the army.

A particularly ugly case of the closed area policy occurred in Kafr Baram, on the Lebanese border, a village inhabited by pro-Israeli Palestinians (the Lebanese-influenced Arabs and the Druzes have always lived in relative peace with the Israelis). Barem is near the Kibbutz Baram, a Zionist-socialist Mapam commune, belonging to that Party's agricultural movement, the Hakibbutz Haartzi. In the fifties, when this movement was still fairly socialist and in opposition to the government, Baram had to expand. It needed land. It was a 'borderline settlement', part of the defence-line formed by these feudal-cooperative fortresses. So the military authorities declared the Kfar Baram lands a 'closed area'. The villagers countered by appealing to the High Court, which in September 1953 gave a judgement allowing them to return to their homes.

*Finally the 'artistic' project was scrapped – as too expensive for the artists and writers.

Suddenly, on 16 September 1953, the planes and artillery of Israel's Defence Army attacked the still empty building of Kfar Baram. The long-range shelling and bombing went on till only rubble, ashes and burning barns were left.

Kibbutz Baram got the land it needed. The villagers were offered compensation and resettlement (mainly as a result of the outcry from liberal circles in Israel), but refused. Only in the late sixties was a satisfactory agreement reached. And the lands of Kfar Baram remained, as is usual in these cases, in Jewish hands.

Without condoning racialist expropriation in the least, one must state that most of the legalistic – but not humanistic – arguments against Jewish 'Conquest of the Earth' have proved to be arrant nonsense. It must be understood that under Ottoman rule decisions – especially about land – were arbitrary and inclined to depend on the giving of *baksheesh* and the bribing of officials. Under the British Mandate attempts were made to regularize the situation by means of comprehensive laws. But this proved extremely difficult. Successive Arab revolts and Jewish armed attacks drove the British Mandate to rely increasingly on Emergency Regulations which 'legalized' such varying methods of oppression as the abandonment of *habeas corpus* and the confiscation of land. It was a heaven-sent opportunity for a settlers' society trying to establish an exclusivist state on the ruins of the Mandate. Here once more imperialism, if not guilty of the crimes of those who followed it, was at least responsible for leaving things in a mess – and, by consolidating its rule on autocracy, for teaching the newly independent state how to oppress minorities in its turn, Britain was responsible for the 'legal education' it gave both Jews and Arabs during the Mandate; and most particularly for the Emergency Regulations.

These Regulations were promptly incorporated in a 'purely Israeli' version by the new government and Knesset. In 1949 they were officially re-promulgated by the Ministry of Defence, and thereafter automatically renewed each year by the Knesset. Some amendments were later added to the original text.

A further means of liberation of the land was the 'Emergency

Articles for the Exploitation of Uncultivated Territories'.* These articles simply allowed the Israeli government to allocate tracts of uncultivated land to whomever it saw fit. The land might belong to a variety of owners – private absentee Arab WAFK, the State itself. On occasion even land still cultivated by Palestinian Israeli villagers came under these articles. The procedure in such cases was as follows: for 'security' reasons an area was declared closed by the Defence Ministry. The villagers were therefore unable to cultivate it. The civil authorities stepped in and allocated the 'newly uncultivated' land to some Jewish Kibbutz or Moshav, usually a neighbouring one, sometimes a purpose-built one. No doubt it was a further step towards the 'liberation of the land'.

Furthermore, in 1949 the government passed a 'Law for the Requisition of Land in Times of Emergency' – such requisition always being justified by 'security'. By 1970 this law had been amended several times. At first it was only permitted to take the land for three years. Then for six. Finally it was stipulated that such land held up to 1 August 1958 belonged to the Jewish State for good. Sometimes compensation was paid to the former owners. In their opinion the compensation was not enough.

According to Sabri Geries, in the 'Triangle' area villages of Um al Fahes, Tayba, Maalia, Bakka el Gharbiyah, Jaljulyah, Kafr Kar, Majdal and Sajur, 136,00 *dunams* of land were taken from Arabs *still living in the State of Israel*. He further claims that some 380,000 *dunams* were transferred from Arab villages to state-ownership by 1962, under the Land Acquisition Law. In addition, some 9,300 complaints have been legally settled to put the Jewish State in possession of another 146,474 *dunams*. In conclusion Geries states: 'We can regard the estimate of one million *dunams* of land expropriated from Arabs *living in Israel* as reasonable and accurate.' Geries is a lawyer. His pan-Arab politics do not preclude a passion for legal exactitude in investigation of the facts. Nor have his statistics ever been seriously challenged by Israeli or other sources.

*Sabri Geries, op. cit., p. 72; and Israel's *Official Gazette*, No. 27, of 15 October 1948, p. 3.

It should be remembered that this analysis does not refer to refugees who escaped or were thrown out. It refers to Palestinians who still for the most part live *within* the boundaries of the State of Israel. In other words: not only ownerless land has been 'liberated', but the land has been liberated from its owners. Before the creation of the State of Israel land was seen by Zionist ideology as necessary for the consolidation of a future state. But once free political and economic institutions had been built, once the frontiers were opened to Jewish immigration from abroad – and while large tracts of countryside were still arid and bare – the only possible explanation for the systematic confiscation of non-Jewish land was the racialist wish of an exclusive settlers' society to push out its 'natives'.

It would be tedious to analyse in detail all the laws and emergency regulations which have made this possible. Sabri Geries does so, and official Israeli sources are freely available. What is important here is to see the pattern and its relationship with the psychological blindness of an ideologically driven society.

Behind the pattern lay two things: first and foremost, the psychological need to disfranchise non-Jews who possessed parts of the land of Israel. As long as Israel is Jewish, this will be its reaction, as inevitable as the nervous system's response to the dictates of the brain. But there were also practical, political considerations, such as determined the establishment of a 'parallel town' above Arab-settled Nazareth, so that thousands of Jewish voters would ensure there was never a purely Arab Nazareth.

The 'Liberation of the Land' still goes on. The Zionist Establishment, firmly entrenched in its belief that the State of Israel must be an exclusively Jewish-ruled organism, has not been content with rule by force and law by majority decision in pseudo-democratic institutions. It has also 'created' facts – facts of Jewish settlement of large areas, facts of expropriation of Palestinian land, facts of industrialization to provide work for the dispossessed Arab villagers.

This policy was not directed primarily *against* the Palestinians. No racialist policy is aimed at first against a minority. The aim at first is always to encourage the strength and independence of the 'pure' majority. Distortion, infection, perversion set in later – when there are signs of reaction against the rule of racialism or when an economic crisis threatens.

*

The Kibbutz is the showcase of Israel. For fifty years it has been the foundation stone of Jewish settlement. The communist-utopian regime of these industrial and agricultural communes is praised throughout the world.

At the end of the 1967 war there were some 230 Kibbutzim, their membership varying from sixty to two thousand. The total population of the Kibbutz communes was only four per cent of the then 2,800,000 people in Israel, but their moral and economic influence was enormous. Their military importance too was very great.

The Kibbutzim employed in 1969 twenty-five per cent of all salaried agricultural workers in the country. They grew and produced about twelve per cent of the gross national product. In 1968 alone the Jewish Agency for Israel, part of the World Zionist Organization, contributed $430,000 to the Kibbutz movement through its various party affiliations. In 1969 this allotment was more than doubled. In addition the Israeli government, through the Ministries of Development, Agriculture and Defence, provided further and substantial funds. The Kibbutzim developed some 12,500 acres (or 50,000 *dunams*) in 1959, besides providing a good example for the less favoured agricultural settlements, such as the Moshav and the collective Moshav.*

Thus, from an agricultural and social angle, the Kibbutz makes a valuable contribution to Israeli society. As far as the ideological value of life in the Kibbutz is concerned, one must restrain one's enthusiasm a little; in an industrial society such as Israel has

* The *Moshav* is simply a government-subsidized village. Often the poorest and most ignorant immigrants, from North Africa, Kurdistan, etc., are directed to colonies of this kind. The *Moshav Shitufi* or collective Moshav, has common institutions and marketing bodies, but the families live separately.

become, Kibbutz life is an improvement on simple military activity and discipline; but it is certainly more restrictive than life in the big cities. Equally it is questionable whether the dividing-up of Israel's agricultural effort into comparatively small units of land controlled by comparatively small units of administration, such as Kibbutzim, is justified. If Israel were at peace, the country could concentrate on industry and import the food it needed from its Arab neighbours, whose produce and labour are much cheaper. Even in existing circumstances many Kibbutzim have gone over to specialized agriculture, such as luxury produce for export, or have tried to create parallel industries to ensure the survival of their way of life under any conditions.

With all this taken into account, the fact remains that the Kibbutz is one of the settler society's principal means of conquest and oppression. It is, in fact, the ideological embodiment of that society. The Kibbutz is also its military outpost, its educational framework, and its school for Spartans. Many organisms and institutions which are beneficial and necessary in times of peace become destructive or oppressive when a country is at war. If one considers the political, military and ideological implications of an armed and almost self-sufficient outpost on a contested border, it seems to be natural that the evolution of Israeli society should tend to deprive the Kibbutz of most of its positive characteristics. Not only did the 'communist-Utopian cell' prove sharply competitive and exploitatory towards the rest of Jewish society, including the workers and new immigrant poor as a whole, but its relationship to the Middle East as a whole also established it increasingly as a tool of colonizing policies, less and less a way of providing absolute communism for the few.

It is not difficult to find dozens of cases of Kibbutzim razing Arab villages and dispossessing the villagers of their land. The first distribution of homes and (unofficial, but later approved) annexation of lands in the wake of the 1967 war was carried out by the outpost Kibbutzim near Ramallah, in the Latrun area. They took over the strategically important, but also rich and fertile, lands belonging to the Arab villages of Yalu, Beit Noowa and Emawas, which were dynamited, and their dwellers driven off. These lands overlook the road to Jerusalem, by which most of the traffic from the coastal area now passes. The incident itself caused one of the few cases of insubordination, during the 1967 war, when a writer, Amos Kennane, who was serving with the reserves, drafted a letter of protest to his military superiors and published it as a leaflet.

(It must be said, on the other hand, that the policy of annexing lands is by no means to the benefit of Kibbutzim alone. In February 1971, for instance, the last inhabitants of the Nebi Samuel village, overlooking the entrance to Jerusalem, were driven off and houses and ruins of that village blown up to make way for a development housing project of the Jerusalem municipality, which was intent upon creating 'facts' such as a Jewish majority in the annexed, eastern part of the town.)

Kibbutz members, it is well known, suffer a disproportionately large share of casualties in the Israeli army. The reason for this is that there are a disproportionately large number of them in the army, and then mostly in combat-type units, a fact which can be accounted for in three ways: (a) the close-to-nature character of his education prepares the Kibbutznik for life in the army; (b) the Kibbutz tends to develop communal and disciplinary aspects of life, and to discourage individual thought and self-determination; (c) the child of the Kibbutz has a direct and proprietory approach to the land, and, deprived by his education of seeing the *fellahin* (the Arab tenant-farmers) as agricultural workers like himself, naturally considers territorial conquest as a kind of extension of his work on the land. After all, what is tilling and reaping if not the subjugation of the land? Is not conquest by force of arms, from a people 'who leave the land a desert' (as is stated again and again in Israel) merely the natural outcome of such a sociological growing-up?

Be this as it may, it is a fact that Kibbutz and Moshav members are the finest soldiers and most active officers in the army of Israel. The famous – or infamous – '101' unit, founded in the early fifties by Moshe Dayan under the command of 'Arik' Sharon, was composed in its majority of Kibbutz and Moshav members. The Parachutists, the *fer de lance* of Israeli mobile power in the 1954–67 era, were also predominantly drafted from among Kibbutz and Moshav members. And so it goes on, all along the line – tank commanders, the Engineers Corps and even military governors and other administrators of the conquered West Bank and Gaza Strip.

Moreover military life – or rather garrison life – has been a characteristic feature of outpost-Kibbutzim since the first settlements were founded. Today, when the defensive sociology of the Zionist State has been replaced by more dynamic, offensive and *conquistador* attitudes, it is no wonder that the Kibbutzim have become forts dominating occupied 'Indian country'. This is *not* due to military necessity. Helicopter-borne units, spies, *agents provocateurs* among the Palestinian population, and an outer ring of military forces have been found perfectly adequate to control the occupied territories. In any case it has been proved that purely military units are less expensive and more brutally effective for this work than Kibbutzim. A military outpost, however, has no permanence, no feeling of belonging. Its men are glad when their tour of duty is over and they are able to go home. For the people of the outpost-Kibbutzim, such as Nahal Yam in the Sinai desert, the settlements of the Golan Heights, and particularly those on the West Bank of the Jordan, conquest means creating a home there. It would be useless to ask these young men and women, after a few years of gruelling sacrifices and blood-letting, just to up and leave. Even if they were forced to do so, the 'return to Jewish land' would keep for them a mystique of its own. This happened after the 1967 war, when new settlements were founded in the reconquered Gush Etzion area, in addition to the old ones, over-run by the Arab Legion and under Jordanian rule from 1948 to 1967. The press and the politicians spoke in tear-stained chorus about Israel's 'right' to that land; without deducing, of course, that if anyone had a *permanent* claim upon any particular piece of land, much of that on which Jaffa and the outer suburbs of Tel-Aviv stand should have been returned to their Arab owners.

A double standard applies to all fields of conquest, but particularly to agricultural land. The 'conquest of the earth' was an axiom before the birth of the State, and still holds most of its emotional appeal today.

In territories occupied 'temporarily' or 'permanently' the tendency to convert the Kibbutz into a Templar-like military settlement grows ever stronger. At the same time the moral – or social – advantages of the Kibbutz are in the process of being debunked. A conqueror's settlement cannot be justified even in Zionist eyes, just because its internal structure is Utopian-communist. When it shows itself to be *kulak*-like in its approach to the country's capitalist economy (dumping of produce to keep up prices, employment of low-waged Arab workers, sale through cooperative organisms at high prices not determined by value but rather by demand) and intolerant of non-conformists in its midst, then the Kibbutz increasingly appears a degenerate cell in a negatively evolving society.

16 The Army

Of all the social and economic elements in the State of Israel, there are only two without which it could not go on existing *as an exclusivist Jewish State*: the external sources of economic aid, nicknamed the '*Schnorr*'; and the Israeli Defence Forces, or Tzahal.

Tzahal is not only an army: it is a state within a state; a security apparatus; an extremely dynamic economic empire; a never diminishing source of managerial manpower for the civil economy; a way of life; the main planning authority in Israel for fields as diverse as agricultural settlement, industrial development, law and policing. But first and foremost for the average Israeli, Tzahal is the main channel of his indoctrination, the symbol of the identity he wears, in fact and in thought, when he feels insecure or knows himself to be under attack. First and foremost Tzahal is the backbone of the New Sparta in the Middle East. During his schooldays, every Israeli child, boy or girl, gets some paramilitary training with the Gadna, the youth battalions affiliated to every school, technical institution, or private educational body. At the age of eighteen they are drafted. Theoretically, girls have to serve eighteen months and boys three years. In practice the reservations of the extreme religious parties make for two forms of discrimination: all boys in a *Yeshivah*, or religious school, mainly concerned with teaching the Torah, the Jewish Law, are exempt from military service; and girls who sign a sworn statement refusing service because of their religious beliefs are equally exempt.

While the *Yeshivah* scholars account for comparatively few cases of draft-dodging by non-zealots, as many as forty per cent of Israeli girls avoid the draft by 'declaring', as it is called in slang. As no more than 15 per cent of the population* votes for the religious parties at election time, it is obvious that religious objection is frequently no more than a pretext. There is, on the other hand, no proviso in Israeli law for conscientious objection. Pacifists may be, and have been, sent to jail, although they are usually treated leniently in prison or sent to an open prison camp called *Maassyahu*. In any case conscientious objectors are few.

The fact that each and every healthy Israeli boy lives in a military organization from the age of eighteen to twenty-one ensures that Israeli society is, by and large, impervious to radical upheaval. At this age certain boys in other countries are going to universities, the centres of ferment. Others are introduced, in the factories, to industrial class-confrontation. They discover dissent, they cut their ties with stringent family set-ups. In universities and industry alike the impact of new information, of cutting off one's family-past and of opportunities for freer sexual experience become linked in the young man's mind with the fact of his being a 'student' or a 'worker'; a member of a group apart, composed of young, 'free' people.

Something similar occurs in Israel through the three-year draft to Tzahal – but in the opposite direction. Discipline, loose but painstaking; the actual use of lethal weapons and the dizzy sense of power this gives; sexual permissiveness and opportunity (in mixed, if somewhat puritan, military camps and even more in Nahal colonial garrison settlements, where women and men work and guard together); membership of an in-group; the quite justified conviction that by serving in the army he is defending the existence of his country; further identification with a beautiful and still savage land from travelling through it more than before – all these factors make the young Israeli forget his feelings of rebellion against society (usually centred on his relationship with his parents and his rejection of the family's old-style Jewish background) and identify himself with the army, that is, with Israel's 'young' society. Add to this the facts that as often as not

*202,208 voters gave their votes to the various religious lists for the Seventh Knesset of 1969, out of a total vote of 1,367,743.

he sees action and that he faces a genuine conflict with genuine enemies intent upon destroying him and his State, and it is easy to understand why, after three years, very few revolutionaries emerge from the Israeli defence forces. When the better-off Israeli finally reaches the university campus at the age of twenty-one or over, he is already a psychologically conservative element of society. After passing through army ranks, most Israelis avoid rocking the boat.

The ever-growing need of a garrison-style settlers' society, attacked from outside and developing consciously or unconsciously the myth of being a state fortress which must survive alone in the face of the whole world, makes for a dynamic growth of the army-complex. Whereas in other countries, this dynamic growth is first of all bureaucratic, and becomes military-industrial only by association of interests, in Israel the army-complex is directly involved in agricultural colonization (garrison settlements of Nahal); and in industrial developments (weaponry, electronics, aeronautics, soldiers' equipment, printing, editing, broadcasting, public building, packaging, food processing, etc.). From turnips to transistors, the military industrial complex is responsible for production and often for sale and distribution.

As often happens, in an embattled society, research, industry and development are accelerated in times of war and stress. This is particularly so in a country without natural resources, where specialized electronics and machinery are a logical means to solvency. Modern warfare needs such specialized electronic and micro-industrial components, and the 1967 war gave an impetus to their development in Israel which twenty years of intermittent 'fighting peace' had not provided. This development was qualitative as well as quantitative. On 26 March 1970 the Minister of Commerce and Industry, Joseph Saphir, told the Knesset that every other worker added to Israel's working force in 1969 had been absorbed by the military industries. Israel's metal industry, in particular, took a leap forward. On 8 March 1970 Professor Don Patinkin, of the Hebrew University, declared that Israel must get some 19,000 engineers during the next decade. Forty per cent of them would work in the machinery, electronics and electronic production industries. A high proportion of the remainder would be mechanical engineers. General Twzi Tsur, Deputy Minister of Defence, said that up to ninety per cent of the ammunition required by Tzahal was met by the military industry, at home. At this point the Israeli military-industrial complex was exporting goods valued at U S $40 million per annum – instead of merely milking the economy.

On 3 March 1970 Hannoch Smith, head of the Manpower Division of the Ministry of Labour, said Israel had now reached a high level of technology: whole industries such as electronics and optics had doubled their volume of output because of the defence needs, during the thirty months since the end of the Six Days War. In a few years Israel's gross national product was expected to reach a standard comparable to that of a European country. The inference was inevitable: far from damaging the interests of the average Israeli, Tzahal and the emergency situation were on the whole beneficial for Israeli development.

In May 1970 the American *Aviation Weekly* reported that Israel was now able to proceed with the manufacture of her own fighting aircraft if the U S did not reconsider its policy of selling only a limited number of aircraft to Israel. (The U S did.)

All these developments went far beyond Israel's economists' wildest dreams on the eve of the 1967 conquests – and of the total French arms embargo which followed. The additional push of military activity, the intellectual need to cope and political rearrangements, all these gave this country a new dynamism in military-industrial development and, as a corollary, in its import-export policy. The fact that all this could have developed, perhaps even further, in peace – on a basis of cooperation and exchange arising of co-existence with the Middle East, was mentioned neither by the Israelis nor by the Arabs, who saw in the fabulous renewed development of Israel just added proof of Israeli militarism. So it was. But it would have been worthwhile, at this point, to draw a lesson from the possibilities at hand, and perhaps to arrive at some wish for collaboration.

*

Israeli society is in love with war and Tzahal: because they give the average citizen a feeling of contradictory safety; because they develop the mind and muscle of the economy and help them fill their pockets; and because war and preparation for war tally with the dynamic development of Israeli industrial life. Furthermore, war **is** the only possibility, when your aim is to live alone in a country where another people lives as well.

The second level of Israeli involvement with Tzahal is social, or class-induced. The army is above all the big regulator of Israeli society. Everybody passes through it, and the fact of completing one's military service with some degree of success is an indication of one's success as an individual. (No employer accepts a prospective employee without first glancing at his Discharge Sheet.) For this reason officers in Tzahal have become the marrow of Israel's managerial and executive classes.

This was inevitable. To be efficient the army has necessarily to be selective, and its officers, especially the high-echelon officers, were therefore better 'human material', as an Israeli idiom puts it. A man who succeeded in becoming a high-ranking officer was of necessity a good manager, director, planner or executive.

Another factor identifying the rising managerial class of the early seventies with former senior army personnel is the early compulsory retirement age in Israel's defence forces. It is unusual for a man of fifty to remain an active-duty general. As a result many excellent officers are released from the forces between the ages of forty and fifty – the ideal years of managerial aptitude.

Moreover, Israel's society being small and cohesive, the army is reluctant to see its former officers unused and underpaid. From a practical point of view it is necessary to prevent most of them from accepting offers from abroad, which a former colonel or general would easily attract from American, West German or other Western industrial enterprises. But an Israeli is rarely freed from reserve duty, and a higher-echelon officer almost never. It is necessary that this reservoir of military brains and brawn should stay in the country to be used in times of war.

In any case, since Tzahal has enormous prestige, and since its command is part of the ruling Zionist Establishment there is a natural affinity of mentality between, say, the leadership of the personnel department of the Israeli defence forces and the higher bureaucrats of the Histadrut's main industrial complexes. For all these reasons a state of affairs had developed by the late sixties in which, as a local wag put it, 'the State and the Histadrut get generals for managers; private firms must put up with lieutenants and majors'. In other words, the prussianization of Israel – a thing dreaded for many years by liberal politicians and theorists in the country – had started to become a fact, an inevitable fact given the sociological and military situation of the Jewish State. In fact, each time a general or colonel passed from active to reserve duty, the new managerial class was automatically strengthened.

This is more than a sociological phenomenon: it is also a social problem. The new managers, the 'officers in business suits', have brought not only efficiency and cool-headedness to their tasks; they have also brought the preconceptions of former military men: the belief that the interests of (Zionist) society come before the welfare of the individual citizen or organization; an authoritarian attitude towards labour; impatience with the often muddled and inefficient democratic processes of law and policy.

More serious than this, however, is the fact that a class has been created which has concentrated an unusual slice of power in its hands. This class, whose conceptions are clearly authoritarian and politically right-wing, is in the ascendance. Without a radical structural change in Israel's economic and ideological set-up there is no hope of checking its influence in the foreseeable future. Thus the prussianization of Israel is the result not only of the continued siege by neighbouring pan-Arab countries; but also and inevitably of the social, war-induced stratification of Israel.

In a sense it is wrong to talk of Israeli military characteristics as 'Prussian', even though striking similarities exist between the Germany of Bismarck's day and after and the Israel of today. In both countries the territorial problem was a main source of national inspiration – and frustration. In both countries the upper echelons of the armed forces became the ideal of manhood, although in quite differing ways. Both countries suffered crushing traumas, which led to the 'Encirclement Syndrome', and, indeed, were also surrounded by hostile nations and dependent for their continued existence as countries on expansion or integration with quite alien concepts and national personalities. In both countries the officers of the army were a privileged class, assured not only of economic privileges but of a place at the top of society as their natural right. Finally, both countries, in their respective times, were passing through the stage of acquiring a strong proud national consciousness.

But there are considerable differences. The Prussian officer caste was bred from a brew of robber-barons, settler-aristocrats, and other hereditary aristocrats, jealous of their feudal privileges and trying to maintain these privileges in the new, imperialistic phase of their country. The Israeli officer's background is more relaxed. He is a native development, a mixture of British cool-headedness, Russian partisan spirit, settler's guile and self-sufficiency. His origins are socially and ethnically mixed (although the percentage of Western-parented senior officers is higher than that of officers from an Oriental background). And if any social factor predominates in this caste, it is birth or education in an agricultural settlement, the Kibbutz or the Moshav. The Israeli officer's brand of Prussianism is a middle-class, popular one; a modern development which can be paralleled, up to a point, in the USSR or in post-Nasser Egypt.

This may need some explanation for those emotionally conditioned against the Soviet Union or the UAR. The development of an officer-caste is not a modern phenomenon. Such a caste existed in ancient Babylon, for instance, and in almost every primitive society from the troglodytes onwards. But in the theocratic and aristocratic phases of human history, whether feudal or imperial, the soldier-leader was subordinated to the traditional, religious, hereditary or feudal leader. Whenever the fighting leader's greater force or deeper intelligence caused him to grasp the reins of civil power – as was bound to happen from time to time – the rule remained dynastic. The dictator took on the role of king or caesar instead of abolishing the hereditary ruling class.

Modern fascism and USSR communism evolved in a different, 'democratic', or rather popular pattern – in the sense of marshalling its power-reserves from among the people's ranks and rejecting dynastic leadership. Natural charisma and popular identification with a mass-symbol replaced the mixture of religious feeling and social idolatry which was, up to a point, the psychological basis of monarchy. Thus the way was opened wide for the rule of naked power, unhampered by traditions or pretexts. The commissar, the bureaucrat, and the war-lord could govern without becoming kings or hereditary rulers. With the growth of twentieth-century society, and with education becoming much more widely spread than in the past, this was in fact inevitable. The absolute rule of tradition was at an end. The rule of opportunity had begun.

When the 'underdeveloped' countries became relatively free from direct imperialist involvement, it was only be to expected that real democracy should not evolve. Indeed, democracy had only the slimmest chance of evolving in such emotionally blighted, economically underdeveloped and culturally subjugated areas of the world as the former colonies and mandates. Whether the institutions of parliamentary democracy existed or not in these countries, they had no practical context in the life of an underdeveloped land. The army, on the other hand, as the only organized, trained, relatively efficient and always powerful element (controlling, as it did, weaponry and intelligence), had an evident role to play. The military bureaucrat emerged as the most vital, and in sociological terms the most 'progressive' force in society.

The warrior had the advantage of a living standard assured him by a society which also gave him such disproportionate autocratic power, and this freed his intellectual potential and his dynamism for other, more sophisticated purposes. They were as often as not political – that is, civilian. Moreover, he had that ultimate luxury of the modern society: freedom of action in all fields. He just had to use this power for non-military purposes.

That an authoritarian, military-trained mind is much more prone to miscarriages of justice, not to speak of the stifling of popular government, did nothing to change the fact: the men nearest to physical power and best trained for decision and action were almost always the ones to take power in underdeveloped areas and formerly foreign-oppressed countries.

In the Arab countries, where the degree of popular education and of Western-intellectual sophistication is comparatively small, the rule of the armed élite has become the obvious gambit of all revolutionary thinkers of the area, from Egypt's late Gamal Abd-El-Nasser to the Baath Party's theoretician, Michael Aflak. In spite of their talk about 'popular' revolutions, even such Marxist-Leninist revolutionaries as the Palestinians' PFLP's Georges Habash and Nayef Hawatmeh of the Democratic Front for the Liberation of Palestine have had to acknowledge the necessity of creating paramilitary cliques, 'revolutionary leaderships'.

In Israel the same thing has happened, although in a quite different manner, appropriate to the very different sociological background. Among all men, but among Jews in particular, there is a need for a small nucleus which stops thinking in abstractions and starts acting according to realistic, if subjective, premises. The Zionist revolution was altruistic and utopian in its beginnings. It produced a Zionist Establishment which was fat, self-satisfied and illogical, and which took its basic ideological premises as holy writ, never to be doubted. To keep things running, men had to appear who while paying lip-service to ideas or ideals, acted on practical assumptions. Without them the country could not have survived in the face of pan-Arab attacks and in a continued isolation which was at the same time self-chosen and imposed from the outside. A structured fighting army is the best possible cadre for realists. In Israel in the 1950s and 1960s it was also essential to evolve one. Militarism was not only an ideal, as in Prussia (in fact, it became an ideal only gradually and against the wish of most old-time utopian Zionists), but a sociological necessity.

On the other hand, the tightly knit chain of command, the day-to-day decisions, and above all the actual life-and-death fighting cured these professional warriors, up to a point, of the sickness of power endemic in more parasitic ruling classes. An

Israeli officer's career is short and fraught with peril. His chances of death are high. As long as he is in full-time active service, he has little opportunity of becoming a parasite. As one Israeli humorist puts it: 'A military dictatorship of really fighting soldiers has at least this to be said for it – some of them get killed.'

It should be stressed that in the early seventies Israel has not yet become a military dictatorship by any means. For one thing, the newly created military-bureaucrat class is still subordinate to the Zionist government, the 'old men cabinets' of David Ben-Gurion (in his seventies when he abdicated), Levi Eshkol (in his seventies at his death in office), and Golda Meir (in her seventies at the peak of her rule). But the military-bureaucrat class does have an unusual amount of power and enjoys much prestige and many advantages.

In the degeneration of a society founded on idealistic goals it is quite incapable of attaining, the army remains the only 'clean', moral and open-minded element. Parliament is neutralized. Economic life is largely parasitic or exploitative. The courts are hamstrung by the lack of a constitution with teeth and the automatic 'guillotine' overruling of the petrified, Labour-controlled Knesset. Education is Jewish-orientated. Police and administration are autocratic. The meagre free press is fighting for its life. In such a society all national and social life suffers. A group of men working on false assumptions, deluding themselves that they are keeping alive the 'character' of the country – which events have irrevocably changed long ago – are in danger of committing sociological suicide. In extreme cases the danger becomes reality. And if one hesitates to mention in this context the more extreme cases, such as Nazi Germany, one cannot but see striking similarities between such diverse countries as Russia in 1917, Congo in the 1960s, and Israel in the early 1970s.

For those trying to stop the rot, the problem is always the same: where to find a nucleus of men free of the corroding disease of degenerate power. Such a nucleus is often found where power is used freely and without calculation, and sometimes in the most amazing situations. During the Algerian War, for instance, while part of the French high command (and its civilian political masters) were rotten to the core, some of the actual fighters, the *paras* and their officers, developed on the battlefield a strange kind of honour. Although their code, based on pride and responsibility, permitted dreadful excesses – torture, killing and oppression – they held in contempt those officers who could be suborned or who used cruelty for private purposes. To do violence from motives of military expediency was right. To use it for private purposes was despicable, in the eyes of these latter-day *condottieri*. No wonder, then, that so many of them found kindred spirits – *des purs et durs* – among their interrogators and indoctrinators in the communist concentration camps of Indo-China where they had served before coming to Algeria. Indeed, the whole conduct of the Algerian campaign reflected an 'infection' caught by French officers in Indo-China, an infection of the kind which crosses frontiers and gives fighting enemies the predominant psychological characteristics of those who fire at them from the other side.

In the Israeli army, for all the sophisticated differences of the society it comes from, similarities have developed with the behaviour of the 'pure hard' *paras* in Algeria on one hand and with the attitudes of the 'young officers' of Nasser's revolt on the other. The differences are basic, of course. Because the links in the chain of command of Tzahal are tighter than those of the French army in Algeria, and because no vast geographical distance has to be crossed, the army itself as well as its General Command remains pure and hard, up to a point. Authoritarianism and corruption are usually swept upwards to where they can develop naturally in the spheres of political and economic power: the government, the political parties, the bureaucrats, the economic mechanism for distributing incoming foreign money, and the all-powerful, all-encompassing syndicalist trade-union complex.

This may help to explain why Tzahal is the only thoroughly efficient organism in the whole of the State. The parties, economic organizations, trade unions, government bureaux and ministries are all not only inclined to corruption and favouritism, but also bureaucratic, sluggish and inefficient.

Signs of degeneration have appeared inside the army too, but again and again this amazing organism has defended itself against them. For instance, over twenty years an administrative apparatus, the military government, has been developed inside Israel for the repression of Israeli Palestinians. Nominally subordinated to Tzahal, it is in fact controlled by the Shin Beit and the higher civilian bureaucrats of the Ministry of Defence and the Prime Minister's Office. When Tzahal took over the West Bank of the Jordan, the General Command gave express orders that military government experts were *not* to be employed as governors of the occupied cities. 'We do not want "rulers"',* one High Command officer is said to have protested. So the Chief of Staff took directly from their armoured cars and from the positions they had conquered the best fighting officers he had, young dynamic 'centurions', presumably 'cleansed by blood and fire', and made them serve as proconsuls of Nablus, Jenin, Gaza and other towns. As it turned out, this policy was successful, in the first phase of Israeli occupation, although it was of course unable to prevent the normal evolution of rebellion, repression and further bloodshed.

In the final analysis, while the politico-economic organisms of the Israeli State are basically parasitic, the army is essential. Indeed it is *the* essential infrastructure of Israeli life. While the State of Israel lives on funds coming from afar, the army is only partially and indirectly affected by them: only as far as approval of the military budget is concerned (a foregone conclusion) or the sociological and class motivations of the military leadership. It has been known for generals and colonels to tour the U S for money for Israel, but there is no serious involvement of the active-duty army superstructure – and even less of the huge popular infrastructure – in the sources of the country's parasitism.

Tzahal stands like a sturdy tree planted in meagre soil. Its roots have not withered. Considered dispassionately, the reason is obvious: of all the nation's organisms, Tzahal alone has clear-cut goals, of which its leaders are consciously aware, and a clear-cut framework enabling it to function at all times; and it must

* *Moshlanim*, in Israeli slang.

succeed – or perish. If the army should fail but once, the Jewish State will collapse.

In spite of deep and sincere grief for the fallen, neither the Arab nor the Israeli leaders really want peace. The Arabs need war and an enemy to salve their broken spirits, and some of them need it to try and create a united, racialist, pan-Arab nation. And the Israelis need war in order to keep a parasitic society going, in the framework of their old, exclusivist Jewish identity. For the Israeli soldier, matters are much simpler. He has always had recourse to the fact that he was 'only obeying orders', that the political issues were decided, blessedly, somewhere above him, in the corridors of political and economic power. Even when he has actively intervened – as some officers have – he has been able to put on the hat of an adviser, counselling those who hold the reins of power so that they can decide the ideological goals for which he and his men are willing to die.

Moreover, as a 'practical man' the army officer can reflect that it is war and a continuous state of national emergency which has developed the country's armoured fists, its economy and its technological expertise. More cynically but no less realistically, he can tell himself that, since civilian bureaucrats are inefficient and often corrupt, all Israel would suffer if real peace came and emergency military rule over so many fields of civilian endeavour had to end.

There are any amount of reasons why war should cheerfully be accepted by the army as something bound to go on almost indefinitely. 'There will be peace – some day', is the most the country hopes for, and this equivocally expressed wish is reflected throughout everyday life and in every sphere of development.

So while enjoying, perhaps unconsciously, the fruits of war and military power, the armed Israeli warrior reveals himself to be a second cousin to the Prussian officer. Equally he shows himself related to the nineteenth-century anarchists: his experience 'proves' to him that only the work of violence is moral and clean.

On a more personal level, the Israeli career officer's interests demand that the situation should continue in the pattern of events up to 1970. His standard of living, his power and his chances of promotion in either the civilian or the military superstructure of the country depend on war. Even if he does not consciously admit such a motive for being a 'hawk', there is no doubt that the personal element influences his natural thinking. The ring closes, the negative sides of belief-inspired and class interests interlock, and the emergence of a war-economy influenced by an officer caste, on its way to replace the 'old men' of the Zionist bureaucracy, becomes a fact.

This is illustrated in another development of the Jewish character. As pressure made intellectuals out of despised pedlars in the Ghettoes of medieval and Renaissance Europe, so now in Israel pressure creates a new type of super-efficient Spartan.

It is too early to make a prognosis of the future militarization of Israeli political power. But there are some signs that the rule of formerly exploited colonial countries by a military caste is not fortuitous nor, as has been thought, only the inevitable result of their being left underdeveloped. Perhaps these countries are precursors of a global trend? The army-bureaucrats seem to be taking over from the political bureaucrats as the latter did, before them, from the non-technocratic capitalists.

17 The Racialism of Belief

Why did a democratic-minded people like the Jews and a liberal-revolutionary movement such as early Zionism bring about a situation charged with so much pain and grief? Can we analyse this development simply in terms of socio-economic evolution? Or must we dig deeper and try to discover how a group, a social entity, behaves in the face of danger?

To answer these questions, indeed to understand the Israeli-Palestinian confrontation at all, we must learn first how *not* to look at the events which have juxtaposed two mutually exclusive beliefs: Jewish Zionism and pan-Arab nationalism. We must not, for instance, look for a 'right' side or a 'wrong' side. Neither must we consider the problem in terms of 'inalienable rights' or 'national rights'. We must ignore what I like to call the 'diabolic theory of history', by which an arch-enemy – a class enemy, an alien enemy from beyond the borders, or a home-grown traitor – is blamed for all the evils of a country.

This is the view adopted, up to a point, by nationalists, by Marxist internationalists, and, in the Middle East conflict, by both pan-Arabists and Zionists: a view justified in their eyes by such undeniable facts as that the Versailles peace treaty bled Germany white after the First World War; that capitalism and imperialism exploit the proletariat at home and abroad; that the Omayyads, Abbasids, Fatimids and Ayyubids fell because of their enemies; that the tribes of Moses had to fight off all other indigenous tribes; and that the Jews of the Diaspora were cruelly persecuted by Christians and Moslems alike, before being almost totally exterminated in Europe by National Socialist racialism.

Beyond question injustice exists and so do the unjust: the

enemy is not a fiction. But this highly selective view of who is guilty ignores several things about the human condition. To begin with, it confines itself to the evil done by a specific group, nation or class to no less specific victims. Secondly, it fails to take into account the chain reaction of evil whereby an oppressed people tends either to return violence for violence or to pass on the oppression it suffers to a victim weaker than itself.

Most importantly, this analysis ignores the fact that human society cannot be held altogether responsible for its actions, being unfit to plead. Since society does not operate rationally – whether in pursuit of 'good' or 'evil' objects, whether oppressing or oppressed – it must be considered insane.

Many profound thinkers have shrugged away the importance of 'psychologism', taking irrational behaviour to be the exception to the rule. But more important than reason in prompting the behaviour of societies are the basic drives of human nature, among which one of the most powerful is fear. Rationally man should be able to live with his fellow men. Yet rarely has the history of the world shown a peaceful meshing of tribes and cultures which have come in contact with one another, a sharing of property and experience. Why is this so? The answer, I believe, should be sought in fear of the stranger. Unfamiliar behaviour, a foreign language, appearance at variance with 'our' standards all contribute to the conviction that 'they' are not, to put it in extreme terms, wholly human.

Modern social thinking including Marxism-Leninism, the main theory of social upheaval of the last two centuries, has no place for fear as a *source* of human action. For these 'materialists', that is, pragmatists hoping to discover that effective action is identical with universal law, fear must surely be a result, not a cause. Were they to revise their thinking to take account of fear, they would arrive at an unworkable theory of revolution. Yet fear is part of the defensive equipment of the 'territorial animal' which is man. From the moment man gave himself territorial rights, and particularly since he developed means of production which he could exploit himself, he has known fear for his possessions and the need to keep others away from his land. It is this fear which set tribe against tribe through history and which lies at the root of nationalism and racialism today. In the light of this truth it is not the exploited but the exploiters, whether they wear the mask of capitalism, of bureaucracy, or of feudalism, who are seen to be the most basic irrational expression of humanity itself.

It is not merely economic interests, however, which are protected by fear but – perhaps more importantly – the identity of a group, tribe or nation. Even when economic interests conflict, assimilation of a conquered or migrating group into an established society is possible, so long as the group is prepared to relinquish its identity. If, on the other hand, it succeeds in maintaining its own language, culture and, above all, beliefs, there can be no assimilation and, in all probability, the stronger party will attempt to exterminate, subjugate, exclude or at least exploit the weaker.

Antiquity provides many examples. So today do the immigration laws of, for instance, Britain or the approach to 'foreigners' of both Islam and Judaism. But the urge to separateness characterizes not only the majority: the wish of the minority – Asian immigrants in Britain, Arabs in Israel, Christians and Jews in Arab countries – to remain separate should not be underestimated. Like the exploiting majority, the exploited minority resists change because it fears a loss of essence, of identity. (It is observable that human pride focuses less on an individual's 'real' qualities of youth, beauty, health, intelligence or creative powers than on what he feels he is – a member of a sect, group, community, nation or race.) Fear is the safeguard ensuring 'we' remain separate from 'them', the compulsive emotion which overcomes the lesser fear of death as it overcomes ethical scruple, permitting 'us' to attack 'them' with a good conscience and despoil them of their land, their possessions, the fruits of their labour.

This brings us to the question of identity. What gives a group its identity? What makes it feel itself a social unit separate from all others?

Common possession of land and common economic interests

are indubitably factors contributing to common identity; but no less important are common patterns of behaviour, whose function it is both to express group identity and, by way of the indoctrination of the young, to guarantee that identity's survival. This indoctrination, usually called education, is not a rational thing, programmed to supply what a child's personal experiences or natural faculties demand. Instead it is based on the experiences of past generations, on what the older generation 'knows' to be 'true', on the religious – that is, irrational and undemonstrable – codes of the group. Derived from a distant past, a society's lore and culture no longer meet the demands of the present but, bolstered by repressive laws, become a constriction preventing change, a rotting bandage infecting healthy growth.

Thus, driven by fear of hunger and uncertainty, society supports itself on the irrational props of 'culture' and 'religion' (or irrational behaviour and unsubstantiated belief), and in the process becomes ever madder as the real needs of its members move ever further from what their patterns of behaviour and belief provide.

Belief, the acceptance of the unprovable, cannot be dismissed merely as a tool of social manipulation developed by ruling castes to keep the masses in subjection (though it is that as well). Basically it would seem to be a response to humanity's need for security in a hostile world. But in the context of social evolution its important function is the division it makes between 'us', the believers, the sons of the One True Church or the Children of the Chosen People, and 'them', the infidels. In this way, religious identification tends initially to be racialist, in that, as one element in the unholy trinity of religion, language and culture, it 'keeps a group together' by making it feel different from and better than all others. Thus it was in primitive societies such as Palestine in 1500 B.C., and thus later in sophisticated ones like those of feudal Europe or of the world of Islam. It would seem that the urge to maintain cultural, religious and linguistic separateness is, like racialism, a basic prop of irrational social behaviour, a means to ensure that society does not change too much.

Exiled by the Babylonian conquest, the people of Israel

learned to adapt its belief to a new purpose: the preservation of a separate society in circumstances which deprived it of political power. But in spite of the efforts to remain aloof, many 'foreign' elements crept into the linquistics and ethics of Judaism. When the fall of Babylon allowed the exiles to return to their Holy Land in 387 B.C., their leaders Ezra and Nehemiah understood that they would have to rely on belief to consolidate once more a separate Jewish identity. The parts of the Torah, or Law, which should become Scripture were carefully selected, on principles well expressed by the Rev. James Parkes, a pro-Zionist Christian: 'The books chosen emphasized the perpetual paradox of Judaism, a particularism which fenced in a particular discipline of life for a single people, and an ethical monotheism of universal significance by which it could be developed.'* In other words: an instrument of belief was developed which not only maintained the separate survival of a given group, but which was also to serve to justify other irrational beliefs and separatist approaches to life.

For the first time religion became an advanced social tool in the hands of the leadership of a group or nation. Parkes explains how it was done: 'The technique was twofold: the religious education already described, and the establishment of the synagogue, providing a centre for regular worship wherever a Jewish community existed. Its combination of prayer, praise and teaching has formed the basis of both church and mosque.'†

We see, then, that the preservation of obsolete laws and precepts was not achieved by the codification of belief alone, but also by the invention of indoctrination. For the first time a systematic link between teaching (the giving of information to the younger generation) and forcing it to believe (forbidding evaluation of the information given) was forged – hopefully to iron out among the young any wrinkle of independent thought or behaviour.

The pattern was set. It was to become that of all monotheistic

*James Parkes, *Whose Land? A History of the Peoples of Palestine*, Penguin Books, 1970, p. 27.

†ibid.

systems, or simplified irrational beliefs in external guidance. Christianity, Islam, Judaism, Dialectical Materialism with its irrational belief in history as predictable, all of them identified education and indoctrination, proclaimed the 'only truth' in their teaching, established places of worship and spiritual enlightenment which were also centres of indoctrination and control. Nationalism too has used schools and churches for its own consolidation; and while it has usually relied on an already existing religion to control the masses, it has at times reached peaks of hysterical conservatism which were (in practice if not in essence) in themselves religious.

With time a rule of thumb developed: the more restrictive a political regime, the tighter the coordination between belief and education. National Socialism reached an apex of irrationality – murderously insane not only in its practices but in its very beliefs. And National Socialism was an ideology which started indoctrination in the kindergarten and ended it in the grave.

But it would be a mistake to see National Socialism as an insane exception to 'sane' humanity. We are all, to a more or less microscopic extent, Nazis. The extremes of National Socialism were simply peaks of a madness which is apparent in all societies: for all societies are ruled by belief, not by analytic logic unfettered by compulsive emotions.

The coupling of indoctrination and communication has been historically disastrous in that it limits the free development of human intellect and endeavour. But in the short term it has generally proved extremely effective. A group convinced it has guidance and is right is more likely to succeed in its military and social programmes. It simply has more stamina and courage, and its brains work better in finding solutions to immediate problems. This, by the way, may help to explain why military thinking, effective under stress in battle, is totally dehumanized in peace – an apparent contradiction which resolves itself when the dialectics of short-term and long-term human activity are contrasted: what is good for the achievement of an immediate goal is usually bad for the attainment of the next stage of development of the individual or the group.

To sum up: Belief creates the socio-psychological conditions necessary for the perpetuation of a separate group or national 'identity'. Besides supplying matter for indoctrination, and thus becoming the kingpin of the mechanism of perpetuation of madness, belief serves a number of purposes in a separatist group, nation, tribe or class:

(a) It provides justification for separateness which never requires definition, belief being indefinable and unprovable.

(b) It provides a pretext for ruthlessness, the ethical justification of non-ethical or anti-social behaviour.

(c) It makes unnecessary the reappraisal in practical terms of a given policy, belief in external guidance, in the deity, in fate and in the need for separateness being quite outside any logical frame of reference.

(d) It permits the separatist to feel he is something special and as opposed to 'them', somewhat more than merely human.

Thus belief is the perfect tool of racialism – which is really only an extreme expression of man's irrational fear of being submerged in a wider identity. The conflict between the individual and the mass, between the victim and his oppressors, between the foreigner subjected to slavery and the owner of the land he tills – this conflict finds expression in belief, the bastard child of fear. Only by eliminating the 'natural' reaction of an individual or a society to archaic fear will men reach the stage at which they can act in accordance with a logical appraisal of their situation and not in obedience to the half-unconscious dictates of a long irrelevant past.

*

For social purposes belief needs a repository, some politico-religious leadership which 'translates' the wishes of the deity into comprehensible political goals selected to ensure the continued existence of the religious 'national' group. At the primitive level of human history, this repository tends at first to consist of both the holder of temporal power and the priest at his side who interprets belief and sanctifies his lord's divinely inspired actions. In the next stage, monarchism, the king tends to seize religious power for himself, to add to the temporal power he already possesses; a development which usually marks a period of consolidation when the purely conquering warlord or purely revolutionary leader is replaced by a ruler of undisputed territory or by the forces of revolution triumphant.

The emergence of the king-priest would seem to be the result of the evolution from small tribe to bigger nation, when the people loses contact with its lord or shaman and is obliged to identify with an abstract entity. Belief in an unseen deity has to be extended to an unseen, or almost never seen, ruler, and the ruler like the deity is invested with sacred significance, a symbol of the community.

At the time of the prophets or of King David, Jewish society operated this system admirably – not because the Israelites differed in essentials from neighbouring communities, each of which similarly had its deities and its politico-religious leadership, but because, possessing in the Torah a more sensible and more elaborate code of precepts, the Tribes of Israel wasted less time in doubt and apostasy and could thus concentrate on consolidating themselves on the foundation of their religion into a nation united against all comers. So, from primitive religious precepts which were a little more progressive and functional than those of their neighbours, the Children of Israel gathered the force to create one of the most thoroughgoing theocracies of antiquity.

There were of course power struggles between the purely religious leadership of the prophets and the politico-religious leadership of the monarchy. But on the whole the arrangement worked remarkably well to preserve an imperialist kingdom, charged by its beliefs to consolidate its religious rule over the biggest territory then imaginable, 'from the sea to the desert', in Yehova's words to Abraham.

Over the course of time the belief-theocracy of the Jews was slowly giving way to a plain absolutist, God-protected monarchy, and it was just their bad luck that Roman imperialism sent them into a second exile before the process was completed, thus leaving them encumbered for two thousand years with the ideological baggage of religious-temporal duality (a duality which, inherited by Christianity, did much harm to Western society as a whole until the age of capitalism relegated religion to a subordinate role). Up to the twentieth century Jewish society remained fixed at this stage of development, still honouring the glories of the Kingdom of David and of the Temple of Yehova as its symbols of nationhood, still bound to a territory it no longer possessed by the belief which identified that territory, and the Jews' possession of it, with heavenly salvation.

In exile the Jewish communities were obliged to shed their leadership, substituting for the king-priest the Rabbi, or teacher, who was neither a priest nor the possessor of much temporal power, but the repository of belief and wisdom, the educator and indoctrinator; and as such he was of greater usefulness to this landless people than king, or priest, or prophet. As a class, the Rabbis remained on the whole 'sane'; the power they did not have could not compound the insanity resulting from hereditary belief.

The more insecure a class, group or nation, the greater will be its reliance on belief. The further that belief is removed from the beliefs of other men, the greater will be the group's emphasis on honour, or duty towards its beliefs. So it was with the Jews of the Diaspora, sustained as a distinct people through centuries of persecution, exploitation and national isolation by belief; and the life experienced outside the Promised Land ensured total belief, total adherence.

A group belonging to a 'God-given' country, held together by a 'God-given' doctrine, living in expectation of a 'God-sent' Messiah, and basing its culture on these beliefs could neither integrate with the societies surrounding it nor win its liberation from oppression on any terms other than those its beliefs dictated. The dual belief in the coming of the Messiah, son of King David, and in the return to the Promised Land precluded a national revolution which would restore to the Jews as individuals a sane and independent life. For uncounted generations the Land of Israel – the basic ingredient of all Jewish prayers, songs, legends and lore – was the only way out. To liberate themselves they needed the New Jerusalem.

The other side of this separatist coin was that the Jews became oppression-prone. It may have been their rootlessness which first kindled in the ideologically and emotionally well-rooted communities amid which they lived the spark of anti-Semitic distrust – the atavistic fear of the cave-dweller confronted by a wanderer trespassing on his territory. Once kindled, the fire was fed with the faggots of religious intolerance, economic exploitation and semantic incomprehension. Moreover, Judaism came to serve as a small-scale but quite accurate mirror of what Christianity could ethically have remained, had it not chosen instead to become an instrument of exploitation, ignorance and terror (as Judaism would itself have become if it had remained a state religion; as indeed it is becoming in Israel today). Religious intolerance, the force which crystallized Western belief-based society, could not co-exist with Judaism. The Jews had to become Judas, 'the betrayers', the hated and despised, if the threat to Christianity's monopoly rule were to be eliminated. Thus, surrounded by alien beliefs and hostile political forces, but stiffened by their own mystic lore, the Jews survived in their separateness, bereft of power, land, or any means of production particular to themselves, a nation in a vacuum.

However, weakened first by capitalism, the role of belief as the main conscious prop of the societies in which the Jews dwelt was finally ousted by the mechanical facts of the industrial revolution. The scene was set for rapid and radical change.

As long as the Jews as a comprehensive whole continued to believe that the Messiah – mounted, according to the popular eastern-Jewish legend, on a white ass – would lead them back in triumph to the Promised Land, they remained a defeated people. But swept along by the storm of change around them, towards the end of the nineteenth century the Children of Israel saw their double goal begin to fade, thus making vital a re-evaluation of their national aim and heralding the Zionist revolution. The white ass was pushed aside by history, and instead of the Messiah appeared a bearded non-believer, Theodor Herzl.

18 Youth and the Future

Although there is not a single political group, in the early seventies, which could take the initiative for the separation of Israel from its Jewish heritage and beliefs, and for the total integration of Israelis and Palestinians, there is something far more significant going on – a generation gap which is fast becoming the partial insurrection of a whole generation. And by this, a truly younger generation is meant: boys and girls under eighteen years of age in the 1973 war.

The Israeli set-up makes the usual Western 'student unrest' a thing unknown in this country. A Zionist-socialist leader once said: 'We do not have time for a students' revolt. At the age when other young people are throwing stones at the police, our young men are at the Suez Canal or on the Golan Heights.' This is accurate – but not the whole story. The truth of the matter is that Israeli students, as a body, are one of the most reactionary elements in the country. At the same time some of the middle-echelon army men are to be counted among the most progressive, and practical-minded, Israelis.

The army man is faced with daily realities and necessities but he does not have to fight for his basic needs: home, food, the usual comforts, transport, health insurance – all these are provided by the State. Even his family is taken care of, should he fall in battle. He can, then, afford to be mildly critical, at times – as long as his criticism is unrelated to the war.

The student, on the other hand, is either fighting two months a year in the reserves, or has just completed three years of army duty. He is cynical, knows the political Establishment to be 'impregnable' to new ideas, and furthermore sees only exclusivist Arab forces on the other side of the border. He also knows that upon completing his studies he will have a good deal of useful knowledge and a position which will be almost automatically allotted to him by the manpower-hungry Establishment. He will have the two necessary attributes: knowledge and Jewishness. In the natural course of events he will be allowed to take his place among the élite of this small country.

Politically, the Israeli student has been indoctrinated from earliest childhood on. He thus reaches his conclusions, out of his own vested interests but without real knowledge or personal experience of the social and military roots of the conflict upon which his society is based. His future, his economic interests and past military indoctrination all tend to add up and force him to ignore 'dangerous' facts such as racialist exclusivety and perennial war. He concludes that the most important thing is to find himself a comfortable niche in the war-ridden, but for him economically easy, set-up.

In the West and the industrialized East, the young worker and the student can afford to tear down society. They know that by so doing the floodgates are not open, and their country will live on. They are, on the other hand, not precisely unaware of the abstract danger of death, upon entering a confrontation with the hostile social framework, but, rather, feel this danger to be rather far-fetched. When some of them are, for instance, killed by police during a demonstration indignation is enormous: an accident has occurred, or rather a murder, not a killing on the front lines, which is a 'normal' occurrence at war. Moreover, they are certainly unafraid of dying as a group, class or nation. In short, they can afford to play the Russian roulette of revolution.

The Israeli students' revolver has six chambers loaded. He cannot afford to play the game. He has also used up most of his stamina in war. He has very likely killed. Emotionally, he 'knows' that only a purely Jewish state can save his existence and that of the community he lives in. He 'knows' the other side is waiting to kill him. He therefore directs his bitterness and hatred of injustice – an inherent part of any young human, before he is brutalized by pain and conditioned by environment – towards the enemy who tries to kill him, and his family, and his people, and in fact his whole country. A similar thing happens to the young Israeli worker, usually of Oriental origin. Only there, cynism and awareness are replaced by simple fear and the satisfaction of having someone still lower to tread upon.

A conflict is thus created between the basic intelligence of the young Israeli and the socio-economic conditions in which he lives. This contradictory set of circumstances cannot endure. Water finds its level, and seeps through the dyke or circumvents it. A process was accordingly becoming apparent in Israel of the 1970s similar to what happened in France after the failure of the 1968 Paris revolt. Since the students and the other young men of post-military age cannot revolt, the violent opposition to death and pain, to injustice and 'tragic destiny', or, as the Israeli Establishment puts it, to a situation 'where there is no choice' passes on to an even younger generation. Where the students fail miserably if understandably, as men and as Israelis, the high-school generation takes up the fight before it has been mentally castrated, before its capacity for independent evaluation has been cancelled by three years of military life and the hope for a niche ensuring social well-being.

Nevertheless, a students' Left wing, of sorts, has started to emerge. It is led by radical new immigrants from the US and Latin American countries, who gained, in 1972, control of the Haifa Students' Union and weekly. A spontaneous movement of high-school protest also began to emerge in 1968, and later became a driving and turbulence-creating force. It was politically conscious and lucid – much more lucid, in fact, than the older radicals it sometimes imitated and from whom it occasionally took ideas without, however, parroting them blindly. This movement was unexpected, city-bred, and articulate. It started by cutting itself off from everybody, from the Right and the Left, from the ISO and from Avnery's movement; and, of course, from the Zionist socialists. It adopted sentiments and ideas from all of them but, after making its selection, mixed these ideas into a heady formula of anarchism, determination to have peace and the wish for complete, free, and non-puritanical expression. It was, in short, a truly original, truly generational phenomenon.

The first strong and organized blow was delivered by a group of high-school students who wrote to Prime Minister Golda Meir, in the spring of 1970, stating that her decision not to accept an offer by the Jewish World Congress leader, Dr Nahum Goldmann, to negotiate with Abd-El-Nasser some possibility of compromise 'jeopardized our wish not to serve in the Israel Defence Forces'. Some sixty boys and girls, aged from sixteen to seventeen – that is, due for military service the year after – protested against the government's refusal even to try to contemplate peace.

The Establishment reacted as one single man. The high-school dissidents were hounded violently. Throughout the country, in schools, schoolmasters went from pupil to pupil, trying to force them to retract. Other schoolmasters signed up, in their classrooms, thousands of other high-school youngsters under the watchful eye of their principals. The students were forced to sign documents pledging their eternal allegiance to Israel's security.

The whole press set upon these 'senseless rebels'. In their schools, the protesters were isolated, even spat upon. Deputy Prime Minister, and Minister for Education and Culture, Yigal Allon, commanded some of the boys and girls to come to his office and tried, personally, to convince them of the error of their ways.

Two further incidents of similar character but producing a more limited response happened when the relatives of two famous leaders made known their anti-extremist viewpoints. One of them was the actor Assaf Dayan, Moshe Dayan's own son, then in his twenties, who declared in May 1970: 'I would be glad if we could hurry as much as possible and return all the occupied territories, Jerusalem and the Golan Heights included . . . this is a price we must pay for a true peace.'

The grandson of Itzhak Sadeh, one of the leaders of the Palmach shock-troops, whose memory is still venerated by Kibbutz-members in Israel, wrote in *Haaretz* in April of that same year: ' . . . There is no escape from the conclusion – hard to swallow, it is true – that the Israeli government does not want peace. This is a terrible, eye-opening and painful conclusion . . .

I cry out because all of a sudden the moral foundations of being an Israeli have been ripped from under our feet. They have been ripped away in a way that does not allow us to close our eyes to the true facts ... the concept "Israeli" has changed, with a sound like thunder on a clear day. We are no longer on the right side of the fence. We are in complicity. This is a bitter moment like none before it.'

The 1971 high-school students were repeatedly active in street-fighting with the police, when demonstrations were called by Siah, Matzpen, Avnery's movement, the Israeli League for Human Rights, and the Committee for Peace and Security. They went – and were beaten up – regardless of the body which organized the protests. They started digging conscientiously in Zionist history, which in a totally insipid and slanted form, is pushed down pupils' throats in Israeli classrooms.

In February and March 1971 high-school pupils also participated in demonstrations against Israeli brutality in the conquered town of Gaza, where women had been stripped, houses sacked when searched, and men beaten up and sent to the hospital by the 'Green Berets' of the Israeli Border Police. In March they demonstrated again in favour of the newly organized 'Black Panther' movement of Israeli 'Black Jews', or Oriental-born youngsters from the slums of Jerusalem. This movement, at once helped on its way and encouraged by Matzpen, was totally spontaneous, understood to keep its independence from other political formations, and took a leaf from the book of the underprivileged American black slum-communities. In 1972 they fought in protest against the expulsion of Bedouin tribes from the southern Pithat-Rafiah area.

All this activity was prepared, in 1968 – by the publication of a whole series of 'underground' magazines edited in the high schools of Tel-Aviv and Jerusalem by independent-minded pupils. Mimeographed pamphlets, bearing esoteric names, carried out a frontal attack on all the values and beliefs of the Establishment up to and including – in a very cautious way – the hallowed defence and army complex. Not only society, the 'set-up' and the party hacks were the objects of these attacks. 'Rabble rule of a blind and fanatical majority' was attacked in *Gaashush*; while the companion-copy of *Naashush* had this to say to its young readers: 'You, the young man who is aware of today's problems – get on your feet and protest! Come out against the idiot leadership which in its profound dumbness has brought us to where we are today. Stop!'

A more personal note was taken by one eighteen-year-old journalist who wrote: 'Israel has fought, in the past, three major wars – in 1948, 1956 and 1967. In all three of them the whole people fought. The (Suez Canal) war of attrition is the first war fought mainly by boys aged 18 to 21.'

The high-school 'underground press' is not submitted to military censorship and deals liberally with sex, education and hashish-smoking, besides its concern with politics. In this sense, it is influenced by the US and British underground press. Its main importance is in the fact that now in Israel, as elsewhere, an alternative culture is being created by the very young.

Not too much, not too soon, must be expected from this generational rebellion against the values of the Establishment. For one thing, pressure against young people, before induction into the army, is enormous and grows all the time; for another, all of them will have to pass the grinding machine of military service, and many of them will have to fulfil unpleasant duties in the Occupied Territories. And this means that they will have to justify to themselves many of the things they have to do, and this, together with the experience of comradeship, of fighting and possibly of losing a comrade under fire, may change the feelings of many or most of them. Some of them are aware of this, eighteen-year-old youths like Giora Neumann who in 1972 went to military jail for his refusal to 'serve in an imperialist army'. Others, of course, will find a more personal way of escape from the nightmare of unending war: 'Hashish-smoking among the young is alarmingly on the increase,' reported the *Jerusalem Post* on 4 November 1970. An official welfare spokesman said he believed there were 36,000 to 48,000 hashish-smokers in Israel. A secret report stated that junior officers and NCOs of the army, stationed in isolated Sinai desert outposts, smoked the drug.

All this being said, it is still probable that this generation will bring forth new, non-affiliated political idealists who, in spite of repression and indoctrination, can fill the gap in the struggle for peace which no party or group could bridge before them. It is doubtful whether anybody belonging to the older, radical generation, the superannuated pseudo-revolutionaries in their thirties, forties or fifties, could fulfil leadership-tasks in this generational revolt, a revolt prompted by clear self-interest, the desire for survival and idealistic disappointment. It is certain, anyhow, that the 'political oldsters' are unable to build a new political framework by themselves. If they will adhere to it, or try to profit from the efforts of the younger fighters, their task may be secondary, in the final analysis.

As we have seen, there is, of course, an important exception to this rule: the intermediate echelons of the Israeli defence forces, youth turned commanders of fighting men. No political prognosis of Israeli realities can be made without considering this force. In the meantime, the army might become a direct factor in Israeli politics. A generation of Israeli 'free officers', Egyptian-style, is a possibility – if a far-fetched one, as they can as easily integrate into the system without overt challenge of the Establishment.

However, it could happen that the younger generation in the army may not agree to a political line pursued by the political leadership of the state. In that case, the intervention of 1967, which brought Dayan to power as Defence Minister, might be repeated – in the opposite direction. Should this happen, peace with an independent Arab Palestine and a *rapprochement* between this Palestine and Israel would finally become a possibility. On the other hand, such an intervention would almost certainly be the death-knell of what remains of Israeli democracy. Given the dynamism of the young generation, the efficiency of the army and the practical priorities and disciplined mind of even the most liberal of Israeli military men, a permanent autocratic regime in Israel is a virtual certainty, once the Israeli defence forces start political intervention.

Even if – as is to be hoped – this does not happen, there is little doubt that the army will play a considerable role, and impress its specific Israeli virtues – and vices – on the younger generation's struggle. Indeed, it could not be otherwise, for the army's lower and middle echelons and the younger generation of the Israeli people are two aspects of one and the same entity. Thus, whatever Israel's future, democracy seems to be losing out.

Either the present state of affairs will continue to exist, dragging the country to its bitter end; or a movement for peace and renewal will replace it, thanks to the revolt of those not yet indoctrinated. Such a revolt could almost certainly lead to rule by military power in Israel. In either case, Israel is in danger of military dictatorship. The future is not bright.

Glossary

Alyah. Wave (of immigrants).
Bamaawak. *Pax Semitica* (see Chapter 7).
Dunam. Quarter of an acre.
Effendi. Arab landowner.
Eretz-Israel. The Land of Israel.
Fellahin. Arab tenant-landworkers.
Gaffirim. Jewish auxiliary police, under the Mandate.
Gahal. Parliamentary block of the Liberal and HERUT parties, up to 1973.
Haganah. Clandestine militia of Zionists in Mandatory times.
Halachic. According to strict religious law.
Havaad Haleumi. National committee of Jews in Palestine.
Herut. Right-wing party founded by IRGUN; now part of the LIKUD (formerly GAHAL) block.
Histadrut. Main trade-union organization.
Ichud. Jewish-Arab peace movement.
Irgun Tzwai Leumi. Clandestine right-wing militia of Mandatory times.
Jihad. Holy war.
Knesset. Parliament.
Koah Yozem. Group of Two Nations.
Lehy (Lohamey Herut Israel). The 'Stern Gang': fighters for the freedom of Israel.
Mafdal (Miflaga Datit Leumit). The Zionist-Religious Party.
Maki (Miflaga Komunistit Isrealit). Name of PKP after the foundation of the State of Israel.
Mapai (Mifleget Poalei Israel). Precursor of the ruling Labour Party.
Mapam (Mifleget Poalim Meuchedet). Left-wing Zionists.
Matzpen. Israeli Socialist Organization, ISO (from the name of its newspaper).
Moshav. A cooperative village.
Mossad Alyah Beit. Organization for illegal immigration during the Mandate.

MPS (Mifleget Poalim Sotzialistit) ('Mopsi'). The Bolshevik party in the 1920s.
Nahal. (Noar Halutzi Lohem) military corps setting up agricultural outposts, these outposts themselves.
Palmach. Israeli shock troops of the HAGANAH in Mandatory times.
PKP (Palestina Kommunistische Partei). Palestinian Communist Party.
Rafi (Reshimat Poalei Israel). Splinter-group of MAPAI with strong nationalist views; founded by David Ben-Gurion.
Rekah. (Reshima Komunistit Hadashah). Pro-Moscow breakaway group from Maki; now the main Communist Party.
Siah. A movement for Jewish-Arab peace, in the seventies.
Shin Beit. (Sherut Bitahon) Secret service.
Tzabra. Native Israeli Jew.
Tzahal (Tzawah Haganah Leisrael) The army.
Yishuv. Jewish Community of Mandatory times.

Index

Index

Index